# POP ART AND CONSUMER CULTURE

American Studies Series
William H. Goetzmann, Editor

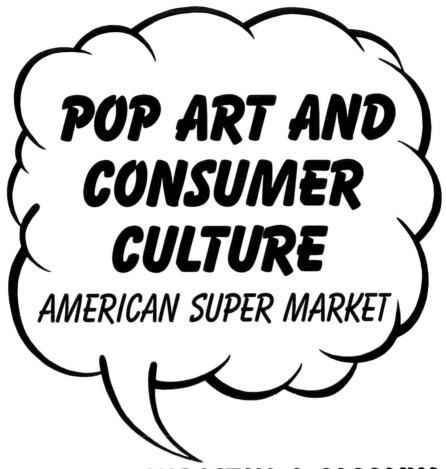

# POP ART AND CONSUMER CULTURE
## AMERICAN SUPER MARKET

## CHRISTIN J. MAMIYA

University of Texas Press, Austin

First Edition, 1992

Requests for permission to reproduce material from this work
should be sent to Permissions, University of Texas Press, Box 7819,
Austin, Texas 78713-7819.

⊗The paper used in this publication meets the minimum
requirements of American National Standard for Information
Sciences—Permanence of Paper for Printed Library Materials,
ANSI Z39.48-1984.

**Library of Congress Cataloging-in-Publication Data**
Mamiya, Christin J.
    Pop art and consumer culture : American super market / Christin J.
Mamiya. — 1st ed.
      p.     cm. — (American studies series)
    Includes bibliographical references and index.
    ISBN 0-292-77653-5 (alk. paper); ISBN 0-292-76440-1 (pbk., alk. paper)
    1. Pop art—United States.   2. Art, Modern—20th century—
United States.   3. United States—Popular culture.   I. Title.
II. Series.
N6512.5.P6M36   1992
709'.04'071—dc20                        91-18892
                                                      CIP

# CONTENTS

# FIGURES

# ACKNOWLEDGMENTS

Working on a lengthy and in-depth project such as this manuscript can be, at times, frustrating and tedious. Despite those moments, the experience of researching, writing, and publishing a book can only be described as singularly rewarding. There are many people who helped make it so by contributing their knowledge, time, and moral support. Their generosity has made this a better book and a more satisfying scholarly endeavor for me, and I thank them all. Many deserve special mention here.

This book grew out of my dissertation, completed at the University of California, Los Angeles. I am indebted to many people there for their contributions at the early stages of this project. In particular, I wish to thank my doctoral committee: Albert Boime (chair), Thomas Hines, Cecelia Klein, David Kunzle, Debora Silverman, and Mary Yeager.

In the subsequent stages of research and manuscript revision, various individuals provided invaluable assistance. Ivan Karp of O. K. Harris Gallery and Leo Castelli of Leo Castelli Gallery granted interviews that afforded me insights into the contemporary gallery scene. Gene Moore of Tiffany & Co. also allowed me to interview him and generously supplied me with previously unpublished photographs. The staff at Leo Castelli Gallery granted me unrestricted access to the material in the Castelli Archives. The staff at the Archives of American Art was most helpful. I appreciate the efforts of Philip F. Mooney, manager, Archives Department of the Coca-Cola Company, Selma P. Kessler of Campbell Soup Company, Rita Rochlen of D'Arcy Masius Benton & Bowles, and Linda Brender of DDB Needham Worldwide, Inc.

Special thanks are due to Shelley Lee of Visual Artists Gallery Association (VAGA) and Katia Stieglitz of Artists Rights Society (ARS) for their patient and efficient assistance in acquiring copyright permissions and photographs. The staff at the University of Texas Press was instrumental in alleviating the stress of publishing, for which I am grateful. In particular, Frankie Westbrook was an exemplary editor; her efficiency, understanding, and perceptive insights were greatly appreciated. Managing editor Barbara Spielman and copy editor Christine Gilbert contributed significantly toward the production of a more polished and compelling book.

The continual support offered by scholars and friends greatly enriched this study. Wendy Kozol deserves special mention; her thorough critical readings of the manuscript at various stages and editorial skill improved this book immeasurably. Thanks are also due to my colleagues at the University of Nebraska–Lincoln who supported this endeavor. Friends such as Elizabeth and Sjoerd Beck helped me to maintain my good humor throughout the preparation of this manuscript; their friendship and enthusiasm sustained me through moments of discouragement, and I extend my sincere thanks. Likewise, the friendship of Mauri and Terry Kearney is greatly appreciated, as is their hospitality on my various research trips to New York.

Finally, I wish to acknowledge the continual support I received from my family and friends. Throughout the preparation of this book they have been a loyal cheering section—for this, I am deeply grateful.

# POP ART AND CONSUMER CULTURE

# INTRODUCTION

*Is Pop Art only an effect of fashion, and thus purely an object of consumption itself?*

—*Jean Baudrillard* [1]

When Pop art first emerged in the United States during the late 1950s, many art critics predicted for this movement a rapid disappearance from the art scene.[2] Most of the established corps of critics expressed their hostility toward Pop art. Wrote Max Kozloff, "The truth is, the art galleries are being invaded by the pinheaded and contemptible style of gum chewers, bobby soxers, and worse, delinquents."[3] Peter Selz commented, "These works leave us thoroughly dissatisfied . . . most of them have nothing at all to say. . . . They are hardly worth the kind of contemplation a real work of art demands."[4]

Yet, much to their surprise, Pop art endured and became *the* art movement of the 1960s. The works of the various Pop artists were soon shown in virtually every major New York gallery, and the Pop artists have continued to enjoy commercial success. Andy Warhol, considered the foremost proponent of the Pop art movement, may well be the most famous American artist of the twentieth century.[5] Indeed, in his obituary of Warhol, critic Robert Hughes claimed that Warhol was the most famous American artist ever, with a "recognizability that almost rivaled Picasso's."[6]

How can we account for the financial and, eventually, critical success of American Pop art, given the dire predictions of many critics and the predominance of abstraction in avant-garde art of the 1950s? This study will demonstrate that the success of this movement was due to the integral relationship between Pop art and American consumer culture, which reached its zenith in the 1960s. Pop art not only depicted and reflected this rampant consumption but also appropriated the mechanisms and strategies of corporate society, ensuring the effective marketing of this movement and its absorption into the matrix of consumer institutions. The focus of this study is the period 1958–1968, which represents the time span from the initial experiments in Pop to its loss of position as the "reigning" art movement.

While consumption has provided a foundation for the capitalist system and thus has a long history, the 1950s and 1960s were a particularly significant period in the history of consumer culture.[7] In its most basic form, a consumer culture is one in which the activities and ethics of a society are determined by patterns of consumption. Rapid urbanization and advancements in technology in the twentieth century were major factors in the development of this consumer culture. Increased bureaucraticization of organizations, growth of the national market, and the expansion of advertising also contributed to the maturation of a consumer mentality.

Most critical, however, for this development was the implementation in the late 1950s and 1960s of policies based on Keynesian economic theory. John Maynard Keynes, the British economist, emerged during the 1930s as a critic of the classical economists whose ideas had influenced economic theory during the first decades of the twentieth century.[8] Keynes objected to their underlying assumptions about market activity (e.g., full employment), which he felt were not natural conditions, as the classical economists had asserted. Keynes believed that this inaccuracy rendered these theories useless in their application to economic policy. In contrast, in developing his ideas, which he set forth in his major 1936 publication, *The General Theory of Employment, Interest, and Money,* Keynes attempted to base his theory on actual market conditions. His focus, unlike that of other economists, was on consumption rather than production as a means to attain economic stability. This theory assumes that the gross national product (GNP) and employment, as reflections of the economy's health, are determined by the level of aggregate demand or total spending in the economy. Thus, in order to ensure a healthy GNP and full employment, consumption must be stimulated. Many economists believe, as Paul Craig Roberts has stated, that Keynes' view is "extraordinary in its emphasis on spending," and another economist even noted: "Keynes said virtually nothing about productivity."[9] The adherence to Keynesian economic theory with its emphasis on spending would clearly be instrumental in the rapid maturation of a consumer culture.

The ascension of John F. Kennedy to the presidency is notable in the history of American consumer culture, since his administration was the first to accept wholeheartedly the Keynesian analysis and to base its decisions regarding both domestic and foreign economic policy on such an approach.[10] The commitment of the Kennedy administration to Keynesian ideas (and therefore to an emphasis on consumption), which was continued by the Johnson administration, is demonstrated by the major influx of economists into policy-level positions in the administration.[11] This commitment is also revealed by the policies enacted and programs undertaken during the 1960s. These policies facilitated the tremendous expansion of multinational corporations, and the fact that the period 1958–1964 represents the greatest period of American foreign economic expansion serves as evidence of this situation. Between the years 1957 and 1962, the value of holdings by U.S. companies in Europe more than doubled, and between 1962 and 1967, they doubled again.[12] As a result of this economic activity and legislation, as early as 1965, economist Milton Friedman declared: "We are all Keynesians now," and Walter W. Heller, chairman of the Council of Economic Advisers under both Presidents Kennedy and Johnson, stated that these two presidents had brought about "the completion of the Keynesian Revolution."[13]

Clearly, on the macroeconomic level, politicians, economic leaders, and business people alike were preoccupied with strategies to encourage mass consumption. Together, these factors contributed to the dramatic maturation of American consumer culture and account for the characterization of the 1960s as consumer oriented.

American culture of the 1960s revolved around issues of consumption not only on the larger scale of governmental policy and legislation, economic planning, and corporate growth, but on the microeconomic level of personal lifestyle as well. Corporations came to rely on the strategy of the planned obsolescence of products, and this, along with the incessant barrage of advertisements, encouraged continual dissatisfaction among American families, whose never-ending quest for the good life increasingly came to be equated with material possessions. Keeping up with the Joneses became an obsession for many, and, on the microeconomic level, consumption (in particular, conspicuous consumption) took on the overtones of a national religion.[14] This orientation was reinforced by the government, which linked the imperative to consume with national military and economic interests.

The pervasiveness of this mentality is evident in the legacy of this period. The generation that grew up during the 1960s has matured into a group often referred to as "yuppies" (young urban professionals) by the popular press. That this age group has been inculcated with the values of consumer culture is clearly demonstrated by a special report on yuppies in a 1984 issue of *Newsweek* that was titled "They Live to Buy."[15] This pronouncement by a mass-circulation periodical that represents, or at the very least addresses, American middle-class culture, reveals how widely this perception has been acknowledged. Not surprisingly, advertisers and marketing executives see this group as "the prize segment of the national market."[16]

While most discussions of consumption and consumer culture focus on the specific economic dynamics and ramifications, it is important to acknowledge that the mechanism of consumption extends beyond issues of money to issues of power. It cannot be denied that consumer culture rewards those in the upper echelons of the corporate structure, for as consumption increases, so, too, do profits. However, as cultural historians Richard Wightman Fox and T. J. Jackson Lears have pointed out, life for most consumers consists of a ceaseless pursuit of the "good life"—a pursuit that serves as a constant reminder of their powerlessness.[17] Because the effects of consumption are so widespread and profound, discussions of consumption must extend to social and cultural aspects as well.

Due to the undeniable impact of advertisements and the compelling nature of consumer practices, consumer culture has contributed to the reinforcement of the established socioeconomic and political hierarchy. This often involves the perpetuation of social stereotypes, ethnic categorizations, and gender roles.

It is within this historical context that Pop art developed. In studying the various facets of the Pop movement, it will become clear that Pop art succeeded not only because it fit into, and reflected, consumer culture but also because it actively entered into the discourse and ultimately deflected or absorbed social and political criticism about this system. While the incorporation of diverse aspects of consumer practices by an art movement would facilitate the ability of that movement to function within a consumer society, it does not ensure its success nor can it automatically be interpreted as support for such a societal system. Indeed, it can be argued that critique that is generated from within a system has the potential for producing far more devastating and effective results than criticism that is aimed at the system from without. However, in the case of Pop art, the movement not only appropriated the images and strategies from consumer culture but also was itself absorbed into the established institutional matrix, thereby rendering it ineffective as a critique and neutralizing any potential for bringing about significant change. The focus of this book, therefore, will be to explore not only how Pop art drew upon the mechanisms, imagery, and ideology of consumer culture but also how it contributed to the legitimation of that very system. As such, this study extends beyond a discussion of formal aesthetic issues and involves both cultural critique and social analysis.

In trying to assess why Pop art was so successful, as in most art historical inquiries, the art works provide the springboard for the investigation. Many studies of Pop art represent attempts to determine or assign specific meanings to the various paintings and sculptures. Often, these discussions revolve around the question of whether these images of contemporary American life represent a positive statement, a glorification or celebration of the consumer ethic, or whether they represent a criticism of the dehumanizing results of such economic activity and an indictment of a society for which standardization, impersonality, and vulgar banality have become the norm. Yet, scrutiny of the images themselves, in conjunction with this debate, demonstrates that the fundamental characteristic of Pop art works is a sense of ambivalence and ambiguity. That is, we can ascertain no concrete or definitive statement either in support of or denouncing consumer activity. However, this line of inquiry is in and of itself Sisyphean, because meaning does not reside within the images themselves. Art and, indeed, all visual imagery encode social values. Because the viewer's reaction to an art work is conditioned by cultural and historical circumstances that predispose him or her to certain readings or that encourage certain interpretations, meaning is derived from the context in which these images operate. Meaning is determined by the interaction between the images and the social environment and is constantly being negotiated. Thus, any attempt to assign permanent, inherent meaning to specific images is a futile exercise. In order to understand the acceptance of Pop art, what must be emphasized is the historical context in which these works were received—that is, consumer culture of the 1960s.

The meaning and power of Pop art images in the 1960s can be attributed in part to the content of the works, which is clearly linked to American consumer culture of that period. From Hollywood celebrities to household appliances and food products, the subject matter of Pop art was immediately recognizable, coming as it did from the realms of advertising, grocery shelves, and movie and television screens. In addition, the visual style and production techniques that were employed in the manufacture of these art works were undeniably linked to the world of marketing, advertising, and mass media. Given that the backgrounds of all the Pop artists included substantial work in commercial art, this connection is not unexpected. Scrutiny of the art works will illustrate the ability of visual representations to mediate, contradict, perpetuate, or reinforce ideological claims presented by consumer culture.

Pop art's links to consumer culture, however, extend beyond the images themselves. Of greater importance in understanding the success of this art movement is the manner in which these works were presented and received. This understanding will be achieved by exploring the roles of other art world participants—the artists, dealers, critics, and collectors—in the establishment of Pop art. In addition to the apparent accessibility of the images, the acceptance of Pop was due to shifts in the equilibrium within this institutional matrix. These shifts made this matrix more compatible with the expanding consumer ideology and practices. Thus, while the influence of the critics waned, the roles of those directly involved in the promotion and sale or purchase of art (i.e., the artists, dealers, and collectors) increased. It was this network that ensured Pop's success by "selling" the art through promotional and marketing techniques derived from corporate practices.

Despite the fact that art has a long history as a commodity, members of the art community have been reluctant to openly acknowledge this aspect. However, it is difficult to deny that the Pop movement benefitted from its links with consumer culture, which made it more easily marketable and therefore more attractive to buyers and the public alike.

Ultimately, what is the importance of this study? Beyond providing a concrete understanding of Pop art, this examination of how and why Pop art succeeded serves as a clear illlustration of the essential intersection between art and the historical circumstances within which it develops. Even further, this study is important because the legacy of Pop art has been profound, particularly in terms of the dynamics of the contemporary art world and the "commercialization of art." The concluding chapter of this book is devoted to addressing this lasting significance of Pop art's intersection with consumer culture. The recent transition from modernism to postmodernism, one of the most prominent developments in twentieth-century art, can be largely attributed to the ascendance of Pop art. By co-opting images and mechanisms integral to consumer culture, Pop art undermined many of the tenets fundamental to modernist doctrine. It can, therefore, be seen as responsible for ushering in the postmodernist era and providing the conceptual foundation for much of contemporary art.

# CHAPTER 1
# *THE RAPID SUCCESS STORY:*
## THE ESTABLISHMENT OF POP ART

*No movement in art history ever established itself so swiftly.*

—*Calvin Tomkins* [1]

Few people expected Pop art to meet with such overwhelming and rapid success. Even in retrospect, critics and art historians express surprise at this occurrence. In her catalog *Blam! The Explosion of Pop, Minimalism, and Performance, 1958–1964* that accompanied the 1984 Whitney Museum of American Art exhibition of the same name, Barbara Haskell states: "Pop Art was thrust almost instantly into the forefront of the art world. . . . Most astonishing was that this notoriety came almost overnight." [2] Considering the hostile reactions of most established critics, this result is indeed surprising. A brief historical overview of the development of Pop will suffice to reveal the rapidity with which the establishment of Pop occurred.

Those artists figuring most prominently in the development of the Pop art movement were Robert Rauschenberg, Jasper Johns, Andy Warhol, Roy Lichtenstein, Tom Wesselmann, James Rosenquist, and Claes Oldenburg. While Rauschenberg and Johns are perhaps more accurately regarded as transitional figures between Abstract Expressionism and Pop art, they are often considered Pop artists because many of their works involve content associated with Pop and their artistic sensibilities correspond with that of the Pop artists. The Pop artists, unlike the Abstract Expressionists who preceded them, did not form a coherent group or closely associate with one another. Rather, each artist developed his style more or less independently of the others, and even after becoming familiar with the work of the other Pop artists, little interaction took place. These artists did, however, share a background in the commercial art world, and all chose to live and work in New York, which represented not only the center of the art world but also of the advertising world—the foundation of consumer culture.

Most of the Pop artists met with remarkable success with their initial public gallery exhibitions. Jasper Johns' one-man show at Leo Castelli Gallery in January 1958, according to one account, "hit the art world like a meteor."[3] In anticipation of the exhibition, Johns' *Target with Four Faces* had appeared on the cover of *Artnews,* which served to fuel interest in the show. The show not only garnered a great deal of publicity but was an overwhelming financial success as well. Of the works exhibited, only two remained unsold at the conclusion of the show. A Dutch dealer named Jan Streep tried to buy the entire exhibition but was told that that was impossible.[4] Alfred Barr and Dorothy Miller purchased works for the Museum of Modern Art, as did several other museum trustees. Important collectors such as Ben Heller, Emily Tremaine, Donald Peters, Mrs. Henry Epstein, and Leo Castelli all bought paintings from Johns' first one-man show. The art world was amazed at the immediate impact of Johns' work, and his debut was one of the most successful in history.

James Rosenquist's initial foray into the exhibition arena was similarly remarkable. Rosenquist developed his signature style based on billboard imagery and format early in 1960, and by the following year, collectors such as Robert Scull, Emily and Burton Tremaine, Philip Johnson, Count Giuseppe Panza di Biumo, and Richard Brown Baker were regular visitors to his studio and purchased paintings.[5] It was no surprise, then, that Rosenquist's first one-man show in 1962 at Richard Bellamy's Green Gallery sold out.

Claes Oldenburg's first one-man exhibition, The Street, was held in 1960. He presented his first major exhibition that incorporated his Pop works the following year. This show, entitled The Store, was deemed a "rousing public success" and was extended a month due to popular demand, despite sluggish sales.[6] The commercial success of his one-man show at the uptown Green Gallery in 1962 attests to the popularity of Oldenburg's work.

Although the response to Andy Warhol's first exhibition in 1960 was not as overwhelming as that accompanying Johns' first one-man show, he did not remain in the shadows for long. His show at the Stable Gallery in November 1962 caused a great sensation and virtually sold out. After that success, Warhol, aided by the silkscreen process that enabled him to produce numerous images quickly, began creating paintings that were "selling . . . almost as fast as he could turn them out."[7]

Roy Lichtenstein and Tom Wesselmann both came to public attention with their Pop art paintings in 1961–1962. Lichtenstein's first one-man show at Castelli Gallery in early 1962 led to the purchase of his works by dealers such as Irving Blum and Ileana Sonnabend, who became influential in Lichtenstein's ascent in the art world. Wesselmann, too, came to the attention of dealers such as Ivan Karp, and soon Wesselmann's work was purchased by Burton and Emily Tremaine, the Buckwalters, Robert and Ethel Scull, Leon Kraushar, and Harry Abrams.

Of the major artists associated with Pop art, Robert Rauschenberg's ascent to prominence met with the most resistance. Initial response to his early exhibitions in the late 1950s was, for the most part, negative. In fact, Rauschenberg's first major American show in 1953 was so poorly received that Eleanor Ward, his dealer, removed the guest book from the gallery because, according to Ward, "so many awful things were being written in it."[8] However, once his work began to receive wider exposure, dealers and, eventually, critics accorded him great stature. By the mid-1960s, Rauschenberg's works were being purchased often before reaching his dealer, for prices between $5,000 and $50,000 a painting.[9]

The rapid ascendance of Pop art is also illustrated by the pervasiveness of works by these artists in major international exhibitions of the 1960s. By 1964, Pop art had established itself as the major art movement of the period and was represented at the Venice Biennales of 1964, 1966, and 1968, the Kassel Documentas of 1964 and 1968, the New York World's Fair of 1964, and the São Paulo Bienal of 1967.

The Venice Biennale is, by all accounts, a major international exhibition and has been considered a weathervane for determining the state and direction of contemporary art. Including works from numerous countries, each with its own pavilion, the Biennale awards coveted prizes to artists selected by an international jury. The American artists represented at the XXXII Venice Biennale in 1964 were: Pop artists Robert Rauschenberg, Jasper Johns, Claes Oldenburg, and Jim Dine, abstractionists Kenneth Noland, Frank Stella, and Morris Louis, and the sculptor John Chamberlain. This Biennale, which soon came to be labeled "the Biennale of Pop Art," caused a great deal of controversy.[10] The heated debate escalated when Robert Rauschenberg was awarded the international grand prize for painting, the first time since the inception of the Biennale in 1895 that the award had gone to an American.[11] This award was considered all the more significant because the United States pavilion, traditionally sponsored by a private institution, was officially sponsored by the U.S. government for the first time in 1964.[12]

The international prizes had historically been awarded to internationally recognized artists with established reputations and extensive bodies of work, so that bestowing the honor on a relatively young artist was considered highly improbable. Indeed, despite the spectacular rise of the Abstract Expressionists in the United States in the 1950s, by the 1964 Biennale they had yet to receive the slightest notice from the jury. This made Rauschenberg's victory all the more stunning.

Other international exhibitions of the same year revealed the degree to which Pop art had taken over the art world. Documenta III in Kassel, West Germany, was, by general consensus, one of the most important modern exhibitions ever assembled. In the words of one critic, Documenta III was "an ideal, comprehensive, imaginary Museum of Modern Art," emphasizing the encyclopedic nature of the exhibition.[13] Because the show had no national framework, as did the XXXII Venice Biennale, and was not organized around specific stylistic concerns, most critics considered Documenta III to be a more accurate reflection of the modern, particularly contemporary, art scene. In addition, no prizes were awarded, which eliminated the behind-the-scene lobbying to which many people objected at the Biennale.[14]

Unlike the Biennale, however, at which Pop art commanded center stage, the only works that could be considered related to the movement were a few paintings by Rauschenberg and Johns. The numerous objections of critics and viewers to the sparse representation of Pop attest to the stature that Pop art had achieved. One critic noted that Johns was "inadequately shown."[15] Another lamented: "Only Rauschenberg, Jasper Johns and Larry Rivers are on show. When one reflects that neither Lichtenstein, Rosenquist, Wessel-man [*sic*], nor indeed any save for Dine and Segal, has been shown in Germany, the omissions become almost ludicrous."[16] Another German critic concurred: "It is a pity that hardly any Pop-Art and New Realism . . . are to be seen."[17] Even critics who were not enthralled by Pop art commented upon the absence of these works. One such critic, in impressing upon his readers the significance of Documenta III, which he predicted would one day be valued as a highpoint in the series, insisted that the omissions were the result of the likes and dislikes of the organizing commission. He noted that "the organizers have, for example, renounced New Realism such as the combine paintings and the vulgar forms of Pop Art."[18] These representative remarks demonstrate the degree to which Pop art had established itself by this point as a major art movement.

Pop art got extensive exposure at the 1964 New York World's Fair as well. Robert Moses, the president of the fair's corporation, vetoed all suggestions of official art exhibitions, claiming that the fair was a straightforward commercial and industrial exposition and that the resources of New York museums made such exhibitions superfluous.[19] Although there were exhibitions of art by various countries in their respective pavilions, art was presented on a very limited scale on the general fairgrounds.

Pop art, however, was highly visible on the exterior walls of the New York State Pavilion. This building was designed by architect Philip Johnson, who retained the right to select the exterior decorations. He commissioned works by Rauschenberg, Rosenquist, Warhol, and Lichtenstein, among others, and visitors to the pavilion were met with large mural-sized examples of Pop art.

The predominance of Pop expanded in subsequent years. Like Documenta III in 1964, the São Paulo Bienal of 1965 caused a stir due to what most critics felt was an inappropriate lack of Pop art works. The São Paulo Bienal was considered by many critics to represent "the most important international exhibition of the plastic arts on the western side of the Atlantic."[20] Held during odd numbered years so as not to conflict with the more established Venice Biennale, the São Paulo Bienal was often compared with its "Mediterranean rival." The 1965 São Paulo Bienal presented an interesting array of styles and images from the numerous countries, but the lack of a substantial representation of Pop art provoked criticism. One critic concluded: "The average quality of the 8th Biennial [*sic*] is quite low: after the 'scandal of Venice' in 1964 and the international recognition given to 'pop-art' through Rauschenberg's Great Prize, Sao Paulo appears as a low-tide session."[21]

The continuing dominance of Pop asserted itself at the XXXIII Venice Biennale in 1966. The United States was represented by four artists: Helen Frankenthaler, Ellsworth Kelly, Roy Lichtenstein, and Jules Olitski. Of the four, Lichtenstein was the only artist associated with Pop. Significantly, his work received the most attention from the press, and he was the only American artist to receive a favorable response overall. In acknowledging that his work was famous the world over, critics remarked that the main reason that Lichtenstein's work had such repercussions was his innovation and his attempt to express something beyond the merely decorative.[22]

Many of the critics considered Lichtenstein a serious contender for the grand prize won by Rauschenberg two years earlier.[23] However, the press reported that objections were voiced to the organizing committee that Leo Castelli, Lichtenstein's dealer, was orchestrating a lobbying campaign amongst influential people to convince the jury to award Lichtenstein the prize. This problem of the behind-the-scene lobbying, and the ensuing complaint that the prizes had nothing to do with the art itself, prompted the press to reevaluate the purpose of and the selection process for the awards. Many, among them Henry Geldzahler, commissioner for the U.S. pavilion that year, suggested that the prizes simply be abolished. Others expressed indignation that such activity would affect the jury's decision. Noted one critic: "Artists must be . . . the opposite of the bourgeois from the moral point of view, and when an artist refuses to accept this caste definition he may as well give up all hope of winning the day at Venice, even if he is a genius like Lichtenstein. . . . To me the idea of not giving the prize to Lichtenstein because maybe who knows where and who knows how and who knows when the dealer pushed his painter, fills me with pity for the jury who thought it up."[24] The prizes that year were ultimately awarded to the Argentine painter Julio Le Parc and the French sculptor Etienne Martin.

The predominance of Pop by this time was so internationally acknowledged that the American contribution to the IX Bienal de São Paulo in 1967 seemed to represent a retrospective of the movement. One part of the U.S. exhibition was devoted to Edward Hopper, who had recently died, and the second part was a survey of art between 1957 and 1967. Among the twenty artists represented were: Jasper Johns, Robert Rauschenberg, Andy Warhol, Roy Lichtenstein, Claes Oldenburg, James Rosenquist, and Tom Wesselmann, as well as other artists associated with the movement such as Robert Indiana, Edward Ruscha, George Segal, and Wayne Thiebaud.

A similar "anthology of Pop" (as the American exhibition of São Paulo was referred to) was presented the following year at Documenta IV at Kassel.[25] All of the major Pop artists were represented, and the catalog contained an essay discussing the movement. The movement had, by then, reached its peak. Rauschenberg and Johns were referred to as "Old Masters," and another critic, whose review of Documenta focused on Pop art, discussed the "difficulty of ageing gracefully."[26]

The Venice Biennale of the same year included none of the Pop artists' work, and because of the stated intention of the Biennale to present new, experimental work, this omission was lauded. Noted one critic: "A virtue of exhibitions [such as the Biennale] . . . is that they can correct misleading or biased views of recent art. And no country's recent art has been quite so one-sidedly represented by dealers and critics as that of the United States. America has produced the main artists of both Abstract Expressionism and Pop Art, and the achievement of these artists has overshadowed the continuing strong figurative tradition in American painting."[27]

The predominance of Pop is reflected as well in the significant and rapid increases in prices that the works commanded. While price is not necessarily an indicator of either quality or ultimate value, it does reflect the interest generated in the works of the Pop artists.

Rauschenberg's works, which met with initial resistance in the late 1950s, were selling for up to $50,000 by the mid-1960s.[28] Johns' spectacular public debut led to great demand for his work. So great was the competition for Johns' works that collectors, upon hearing that Johns was about to begin a new painting, would buy it before any pigment had been applied to the canvas.[29] The prices for Johns' paintings were pushed even higher by his relatively limited output and by the fact that in 1954 he had destroyed all of his art still in his possession, restricting even further the availability of his works.[30] Lichtenstein's paintings met with a similarly meteoric ascent in price. For example, *Big Painting #6*, which was sold for several thousand dollars when it was completed in 1965, was auctioned off for $75,000 only five years later.[31]

The appeal of Pop art has persisted to the present, as is revealed by the consistently increasing prices garnered by these art works. At a 1986 Sotheby's auction, Johns' *Out the Window*, which Robert and Ethel Scull purchased for $2,250 in 1960, sold for $3.63 million, the highest price ever paid for a contemporary work of art.[32] By 1987, seven of the top ten highest priced contemporary works of art sold at auction were by Pop artists (Rauschenberg, Johns, and Warhol). In 1982, Kenneth S. Friedman, publisher of *Art Economist* newsletter, named Rauschenberg, Johns, Warhol, and Lichtenstein as among the handful of artists to gross more than $1 million a year.[33]

Pop art's ascent to prominence in the late 1950s and 1960s was dizzying, and despite the fact that it is no longer the reigning art movement, it has lost little of its luster and cachet. The remainder of this book will explore why this phenomenon came about, and, ultimately, what effect this has had on the contemporary art scene.

# CHAPTER 2
# *POP ART AND CONSUMER CULTURE:*
## CORPORATIONS AND THE IMPERATIVE TO CONSUME

*So I geared myself, like an advertiser or a large company, to this visual inflation [in a commercial society].*

**James Rosenquist** [1]

Between the years 1958–1964, the United States witnessed an explosion in the size and geographic diversity of American corporations. This fact contributes substantially to the explanation of why Pop art succeeded. Despite the fact that much of this expansion took place abroad, especially in Europe, the efforts of these American firms to widen their markets was so overwhelming that it solidified the control of the American economy by the large, multinational corporations. So pervasive was the corporate presence that it resulted in the entrenchment of the corporate mentality in the American public psyche. As an apparatus crucial to the expansion effort, advertising assumed a position of critical importance during this period. Its ubiquity not only ensured the corporate dominance but also further legitimized the marketing practices developed by these corporations. When Pop art (which derived most of its imagery from advertising) emerged on the scene, a climate thus existed into which Pop art fit comfortably, both visually and conceptually. This lent an immediacy to the works and partially accounts for their acceptance.

More important to the success of Pop, however, was the fact that the Pop movement appropriated the mentality that was fundamental to mass production and utilized the strategies that had brought about corporate dominance. In this manner, Pop art did more than reflect consumer culture—it brought about a realignment of the cultural community so that it was more consistent with corporate models, and in so doing, it contributed to a validation of that very system.

The growth of American business was facilitated by a number of intersecting factors, many of which were the result of the postwar climate. The postwar period had seen a spending boom, due to the savings accumulated during the war and the renewed availability of previously scarce goods. Not surprisingly, this boom slowed during the 1950s. The recessions of 1957 and 1960 in particular made American companies painfully aware of the precarious condition of the country's economy. The 1960s were witness to a more concerted attempt on the part of corporations to stabilize and increase their market shares.

The U.S. government (specifically, the Department of Justice) had, since the war, made it increasingly difficult for companies to expand their market shares through mergers or acquisitions. This attempt to discourage monopolies also gave rise to more calculated efforts to introduce new product lines and to increase advertising expenditures in order to convince the American consumer to purchase the goods that were flooding the market.

The domestic economic situation contributed to overseas (particularly European) expansion as well. American corporate expansion had been evolving since the aftermath of World War II, when the U.S. government encouraged American companies to invest abroad, hoping that a flow of investment funds would reduce the level of official loans and grants required to hasten Europe's economic recovery.[2]

Many corporate executives and economists believed that the American market was approaching a saturation point. For that reason, the geographical expansion of markets became a logical maneuver. In addition, the legal anti-monopoly restrictions made foreign expansion the best prospect for further growth.

These conditions encouraging foreign expansion represent only one side of the economic equation. There were also a number of factors that made Europe an attractive environment for investment. Europe provided: (1) an insatiable demand for goods that U.S. companies could satisfy, (2) an abundant supply of cheap labor, and (3) substantial incentives (such as financing, tax advantages, transportation subsidies, and the construction of facilities) to encourage foreign investment.[3]

Another major stimulus to the expansion of the multinational corporations was the formation of the European Economic Community (or Common Market) in 1957. Originally consisting of Belgium, France, Italy, Luxembourg, the Netherlands, and West Germany, the EEC was based on the idea of the customs union. One of the first actions taken by this organization was to legitimize conversion of their currencies into the dollar, a decision that reflected their new strength and confidence.[4] This allowed American businesses to repatriate their profits from overseas enterprises, providing a strong incentive for multinational expansion.

All of these factors contributed to making 1958–1964 the greatest period of American foreign expansion. The creation of monolithic companies not only reinforced the ideal of consumption by increasing the availability of products, but this expansion also led to greatly increased advertising budgets. Because many believed that the American market was reaching its saturation point, product advertising became not only more insistent and pervasive but, to many, more strident in tone as well.

The role of advertising as the most visible and, arguably, the most effective weapon in the corporate arsenal to promote consumption makes an exploration of the function and mechanism of advertising critical to an understanding of consumer culture. It is through advertising that the ideological claims of consumption are reinforced. Moreover, advertising has become one of the most representative institutions of American consumer culture. As Daniel Bell observed in *The Cultural Contradictions of Capitalism*, "[a] consumption economy . . . finds its reality in appearances."[5]

Defining the function of advertising has been problematic since its widespread use around the turn of the century, and this debate has grown more heated over the years. The companies and the advertisers themselves, for obvious reasons, have ascribed a straightforward and beneficial function to advertising. Their claim has been that it provides information that aids consumers in making educated decisions about purchases. While the provision of information about goods and services is clearly of value, most critics and social observers have expressed the opinion that advertising has extended the scope of its goals far beyond mere product information.

One of the major criticisms with which advertisers have often been confronted has been the claim that advertising functions not merely to satisfy consumers' desires by supplying needed information but also that the institution has actually been responsible for the creation of such desires by means of psychological manipulation—exploiting the fears and anxieties—of the buying public.

To some critics, advertising has a deeper purpose. Advertising, they argue, has functioned not merely to promote products but rather to promote the corporations themselves and the corporate mentality. An example of such promotion is the increasingly popular corporate sponsorship of art exhibitions and cultural events, the financial underwriting of publications, and the sponsorship of large-scale public events, such as the Olympics. In such cases, the corporate name is liberally mentioned and credit is given whenever possible, yet nowhere do the names of specific products appear. This type of corporate activity can be categorized as public relations rather than advertising per se, but it clearly serves the same purpose—to increase sales.

There is no consensus regarding the exact function of advertising, but it can clearly be seen as a form of publicity and promotion. How does advertising accomplish this? We need an understanding of the strategies employed by advertising because these same strategies were utilized by the Pop artists at the same time that their works were being absorbed into the consumer network.

The pervasive influence of advertising was facilitated by the destruction of firm social foundations that was a result of the urban-industrial transformation of the late nineteenth and early twentieth centuries. The anxieties that resulted from rapid urbanization are evidenced by the plentiful advice columns in magazines and newspapers as well as by the increasing number of self-help and "how-to" books. Due to the increasingly impersonal quality of urban life and the growing reliance on outward appearances, material possessions became the basis for the determination of success and self-worth. Consequently, making appropriate selections of goods and services acquired critical importance. Advertisers capitalized on the insecurities of and provided direction to American society by promising a cure to every problem. One ad executive declared: "The cosmetic manufacturers are not selling lanolin, they are selling hope. . . . We no longer buy oranges, we buy vitality. We do not buy just an auto, we buy prestige."[6] Despite its grandiose promises, advertising ultimately failed to deliver, since its goal was to induce perpetual consumption. As a result, the consumer's dream of the good life remained ever elusive.

In the 1950s, the carefully orchestrated strategies utilized by advertising were further refined and focused on "market or motivational research." This field was examined (and publicized) in Vance Packard's landmark study of 1957, *The Hidden Persuaders*. The book was replete with concrete examples of attempts by various companies to create markets for their products through psychological manipulation. Louis Cheskin, the head of a Chicago research firm in the 1950s and 1960s that provided such research for advertisers, explained that: "Motivational research is the type of research that seeks to learn what motivates people in making choices. It employs techniques designed to reach the unconscious or subconscious mind because preferences generally are determined by factors of which the individual is not conscious. . . . Actually in the buying situation the consumer generally acts emotionally and compulsively, unconsciously reacting to the images and designs which in the subconscious are associated with the product."[7]

It was through this kind of research that advertisers were able to orient their advertisements to encourage purchases of their products or services by focusing on people's fears and anxieties.

Advertisements, by addressing these very issues, and due to their persuasiveness and careful presentation, served to inform the viewer or reader's perception of appropriate modes of behavior. Advertising, given its ubiquity, created a social world into which one gained admittance through consumption. It is for this reason that sociologists such as Daniel Bell have ascribed to advertising a social function similar to that of family, church, and the educational system.[8] These institutions functioned to induce acceptable behavior and values. To a large extent, advertising has assumed that function.

Advertising can thus be seen as an agent of social control. While there are social critics who question the effectiveness of ads and commercials, this is a difficult position to defend, given the irrefutable pervasiveness of advertising. By the late 1960s, for example, the average television viewer was exposed to more than forty thousand commercials a year.[9] Indeed, the Secretary of the Department of Health, Education, and Welfare at the time pointed out that the average human being over a productive life span watches television commercials for more hours than he or she ever spends in school.[10]

Advertising's powerful impact on our society is revealed by consumers' tenacious belief (or, at least, persistent optimism) in the promise of advertising, despite the fact that on a rational level, consumers are aware of the distorted claims of advertisements. Due to this enduring underlying faith, it is not surprising that the institution is often referred to as a religion. Advertiser James Rorty, who worked for the firm Batten, Barton, Durstine, and Osborn in the early 1930s, published a Marxist critique of the advertising industry in 1934, titled *Our Master's Voice: Advertising*. In it, he claimed that "advertising . . . becomes a body of doctrine."[11] Other social observers concurred. Ann Douglas contended in her 1977 publication *The Feminization of American Culture* that advertising is "the only faith of a secularized consumer society."[12] These references to advertising as a form of religion take on greater import when one notes the disproportionate number of successful advertising agents who came from strict, religious backgrounds. Claude C. Hopkins, Helen Lansdowne Resor, Bruce Barton, Rosser Reeves, and David Ovilgy, among others, were all raised in households in which religion was of paramount concern. Their success in the field of advertising can perhaps be attributed to their ability to reconcile the fervor and passion of religion with the goals of corporate culture. Historian T. J. Jackson Lears has concluded that Barton, one of the founders of Batten, Barton, Durstine and Osborn—still one of the largest advertising agencies in the world—was able to combine a certain religiosity with an ideology of consumption and, in so doing, retailored Protestant Christianity to fit the sleek new corporate system.[13]

The industry's various critics and supporters have grown more vocal over the years, in response to the continuous expansion of the advertising industry. The late 1950s and 1960s saw a substantial increase in advertising expenditures. While the leading national advertiser in 1960, General Motors Corporation, spent over $66.3 million on advertising in that year, by 1968 Proctor & Gamble Company was spending $196.3 million, an increase of 200 percent in just eight years.[14] Magazine publishers saw a 150 percent increase in advertising revenue in the decade between 1958 and 1968, and advertising revenue for network television rose almost 250 percent during the same period. By 1968, the amount of money spent on television advertising, roughly $3.1 billion, was twice the budget of the poverty program.[15]

Advertising provided an environment replete with ads that, as social material that informs behavior patterns, served to encourage self-fulfillment through consumption. Because this strategy justified and affirmed the authority of corporate culture, advertising played a critical role in perpetuating the mechanisms and ideology of consumption.

This maturation of corporate and advertising strategies was a widespread national phenomenon. However, there were certain industries that provided highly visible leadership in this regard. Among such industries were the automobile and food and beverage industries. Given their predominance in the American economy and high visibility during the 1960s, it is not surprising that images derived from their advertising appear frequently in Pop art works. Rather than provide a refuge from the incessant barrage of ads, art galleries and museums with Pop exhibitions were transformed into extensions of the consumer environment. Most studies of Pop art have discussed, indeed, have focused on, this aspect—that Pop art excerpted images from the surrounding society. However, my goal here is to demonstrate that the visual quotations (both in terms of content and form) that surface in Pop art are much more specific and historically grounded than has thus far been acknowledged, thereby making the connection with consumer culture more concrete and fundamental to an understanding of the Pop movement. Later chapters will demonstrate how the relative ambiguity of the Pop images and their incorporation into the consumer network negated any potential critical stance toward this ideology of consumption.

## AUTOMOBILES

The growth of the automobile industry has been perhaps the most significant development in twentieth-century American history. Increased mobility affected to a momentous degree not only the physical character of American culture in terms of urban planning and lifestyles but also the psychological orientation of the country. In a society that has increasingly depended on outward appearances and material possessions as personal evaluative criteria, the automobile has occupied a unique position as a major symbol and as an active agent in socioeconomic relationships. Ed Mullane, an auto-industry executive, echoed the beliefs of many when he stated:

"When I grew up . . . the automobile was the one product that universally signified success in America."[16] One foreign car company addressed this aspect directly in its ads: "In the thirties and forties, in the U.S., the automobile began to change. Instead of remaining a practical and efficient means of transportation, it became a symbol of wealth and power."[17]

Despite its global appeal, the automobile has been closely identified with the United States, especially in terms of its usage. As the railroad was to England in the nineteenth century, and electronics to Japan in the 1960s, so was the automobile for American consumers the product "that corresponded best to a most ecstatic moment of national development."[18] So entranced was the American public with the automobile during the early years of the twentieth century, beginning with the pioneering efforts of Henry Ford in mass production, that by the mid-1950s market saturation had been reached.[19]

The ascendance of Pop art coincided with an important juncture in the history of the automotive industry, which had managed to sell more passenger cars in America than there were households. Having achieved market saturation, the industry sought ways to expand that market. This expansion required a fundamental reappraisal of marketing goals and methods. Albert Sloan, president of General Motors during the 1920s and 1930s and one of the most influential men in the history of the automotive industry, claimed that the late 1950s and early 1960s "saw the most dramatic change in the car market since the 1920s."[20] No longer were the car manufacturers satisfied with one car per household—their new goal was at least one car per individual driver. This new market assault in the 1960s involved no new technology and as such remained purely on the level of production engineering, marketing strategy, and advertising. As one historian explained: "It was the golden age of the automobile *industry*, not of the automobile."[21]

In an attempt to increase sales, Detroit had streamlined its operations sufficiently that the time required to get an automobile from the drawing board to the showroom floor was reduced from three years to six months. This allowed the companies to entice consumers with a plethora of models. However, the frenetic and perhaps excessive efforts of the automobile companies to convince the American public to buy their products were less than successful. Claimed one historian: "When the history of the automobile is written, scholars will necessarily focus careful attention on the crucial period of the late sixties. . . . During that period the largest industry the world had ever known . . . began to die."[22] Thus, the late 1950s and 1960s represented a critical watershed era in automotive history, between the saturation of the market and the decline of the industry, during which time advertising and marketing were of paramount concern.

The image of the automobile appears repeatedly in Pop art. These art works addressed various aspects of the marketing efforts of the U.S. auto-motive industry, as represented by General Motors, Ford, and Chrysler cor-porations, the three dominant firms.

In each of his collage-formatted paintings, James Rosenquist assembles images from the contemporary American environment. The automobile is an integral part and appears as it would in billboards and advertisements of the time—with an emphasis on styling and design. "My metaphor, if that is what you can call it," stated Rosenquist, "is my relations to the power of commer-cial advertising which is in turn related to our free society, the visual inflation which accompanies the money that produces box tops and space cadets." [23] The cars in Rosenquist's paintings are sleek, shiny, and abstracted from the environment. They appear without occupants and float on the canvases with-out reference to their function as transportation. Significantly, they are all American-made cars.

Rosenquist's works do intersect with advertising on other levels beyond the relationship between the visual presentation of his paintings and the vi-sual impact of advertising. Because the utility role of the automobile was a given by this time, most advertising campaigns centered instead on the less tangible, psychosocial function. Rosenquist's work addresses this approach by juxtaposing other items of consumption to the automobile. In works such as *I Love You with My Ford* (1961; fig. 1), the canvas is equally divided between the 1950 Ford at the top, clearly identified by the grille work and Ford em-blem, the central image of the sensuous face of a woman, with the focus on her slightly parted lips, and the bottom panel, which consists of a mass of canned spaghetti. All of these items are presented as consumable goods, and their juxtaposition refers to the marketing strategy prominent at this time that involved endowing the product with attributes aimed at improving the consumer's sense of self-worth and esteem, thereby encouraging purchase of the product.

Buick, for example, promised: "It [a Buick car] makes you feel like the man you are," [24] appealing to the masculine desire for virility. General Motors claimed that the Lincoln Continental "distinguishes you among fine car own-ers. It is the luxury motor-car that stands apart from all other cars. As an expression of individuality, good taste, accomplishment. As a reflection of a way of life . . ." [25] Ads for the Chrysler New Yorker insisted that "a New Yorker commands respect without looking ostentatious." [26]

In automobile advertisements, women were often placed next to the cars for associative effect, as Rosenquist has done in *I Love You with My Ford*. The selling power of sexual suggestion had long been established, and because the automobile industry during this period had so few technological innovations to promote, this strategy became more pronounced. Ads, such as that for the

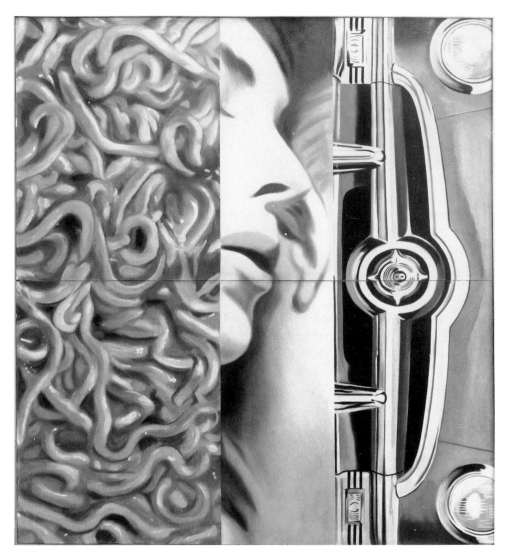

**Figure 1. James Rosenquist, *I Love You with My Ford,* 1961**
Oil on canvas, 82 3/4″ × 93 1/2″
© 1989 James Rosenquist/VAGA New York
Courtesy Moderna Museet, Stockholm
Photo: Statens Konstmuseer, Stockholm

1956 Pontiac (fig. 2), proliferated during the 1960s. In the Pontiac ad, the image of a woman overlaps a photograph of the interior of the 1957 Pontiac. It is visually clear that the woman is not in the car, but she is attired in a dress that mimics the interior decor of the car, thereby reinforcing the association of automobile and woman. The sexual innuendo is further enhanced by the carefully worded caption: "The 'Off-the-Shoulder' Look—just *One* of the wonderful new *Firsts* in the '57 Pontiac." The woman wears a dress that bares one of her shoulders, and on the surface, the caption merely points out the styling (and stylish) similarities. However, the caption could also be read as a subtle pun referring to the backseat sexual initiation for which automobiles had become legendary.

Beth Bailey, a historian who has chronicled the transformation of American courtship, recounts various anecdotes of the late 1950s and 1960s that reveal that at least for the younger generation, cars had come to represent the best opportunity for sexual privacy. She notes that many colleges and universities had instituted regulations against students owning cars specifically for this reason and cites an instance in which students at a midwestern university launched a campaign against what they perceived as an unfair restriction.[27] One student admitted that the issue was not transportation, but privacy: "We wouldn't care if the cars had no wheels, just as long as they had doors."[28]

Automobile ads of the late 1950s and 1960s played on this function of cars, and it is this aspect that provides an added dimension to Pop art paintings such as *I Love You with My Ford*. Rosenquist utilizes this same montage effect in *Lanai* (1964; fig. 3). Here, a Buick Skylark has been placed in the center of the mural-sized painting. Framing the car on either side are a plate of glistening cling peaches on the left and a nude woman kneeling over the edge of a swimming pool on the right. As in *I Love You with My Ford*, Rosenquist has juxtaposed cars, food, and women. Unlike the clearly delineated boundaries of the images in *I Love You with My Ford*, the edges of the component elements in *Lanai* overlap and blend into one another, suggesting to a greater degree that this is to be read as a composite image rather than as isolated fragments.

Roy Lichtenstein, in *In The Car* (1963), presents an image that, while conceptually similar to Rosenquist's works, is visually the antithesis of those paintings. Lichtenstein does not focus on the automobile itself; all that is visible is part of the window at the right, thin borders of the car roof and door at the top and bottom of the painting, and the steering wheel. Unlike Wesselmann and Rosenquist, Lichtenstein portrays the occupants and draws attention to the psychosocial associations of automobile ownership. Numerous studies have conclusively shown that automobiles "are heavily laden with

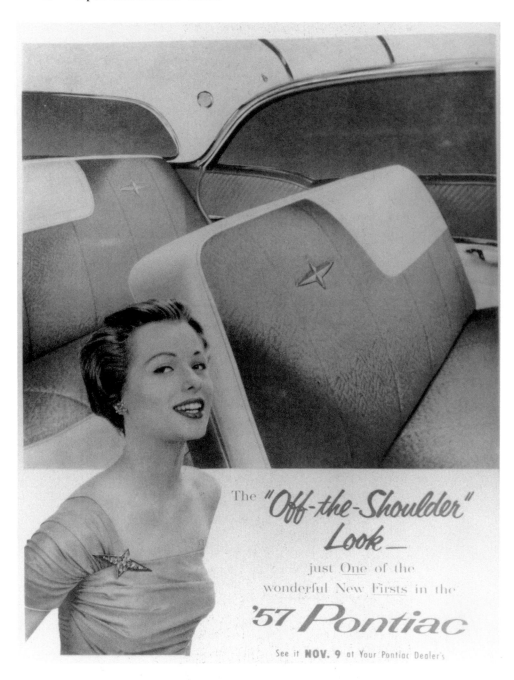

**Figure 2. Pontiac ad, 1956**
Courtesy Pontiac division

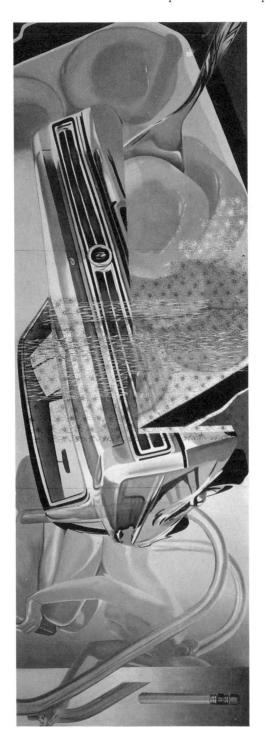

**Figure 3: James Rosenquist, *Lanai*, 1964**
Oil on canvas, 62″ × 186″
© 1989 James Rosenquist/VAGA New York
Courtesy Leo Castelli Gallery, New York
Photo: Rudolph Burkhardt

social meaning."[29] Lichtenstein's car contains a young couple—a clean-shaven man in a neat business suit and a blonde wearing a fur coat and large pearl earrings. Their attire and somewhat haughty expressions suggest an upwardly mobile, status-conscious couple whose car is no doubt a means of achieving as well as conveying their social and financial success. That they are going places, both literally and figuratively, is demonstrated by the horizontal lines that indicate movement and speed. The social implications of automobile ownership became an important element in marketing strategy, and *In the Car* addresses this issue.

Automotive styling and design are the focus of other Rosenquist paintings. *Pad* (1964; fig. 4) includes an angel food cake, a light bulb, an Air Force insignia, and the back end of a 1959 Cadillac. In emphasizing the tail end of the car, the most characteristic part of that model, Rosenquist has focused on a specific design element that perhaps best embodies the concepts and mechanisms of marketing strategies of the 1950s and 60s: the tail fin.

The tail fin was designed in the late 1940s by Harley Earl of General Motors to resemble the Lockheed P-38 Lightning, a fighter plane utilized during World War II. The tail fin was first introduced on the 1948 Cadillac but was not enthusiastically received until the early 1950s. Once it became associated with the Cadillac and therefore a "form of visible prestige marking for an expensive car," according to Earl himself, other manufacturers began to add tail fins to their cars.[30] By the late 1950s, the tail fin appeared in some form on virtually every new car in America. The pinnacle of this design element, which is seen by many automotive historians as *the* symbol of this era, was reached with the 1959 Cadillac, pictured by Rosenquist in *Pad*.

The tail fins themselves served no engineering function, although some models did have taillights in the fins. Rather, this element functioned as a sign of association with wealth and social standing because of its initial identification with the Cadillac. Pierre Martineau, director of research at the *Chicago Tribune*, pointed out that "the automobile tells who we are and what we think we want to be. . . . It is a portable symbol of our personality and our position . . . the clearest way we have of telling people of our exact position. [In buying a car] you are saying in a sense, 'I am looking for the car that expresses who I am.'"[31] Of all styling features, the tail fin became the automotive representation of those aspirations.

The popularity of the tail fin can also be attributed to the fascination of the American public with space exploration and aeronautics. The clearly visible derivation of the tail fin from the jet fighter reinforced the image of the automobile as an embodiment of speed and progressive technology. The national furor over the launching of Sputnik in 1957 and the rush to compete created a climate that encouraged the worship of what Chrysler Corporation

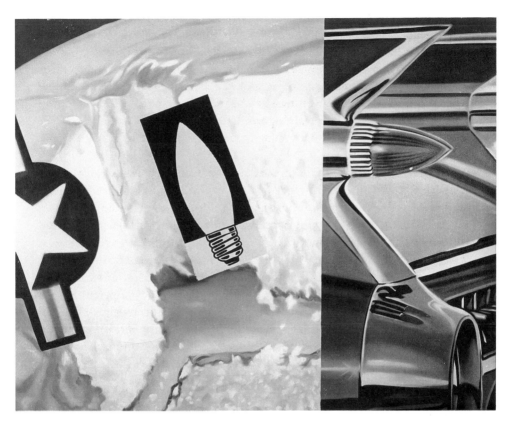

**Figure 4. James Rosenquist,** *Pad,* **1964**
Oil on canvas, 76″ × 62 1/4″
© 1989 James Rosenquist/VAGA New York
Courtesy Leo Castelli Gallery, New York
Photo: Rudolph Burkhardt

advertising termed "the new shape of motion."[32] Jets, rockets, and planes quickly became the sources for automotive design.

This public interest in space exploration that was exploited by automobile manufacturers was not solely the result of the symbolic qualities that were associated with such a scientific enterprise and that were embodied by such designs. Space exploration and its concomitant symbols were also attractive because they were being promoted in the early 1960s as part of the government's program to increase consumption through government expenditures. The interest in space, consumer culture, the incorporation of design elements derived from space technology, and the appearance of references to these design elements in Pop art are thus interrelated.

When Kennedy assumed the reins of office in 1960, he was faced with an increasingly dismal economic situation. In attempting to combat this recession within the guidelines of Keynesian principles, Kennedy searched for an acceptable channel for increased government expenditures. The space program provided such a vehicle. This program (specifically Projects Mercury, Gemini, and Apollo) had propaganda and military value in the aftermath of the Cold War and the so-called "crisis of national purpose." It also provided an ideal opportunity for extensive government spending that was acceptable to the various strata of American society. One economist welcomed the program because it "promises not only scientific knowledge and strategic import, [but] it will also ultimately pump some $40 billion into the economy."[33] Virtually all studies of the space program focus on its scientific or ideological function, and economics was not listed by the government advisory committee as one of the principal motivations for the program.[34] Given the domestic economic situation, however, the government was concerned about the impact such an undertaking would have on the economy. It was clear that a program of this scope would mean additional jobs, and Congress wholeheartedly supported appropriations for national defense and prestige that also provided a stimulus for the economy.[35] The space program, although not instituted for reasons that were primarily economic, was undoubtedly seen as a contributing factor to the stabilization of the economy through government expenditures.

Although the government supported the funding of space exploration, the public did not necessarily agree. Polls conducted after President Kennedy announced his plans for a lunar landing showed that 58 percent of the public opposed it.[36] Public acceptance of and support for the proposed space program became a goal of the Kennedy and later the Johnson administrations. The promotion of the space program that ensued is visualized by Robert Rauschenberg's painting for the 1964 New York World's Fair. Highly visible on the exterior of the New York State Pavilion, this large-scale (approximately 10' x 8'), collagelike painting includes a repeated photograph of Kennedy, gesturing forcefully while making a point. Surrounding Kennedy are various photographs silkscreened onto the canvas of astronauts floating in space, a space capsule floating in the ocean, and a diagram of a lunar landing. It would be difficult for those entering the pavilion, particularly Americans who had been inundated with media stories about the proposed space program, to avoid making the connections between these various images in Rauschenberg's painting.

The extensive promotion of the space program (of which one might consider Rauschenberg's painting part and parcel) by government officials and the prominence of press reports on the proposed program did generate wide-scale public interest.[37] Corporations, especially car manufacturers, were quick to capitalize on this interest and translated the space imagery into car design.

In *Pad*, Rosenquist's blatant focus on the tail fin element calls attention to these intersecting aspects. In addition, his juxtaposition of the tail fin with an Air Force emblem, as seen on jet fighters, points to the participation of the military in the construction of the consumer culture represented by the car in the 1960s. This interaction surfaced not only in terms of the actual economic ramifications but also in terms of the use of military symbols in the design of consumer goods—a use that ultimately buttressed both the ideology of consumption as well as the prevailing military ideology.

Like Kennedy, Lyndon Johnson searched for acceptable channels for increased government expenditures. Such a channel was provided by the Vietnam War, which was indisputably the major stimulus of the economic boom between 1964 and 1968.[38] This armed conflict was successful in generating economic activity for two reasons. First, according to economic historian David Horowitz, it was acceptable to wealthy capitalists and corporate executives. This group had long resisted the use of governmental funds (i.e., taxes) for socially useful investments, such as education, health, housing, culture, and recreation, since these goods and services were already available to them. Military expenditures, on the other hand, provided corporate interests not only with a virtually limitless market for their products but also with protection of such investments and markets.[39] The government feared that antagonizing these wealthy capitalists by greatly increasing the rate of socially motivated investments would likely have led to a decline in the profitability of further investment in private enterprise and therefore sought another alternative. The Keynesian solution to the stagnation and depression-bound system, concludes Horowitz, turned out to be not a welfare state, as liberal ideology proclaimed, but a warfare state.[40]

Second, the Vietnam War pulled the economy out of its lingering recession because of the vast demand for goods and services that it necessitated. Upon examining the difference between an economy based on military expenditures and a war economy, it becomes clear that simply increasing the defense budget would not have sufficed, or at least would not have had the dramatic impact that the Vietnam War did in sustaining the expansion of the American economy. In her study *America and the Crisis of World Capitalism*, Joyce Kolko notes that an economy based on military expenditures results in vertical spending—heavy on technology, high salaries for skilled scientists and engineers, and high profits for a few companies with defense contracts. In contrast, a war economy has a horizontal effect in that the types of goods and services required and the quantities needed are vastly multiplied. As a result, massive amounts of basic materials such as steel, textiles, and paper are essential.[41] In addition, demands for labor obviously rise, leading to a drop in unemployment. Statistics produced by the U.S. Department of Labor estimated that the escalation of the Vietnam War created more than one million jobs during the period of 1965–1967, which accounted for 23 percent of the total increase of more than four million jobs since 1965.[42]

A war economy would therefore be far more effective in stimulating an economy than a federal budget heavily weighted toward defense expenditures. This argument is supported by the fact that even before the sustained entrance into the Vietnam conflict, military spending dominated the federal budget, and yet recession was not averted.[43] Indeed, many critics of U.S. involvement in Vietnam charged that U.S. participation was primarily economically motivated. Noting that the war caused increased costs, labor demand, and prices, thereby increasing the GNP, Senator Stuart Symington asked Assistant Secretary of Defense Robert N. Anthony during a meeting of the Joint Economic Committee of the U.S. Congress: "Do you think this philosophy would justify . . . claims on the part of some people in this country as well as in other countries, that we are promoting a war economy to maintain economic stability?"[44] That both Congressional leaders and the military felt compelled to respond to such questions suggests that the claims carried some force, and ultimately, legitimacy.

The placement of the Air Force emblem, abstracted from a jet fighter, next to the tail fin in *Pad,* makes visible the connections between the military and consumer culture. The tail fin was just one of many design elements that was derived from military and space imagery. By utilizing such elements in the design of consumer goods, corporations reinforced the economic imperatives and ideological claims of military intervention. This corporate strategy was logical, since many of the companies most closely associated with consumer products (e.g., General Electric, Westinghouse, Goodyear, and Chrysler) were also major defense contractors.[45] Ads for Westinghouse defense hardware, for example, were often sandwiched in between ads for Westinghouse refrigerators or light bulbs, and in each case, the slogan was the same: "You can be sure if it's Westinghouse."[46] For this reason, Rosenquist's presentation of a light bulb next to the military emblem and tail fin is very appropriate, as the American public would have been likely to have seen such a juxtaposition during the 1960s in advertisements.

Through this intersecting web of governmental economic imperatives, military imperatives, space technology, and consumer products, the import and claims of each could be strengthened. Purchasing a car that had the sleek styling of a jet fighter or rocket, and which had been marketed as demonstrating taste and elegance, could serve to promote the military and space programs, even if only by contributing to the proliferation of military and space imagery. Conversely, support for military action in Vietnam or for an ex-panded space program would probably compel a consumer looking for a car to buy one such as the 1959 Cadillac that, through its design, could be seen as celebrating such programs of national interest.

The obsession during the late 1950s and 1960s with advanced aircraft de-sign translated into automotive styling is the subject of another Rosenquist painting, *Air Hammer* (1962; fig. 5). In this work, parts of two cars are jux-taposed, excerpted so as to give the viewer few clues as to the exact make and model of the cars. Both cars are white, on a softly modulated, light gray, ambiguous background, which serves to focus all attention on the styling details on the sides of the cars. The graceful curves of painted steel and chrome, like the tail fin, were characteristic elements of this era. Designers utilized the parabolic form as an abstraction of speed, and it became a familiar sight in countless variations on cars during this period. *Air Hammer* promi-nently displays this shape to the exclusion of other elements, thereby bringing visual concepts from automotive design into the realm of art.

Tom Wesselmann's incorporation of car imagery into his works, like Ro-senquist's, addresses the marketing strategies of the automobile industry. Un-like Rosenquist, however, Wesselmann focuses on a foreign car: the Volkswa-gen. The impact of this German-made car on American automotive thinking was immense, and perhaps more than most cars, the Volkswagen resonated with symbolic meaning.

By 1959, foreign cars comprised 10 percent of the American car market. Detroit's introduction of compact cars during the 1960s was in response to the popularity of cars like the Volkswagen Bug. In fact, by 1972 the Volkswa-gen was the second-best seller in history, and one historian pointed out that in contrast to the confusing proliferation of American cars, "Nobody has been able to *avoid* knowing what a Volkswagen is."[47] Automaker John De-Lorean explained what he termed the "mystique" of the Volkswagen: "The foreign-car buyer has an image of craftsmen in the Black Forest, building cars by hand."[48] This popularity was instrumental in altering the course of Ameri-can automotive history by forcing Detroit to follow Volkswagen's pattern.

The Volkswagen Bug and bus were also symbols of the rebellious youth culture of the 1960s. In its attempt to expand its market, the American auto-motive industry had targeted the youth market as a group of potential buyers and had undertaken extensive research in developing cars designed specifi-cally to appeal to this group.[49]

Despite the attendant publicity and advertising that accompanied the introduction of these cars, their sales were dismal. Rather, the car that be-came the symbol of the disaffected youth of the sixties was the Volkswagen (preferably decrepit). To many historians, the Volkswagen was a "precise

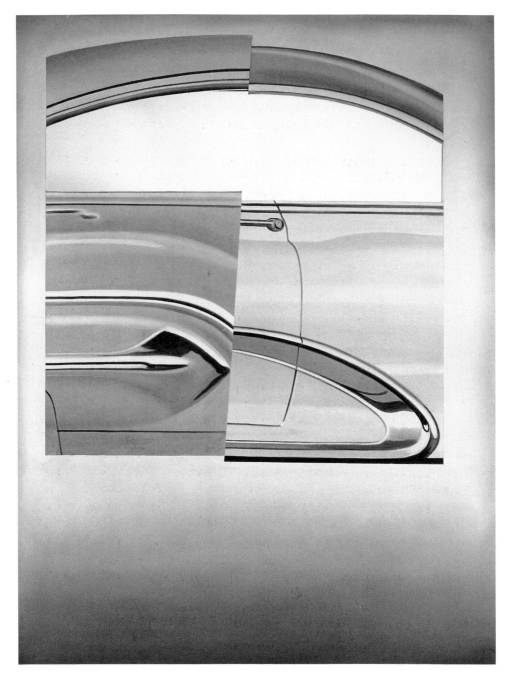

**Figure 5. James Rosenquist, *Air Hammer,* 1962**
Oil on canvas, 77 3/4" × 64 1/2"
© 1989 James Rosenquist/VAGA New York
Courtesy Leo Castelli Gallery, New York
Photo: Rudolph Burkhardt

metaphor for the changing market reality."[50] As a statement, the Volkswagen conveyed the disillusionment of the young generation with the "Establishment" and represented the antithesis of the corporate mentality. Its foreign origin and its low cost were probably also factors in its selection as a symbol of the rebellion against corporate America. Given the message underlying the popularity of the Volkswagen, Detroit's efforts were doomed from the start, originating as they did from the very mentality that was the object of youthful scorn.

Although the appearance of the Volkswagen in Wesselmann's works could possibly be interpreted as a reference to the rejection of the American corporate system that encouraged continual consumption, it also illustrates that ideologies, no matter how entrenched and established, cannot exist for extended periods of time without challenges; no ideology is completely hegemonic. As a symbol of the rebellious youth culture of the 1960s, the Volkswagen represented just such a challenge. What is interesting to note, however, is how quickly Detroit responded to such opposition and how rapidly Volkswagen (as a company) was assimilated into the corporate culture. In order to meet the demand for cars, Volkswagen opened factories in the United States and was soon structurally indistinguishable from the other automakers. Despite the symbolic and market challenges it presented, it was impossible for Volkswagen to remain outside the ongoing activity and established channels of consumer society, and its ultimate absorption into that matrix provides vivid illustration of the power and dominance of consumer culture.

The Volkswagen appears in a number of Tom Wesselmann's works: *Still Life #29* (1963; fig. 6), *Landscape #1* (1964; fig. 7), *Landscape #2* (1964; fig. 8), and *Landscape #5* (1965; fig. 9). Its presentation varies from fragments of the car (*Still Life #29* and *Landscape #1*) as in Rosenquist's images to full frontal (*Landscape #2*) or side views (*Landscape #5*). In each case, however, the automobile is clearly identifiable as a Volkswagen. Even in fragmented form, as in *Still Life #29*, the car is easily recognized. In *Landscape #1*, where the visual image is truncated so that only a small part of the car appears, Wesselmann has painted "VW 1963" on the license plate to ensure identification of the car. This recognition factor in Wesselmann's work addresses one of the reasons for the appeal of the Volkswagen to the youth group; due to its distinctive design, the Volkswagen could not be mistaken for any of the American-made cars.

Volkswagen emphasized this aspect in their promotional campaigns. In one ad campaign, the company asserted: "Our little car isn't so much of a novelty any more. . . . Nobody even stares at our shape." Wesselmann reiterates this singularity of design in his paintings by faithfully reproducing Volkswagen Beetles in all of his car paintings. Aside from this singularity of design,

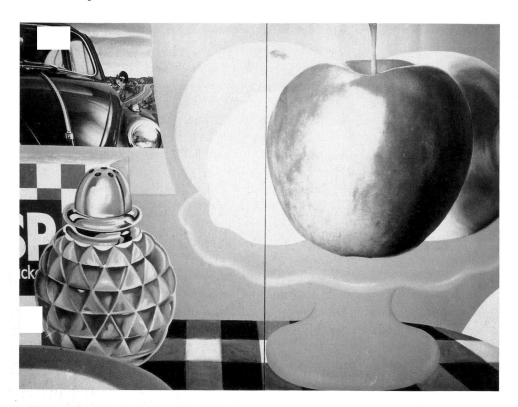

**Figure 6. Tom Wesselmann, *Still Life #29,* 1963**
Oil and collage on canvas, two sections, 108″ × 144″
© 1989 Tom Wesselmann/VAGA New York
Courtesy Sidney Janis Gallery, New York

more specific visual parallels between Volkswagen ads and Wesselmann's paintings are apparent. For example, the car in *Landscape #2,* depicted frontally, visually mimics the Volkswagen in the ad campaign "Why so many Volkswagens live to be 100,000," which advertised their 1966 model (fig. 10). Wesselmann's prescient depiction (the painting was produced in 1964, two years before the ad appeared) indicates his thorough grounding in and understanding of advertising techniques and strategies.

The Volkswagen in *Still Life #29,* although cropped, is virtually identical to the Volkswagen as it appeared in the company's "Lemon" ad campaign (fig. 11). The company designed this campaign to convey how carefully each car was inspected before it was allowed off the assembly line. The company missed no chance to emphasize its foreign roots; in the text underneath the

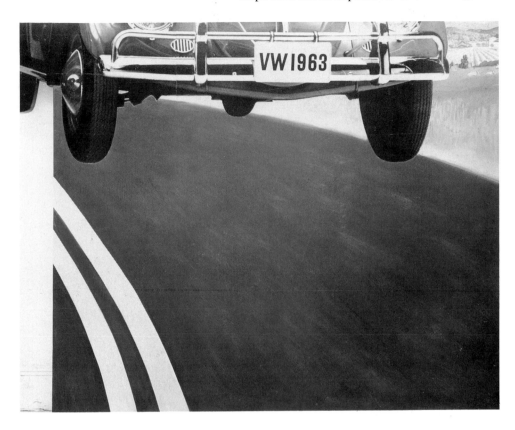

**Figure 7. Tom Wesselmann, *Landscape #1*, 1964**
Oil and collage on canvas, 72″ × 91″
© 1989 Tom Wesselmann/VAGA New York
Courtesy Sidney Janis Gallery, New York

photograph of the car, Volkswagen boasted that "VW inspectors run each car off the line onto the Funktionprüfstand (car test stand)."

Wesselmann's insistent images of Volkswagens do not in and of themselves make a strong, clear statement about disaffected youth in the 1960s or automotive marketing strategies. Visually, they neither affirm nor critique the dominant imperative to consume. They do call the viewer's attention to the complex marketing and ideological issues with which car manufacturers were grappling. The eventual presentation of these works through channels dominated by the corporate mentality negated any definitive critical reading of these works.

Other Pop artists turned to issues that exposed the less-attractive aspects

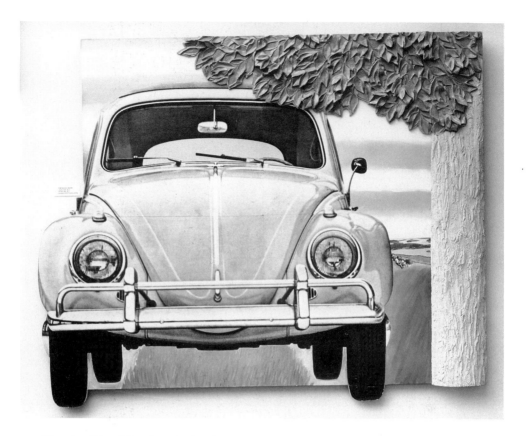

**Figure 8. Tom Wesselmann,** *Landscape #2,* **1964**
Oil, collage, and assemblage on canvas, 75 1/2″ × 94″ × 3″
© 1989 Tom Wesselmann/VAGA New York
Courtesy Museum Ludwig, Cologne

associated with increased use of automobiles, such as traffic congestion, parking problems, and accidents. Automobile manufacturers sought to minimize the danger and inconvenience of car ownership, and by focusing in their ads on the important psychosocial reasons for purchasing a car, they managed to counteract the all-too-grim reality. That these images surface in Pop art speaks to the constant potential for challenge to the imperative to consume.

In his series of silkscreened paintings of car crashes, Andy Warhol conveys the potentially horrendous result of car ownership. With ever-growing numbers of cars on the roads, the number of traffic accidents was rising correspondingly.

Warhol utilized graphic press photographs that he transferred photome-

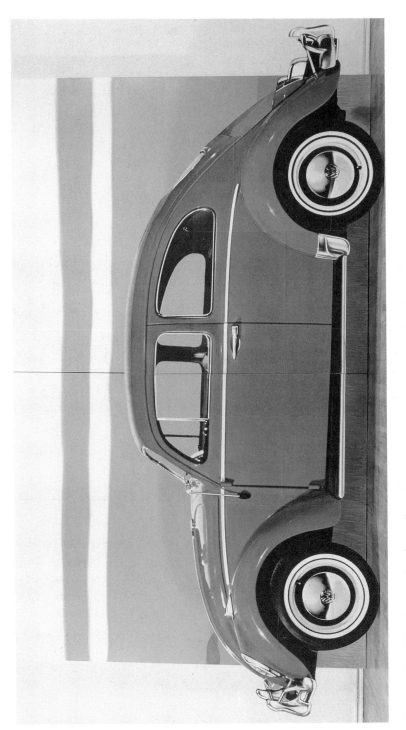

**Figure 9. Tom Wesselmann,** *Landscape #5,* **1965**
Oil, acrylic, and collage on canvas, two sections, one free-standing, 84″ × 144 1/2″ × 18″
© 1989 Tom Wesselmann/VAGA New York
Courtesy Sidney Janis Gallery, New York

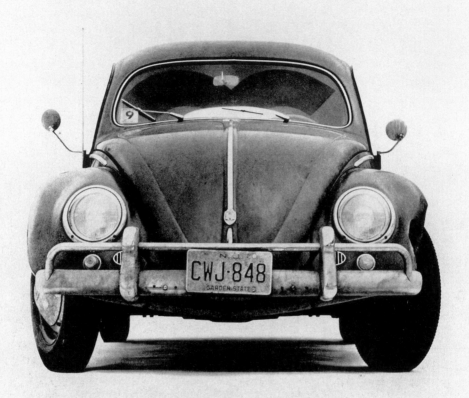

## Why so many Volkswagens live to be 100,000.

The Volkswagen isn't the kind of a car you trade in after a year or two.

It's designed and built for keeps.

The piston speed in a Volkswagen is slower than it is in many other cars. That means less wear. Engine friction and stress are so low that the VW's cruising speed is the same as top speed!

Continuity in making the same basic model year after year has led to Volkswagen's quality of assembly—the kind that a $5,000 car would be proud of; to say nothing of a car that sells for $1,585.*

Just to give you an idea: A Volkswagen is so airtight, it's a good practice to open the window before you slam the door. Even after

you've had it for several years.

So. If you own a '61 or '62 VW that you've taken good care of, why would you want to trade it in for a '66—which looks just like it?

You wouldn't.

You'd keep it, and have the pleasure of seeing 99,999 on your VW's odometer turn to 00000.

Figure 10. Volkswagen ad: "Why so many Volkswagens live to be 100,000"
© Volkswagen of America, Inc.
Courtesy Volkswagen of America, Inc.

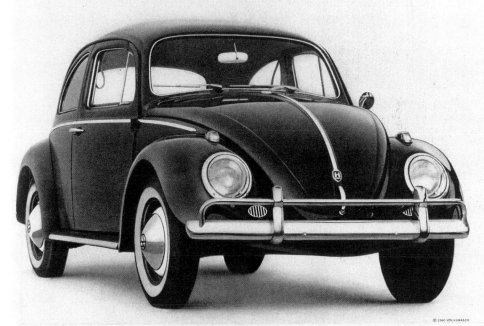

# Lemon.

This Volkswagen missed the boat.

The chrome strip on the glove compartment is blemished and must be replaced. Chances are you wouldn't have noticed it; Inspector Kurt Kroner did.

There are 3,389 men at our Wolfsburg factory with only one job: to inspect Volkswagens at each stage of production. (3000 Volkswagens are produced daily; there are more inspectors than cars.)

Every shock absorber is tested (spot checking won't do), every windshield is scanned. VWs have been rejected for surface scratches barely visible to the eye.

Final inspection is really something! VW inspectors run each car off the line onto the Funktionsprüfstand (car test stand), tote up 189 check points, gun ahead to the automatic brake stand, and say "no" to one VW out of fifty.

This preoccupation with detail means the VW lasts longer and requires less maintenance, by and large, than other cars. (It also means a used VW depreciates less than any other car.)

We pluck the lemons; you get the plums.

**Figure 11. Volkswagen ad: "Lemon"**
© Volkswagen of America, Inc.
Courtesy Volkswagen of America, Inc.

chanically, unchanged, to the silkscreen. Works such as *Green Disaster #2* (1963; fig. 12) and *Saturday Disaster* (1964; fig. 13) present grotesque images of smashed cars and limp, mangled bodies. The repetition of the grisly scenes both within single canvases and in series of paintings impresses upon the viewer the disturbing frequency of such tragic events as well as the extensive coverage these occurrences were accorded by the news media.[51] Public awareness of the potential dangers of automobile operation increased through such images and through publications such as Ralph Nader's *Unsafe At Any Speed* (1966). The National Traffic and Motor Vehicle Safety Act, which established a new federal agency to set safety performance standards, was passed in 1966, and the Department of Transportation was created as a cabinet-level organization during that same year.[52]

The unavoidable congestion that accompanied the masses of cars on the roads led to the launching of the Interstate Highway System in 1956, but by 1960 it was clear that the problem could not be so easily solved. Adequate parking was also a nagging concern, both for drivers and urban planners alike. Car-to-car contact, whether the result of bumper-to-bumper traffic, tight parking accommodations, or traffic accidents, was becoming a more frequent occurrence that had to be factored into planning by the car industry, city officials, and automobile owners. This aspect is the subject of James Rosenquist's *Car Touch* (1966; fig. 14). The work consists of two shaped canvases—the one on the left representing the front end of a Buick, the one on the right, the back end of a Cadillac. Rosenquist excludes any reference to locale and provides no other clues as to the context in which these cars exist. The canvas panels, however, are mounted on motors, which, when turned on, cause the panels to converge and separate, bringing the bumpers together—hence, the title. The limited visual information and the action of the two parts of the painting focuses attention on this act of convergence. Production of this work in 1966, concurrently with the passage of the National Traffic and Motor Vehicle Safety Act and the publication of Ralph Nader's book, along with the publicity that accompanied them, would prompt such an interpretation of this painting. Unlike the graphic, highly emotional images of Warhol's car crashes, Rosenquist presents similar issues in a visually abstracted manner, which makes the painting more ambivalent and perhaps even amusing.

Given the carefully orchestrated and incessant attempts by the American automobile industry to persuade consumers to purchase their products, the repeated appearance of cars in Pop art images is not surprising.[53] As a corpus, these images address many of the issues surrounding the marketing practices, attendant symbolism, and results of the expanding automobile culture. It can be argued that the blatant appropriation of both content and formal strate-

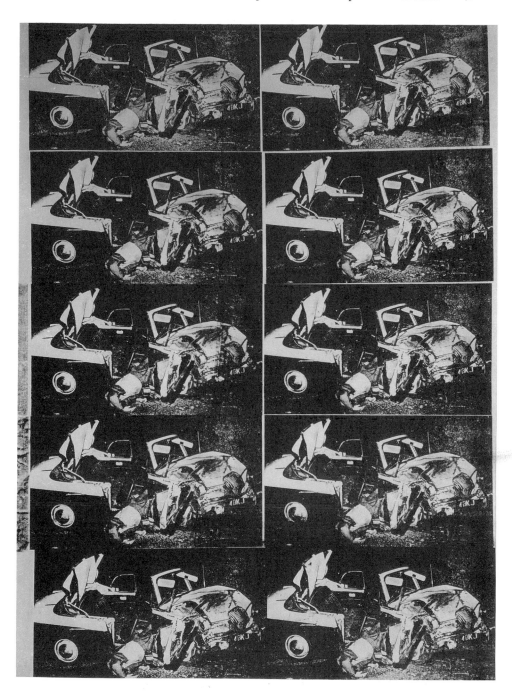

**Figure 12. Andy Warhol, *Green Disaster #2, 1963***
Silkscreen ink on synthetic polymer paint on canvas, 107 1/3″ × 79 1/8″
© 1990 The Estate and Foundation of Andy Warhol/ARS New York
Courtesy Leo Castelli Gallery, New York
Photo: Rudolph Burkhardt

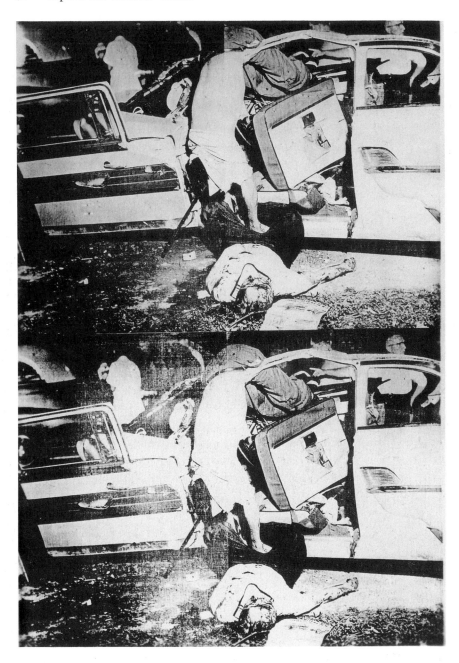

**Figure 13. Andy Warhol, *Saturday Disaster,* 1964**
Synthetic polymer paint and silkscreen enamel on canvas, 118 7/8″ × 81 7/8″
© 1990 The Estate and Foundation of Andy Warhol/ARS New York
Courtesy Rose Art Museum, Brandeis University, Waltham, Massachusetts; Gevirtz-Mnuchin
Purchase Fund, by exchange

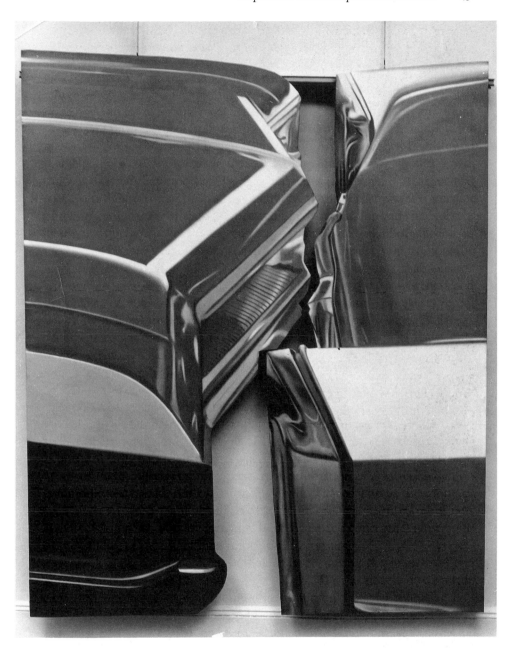

**Figure 14. James Rosenquist, *Car Touch*, 1966**
Oil on two motorized canvas panels, 88″ × 74″
© 1989 James Rosenquist/VAGA New York
Courtesy Leo Castelli Gallery, New York
Photo: Rudolph Burkhardt

gies from advertising efforts prompted viewers to read these art works as they did the ads themselves, rendering less plausible any interpretations of these art works as critical of consumer culture.

## PROCESSED FOODS

Like the automobile industry, the food and beverage industry spearheaded the expansion and maturation of American consumer culture. The accelerated pace of life that resulted from faster modes of transportation, telecommunication systems, and technological advances made the need for convenience foods acute. People no longer felt that they had the time to spend long hours shopping for fresh products, preparing and eating meals. Products and services that could be presented as timesaving were eagerly embraced.

The 1960s were years of great expansion in the field of processed foods. There were extraordinary increases in both the number of products available for purchase in supermarkets and the size of the companies that manufactured such products. Because of the profitability of the food-retailing business in the postwar years, grocery-store chains proliferated. These expanded to warehouse scale to accommodate the plethora of products; complained one industry insider: "Today's supermarket has become a stupormarket."[54] Appropriately, studies done in the late 1950s demonstrated that upon entering supermarkets, most shoppers descended into a hypnoidal trance, the first stage of hypnosis.[55]

The food companies themselves expanded as well. In an attempt to reduce costs, manufacturers diversified into farming to gain control over raw materials and into different processing fields.[56] The result was the development of huge food conglomerates. Statistics in 1963 revealed that of the 32,153 food manufacturing corporations, the 50 largest (.15 percent of the industry) controlled over half of the industry's assets and made 61 percent of the profits.[57]

So explosive was this growth of food firms and the bewildering array of products in the late 1950s and 1960s, that in 1964 Congress felt compelled to appoint a new agency, the National Commission on Food Marketing, to study the industry. The committee was charged with examining the directions in which the food industry was headed, in order to determine the effect on the individual consumer. Part of this effort involved the scrutiny of the balance of power and the nature of competition in the field. The commission concluded that this balance had indeed shifted noticeably toward the mammoth, aggressive food manufacturers and retail chains at the expense of the consumer.[58] Reported the commission: "When a few large firms dominate a field, they frequently forbear from competing actively by price; competition by advertising, sales promotion, and other selling efforts almost always increases; and the market power inescapably at the disposal of such firms may be used to impose onerous terms upon suppliers or consumers."[59]

The dizzying selection of prepared products on supermarket shelves was enticing to shoppers who saw the convenience offered as a valuable asset. Many were therefore willing to pay the higher prices that accompanied these goods, assuming they were getting new, improved products. However, the late 1950s and 1960s in the food industry, as in the automobile industry, represented a period of marketing emphasis rather than significant engineering or technological advances. The price increases that the consumers encountered in supermarkets were due to marketing costs rather than expenses related to product development.[60] In 1965, E. B. Weiss, a marketing expert who surveyed the industry, reported that "at least 80 percent of new products aren't new products at all. They are simply modifications—and minor modifications at that—of existing products."[61] Concern over this emphasis on packaging and presentation rather than product led Congress to enact the Fair Packaging and Labeling Act in 1966, which was intended to protect the American consumer from manipulative marketing practices.

Regardless, few people could resist the allure of the abundance and prosperity represented by the overflowing shelves in the grocery stores. Pop art, correspondingly, is replete with images of products from the supermarket environment. These works extract images from the world of canned, processed, mass-produced foods, and, on both the visual and conceptual levels, duplicate the advertising of these products.

Claes Oldenburg's *The Store* (1961; fig. 15) and Andy Warhol's various boxes (e.g., Mott's apple juice, Kellogg's corn flakes, Campbell's tomato juice, Brillo soap pads, Del Monte peach halves (1963; figs. 16 and 17) focus on the environment in which these products are found that visually promotes a consumptive mentality. Oldenburg's *The Store* (which has since been dispersed) was an environment of plaster reliefs and three-dimensional objects of food and clothing, which was described by art critic Barbara Rose in affirmative, positive terms, as: "friendly, colorful, open, full of the gratification of good things to eat and wear."[62] Displayed in a nongallery space specifically rented by Oldenburg for his own work, *The Store* bombarded the visitor with an avalanche of art objects as products.

Some of the objects were plaster forms painted with tempera, while others were plaster-coated chicken wire and muslin and were painted with commercial house-paint enamel. The roughly shaped, nonillusionistic objects, in contrast to the clarity and visual similarity (between product and art work) of Rosenquist's and Wesselmann's work, raise the issue of art as commodity.

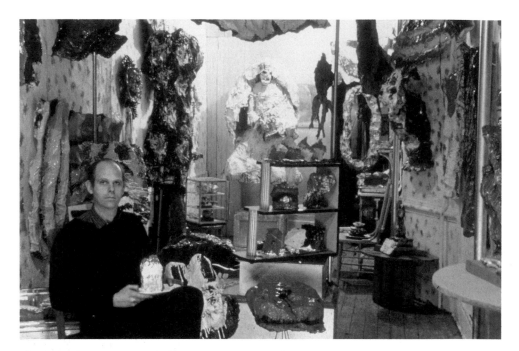

**Figure 15. Claes Oldenburg,** *The Store,* **1961**
Plaster-soaked muslin over wire frames, painted with enamel, various sizes
© Claes Oldenburg
Courtesy Claes Oldenburg
Photo: Robert R. McElroy

In making a formal distinction between the art works and the products that served as their inspiration, Oldenburg revealed "the true function of art in a materialistic society," since the works could not be mistaken for the original consumer products but had to be acknowledged as art for sale.[63] He extended this conceptualization by placing *The Store* under the direction of the "incorporated" Ray Gun Manufacturing Company. Oldenburg, identified on the official company stationery as the president of the firm, was also its only employee.[64] In going beyond the visual parameters of the art works and their exhibition, Oldenburg created a metaphor for the corporate structure and the process by which products are marketed.

As opposed to Oldenburg's clear visual distinction between food product and art, Andy Warhol's boxes blurred that distinction by coming as close as possible to the original cartons themselves. The boxes of Brillo soap pads, Del Monte peach halves, Kellogg's corn flakes, Campbell's tomato juice, and Mott's apple juice, exact replicas of the original boxes in size and design

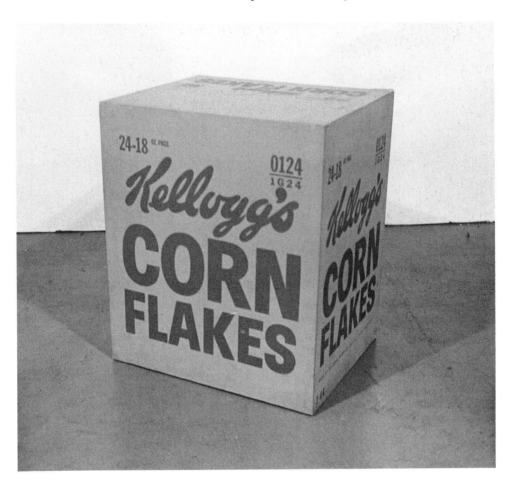

**Figure 16. Andy Warhol, *Kellogg's Box (Corn Flakes)*, 1964**
Silkscreen ink on wood, 27″ × 24″ × 19″
© 1990 The Estate and Foundation of Andy Warhol/ARS New York
Courtesy Leo Castelli Gallery, New York
Photo: Marianne Barcellona

format, visually duplicate the large cartons in which products must be shipped to meet the ever-growing demand for goods. The sole difference between the real supermarket cartons and Warhol's versions is that while the actual objects are constructed from cardboard, Warhol's are wooden, rendering them useless as shipping cartons.[65]

Warhol further encouraged this blurring of the lines between food product and art object by displaying the boxes in a manner reminiscent of grocery

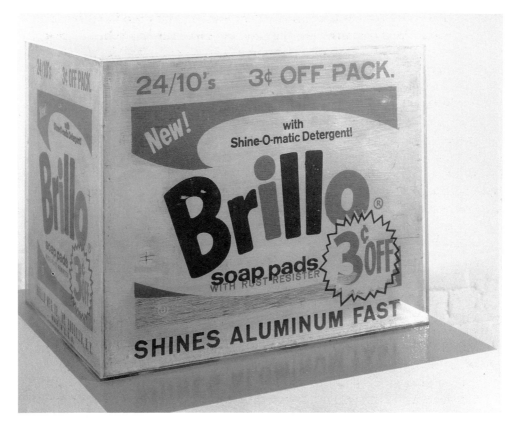

**Figure 17. Andy Warhol,** *Brillo Box (Soap Pads),* **1964**
Silkscreen ink on wood, 17 1/8″ × 17 1/8″ × 14″
© 1990 The Estate and Foundation of Andy Warhol/ARS New York
Courtesy Leo Castelli Gallery, New York
Photo: Dorothy Zeidman

warehouses. Shown at the Dwan Gallery in Los Angeles in February 1964 and at the Stable Gallery in New York in April 1964, the boxes were densely stacked throughout the galleries, making movement through the exhibition difficult. The responses to this display reveal that the analogy to a stockroom was forcefully made. One observer asked: "Is this an art gallery or Gristede's warehouse?"[66] Critic Sidney Tillim described the Stable exhibit as "a very neat warehouse,"[67] and critic Lawrence Campbell compared it to "the storage room of an A & P."[68] Dealer Eleanor Ward described a woman who "came in . . . took one look, and ran out . . . screaming. She said that it reminded her of her mother's grocery store."[69]

Other Pop art works focused on the various foods produced by the monolithic food corporations. The products of certain companies appear with great regularity in Pop art, among others, those of Del Monte, Coca-Cola, Pepsi-Cola, and Campbell Soup. The inclusion of the goods of these specific corporations in Pop art works was due to their predominance in the consumer environment and, more specifically, to extensive ad campaigns that were waged in the early 1960s. The same fifty oligopolistic food companies that controlled the market, among which Del Monte, Coca-Cola, Pepsi-Cola, and Campbell Soup ranked very high, accounted for more than 80 percent of advertising in all media, and 90 percent of food advertising on television.[70] This statistic simply reiterates the important role that advertising played in determining market control. Artists such as Tom Wesselmann wrote directly to advertising agencies and requested material for use in their work, revealing a very concrete link between the high-intensity advertising efforts and Pop art. A closer examination of these specific corporations and the depiction of their products in Pop art works reveals further the intersection between this art movement and consumer culture.

Del Monte, the largest processor of fruits and vegetables in the world, was quick to realize that expanding into related areas of farming, transportation, and distribution and storage was extremely profitable. By the beginning of the 1970s, the chairman of Del Monte Corporation could boast: "We literally begin with the seed and end at the grocer's shelf."[71] This expansion was accompanied by massive advertising campaigns. In its advertising, Del Monte impressed upon the consumer its vast and ever-expanding array of products by claiming that it met your needs "from womb to tomb."[72] Del Monte also assured the supermarket executives of the effectiveness of this advertising: "Del Monte advertising was designed to make a shambles of your displays. Night after night we talk to your customers—we reach 9 out of 10 households on NBC and CBS TV networks during prime time plus local TV in the top 20 markets."[73]

In works such as *Still Life #14* (1962; fig. 18), *Still Life #19* (1962; fig. 19), and *Still Life #24* (1962; fig. 20), Tom Wesselmann alludes to the pervasiveness of Del Monte imagery in the urban environment. In each painting, a can or bottle of a Del Monte product appears prominently, with its logo clearly legible and recognizable. The actual food product is never shown, for Del Monte, in its ads, was aiming for immediate recognizability of its package on the supermarket shelves. In like manner, all that is visible in *Still Life #19* are the Del Monte logos on the bottle and can, suggesting that the brand name was all one needed to know in making a purchasing decision.

In each image, Wesselmann also juxtaposes the canned goods and the

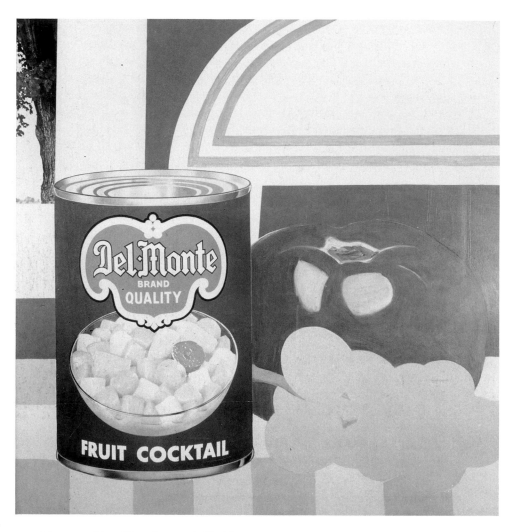

**Figure 18. Tom Wesselmann, *Still Life #14,* 1962**
Acrylic and collage on board, 48″ × 48″
© 1989 Tom Wesselmann/VAGA New York
Courtesy Sidney Janis Gallery, New York

convenience they represent with fresh fruits and vegetables—an ear of corn, a banana, a tomato, grapes, apples, and a melon. In *Still Life #14,* for example, the flat, unmodulated depiction of the tomato and grapes contrasts sharply with the crisply delineated edges of the fruit cocktail label. This causes the fresh fruits to flatten out and visually recede into the background, rendering the can as the focus of attention, suggesting a greater corporeality and a

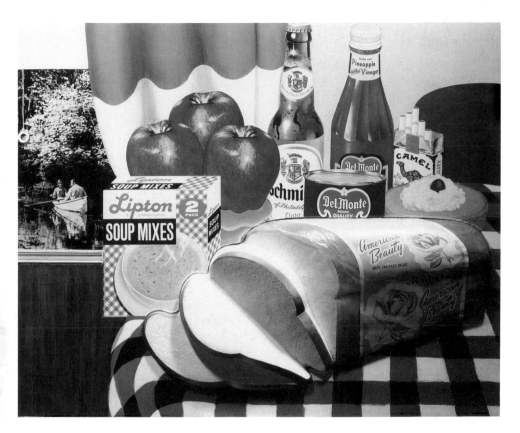

**Figure 19. Tom Wesselmann, *Still Life #19*, 1962**
Mixed media and collage on board, 48″ × 60″ × 5″
© 1989 Tom Wesselmann/VAGA New York
Courtesy Sidney Janis Gallery, New York
Photo: Eric Pollitzer

heightened taste experience as well. This was precisely the kind of thinking encouraged by Del Monte.

Andy Warhol also painted an image of a Del Monte can (*Peach Halves*) in 1960 (fig. 21). Revealing the influence of Abstract Expressionism, the ostensibly incomplete painting consists of a single can with an unfinished label accompanied by dripping pigment. Despite the lack of an identifiable context or background, and the inchoate nature of the label itself, the image retains its immediate recognizability, a quality vital to the success of any mass-marketed product.

This depiction of a solitary can belies the mass quantities of these cans that flooded the market. This issue was addressed by Warhol's wooden car-

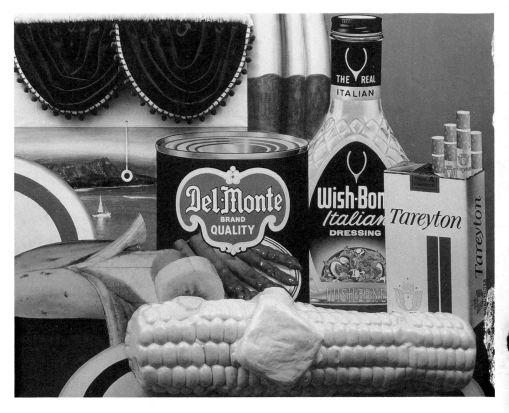

**Figure 20. Tom Wesselmann,** *Still Life #24,* **1962**
Mixed media, collage, and assemblage on board, 48″ × 60″ × 6 3/4″
© 1989 Tom Wesselmann/VAGA New York
Courtesy Sidney Janis Gallery, New York
Photo: Rudolph Burkhardt

tons, some of which are replicas of boxes of Del Monte's peach halves. As previously discussed, these sculptural objects gave form to the infinite availability of these products. In his various works, Warhol presents different facets of the production and marketing processes.

Like Del Monte, Coca-Cola and Pepsi-Cola were involved in extensive marketing efforts in the 1960s. This was the result of fierce competition for the lucrative soft-drink market—in 1960 alone, the American public spent close to $2 billion for cola drinks.[74] Between them, Coca-Cola and Pepsi-Cola controlled 85 percent of this market, yet they were engaged in a "worldwide war" in the early 1960s.[75] While Coca-Cola had always been dominant, the crucial nature of their advertising campaign during this period is revealed by

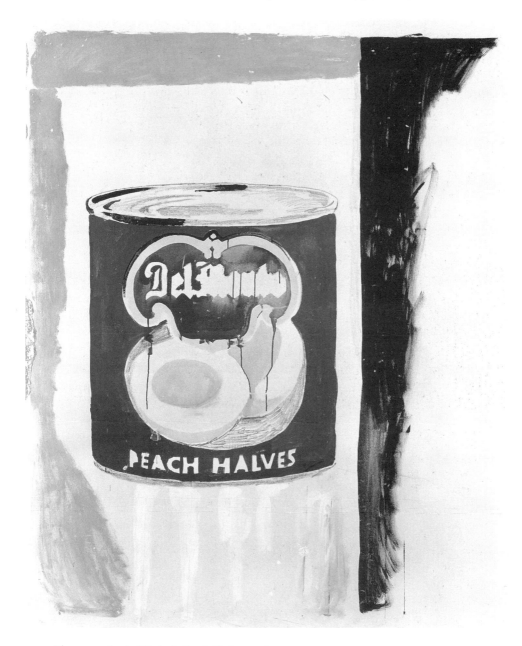

**Figure 21.** Andy Warhol, *Peach Halves*, 1960
Synthetic polymer paint on canvas, 70″ × 54″
© 1990 The Estate and Foundation of Andy Warhol/ARS New York
Courtesy Staatsgalerie Stuttgart

their slogan introduced in 1960: "No wonder Coke refreshes best." This marked the first time in over a generation that any of Coca-Cola's ads contained either a comparative or superlative, a clear reference to the present competition.[76]

In 1961, Coca-Cola poured $50 million into their advertising campaign, while Pepsi spent about $34 million.[77] Warhol refers to the omnipresence of these ads in *Close Cover Before Striking (Coca-Cola)* (1962; fig. 22) and *Close Cover Before Striking (Pepsi-Cola)* (1962; fig. 23). That these works are identical in format except for the slogans and logos and were produced by the same company (the American Match Company) suggests the parity between these two firms, which were literally going head-to-head over the beverage market. The focus in each image is the distinctive logo, and no mention is made of the qualities that made each drink desirable. The manufacturers were mainly concerned with name recognizability and with keeping their product in the public eye.

Although these two soft-drink companies, like most large corporations, advertised through a variety of media, including TV, radio, and the print media, Warhol chose as his subject possibly the most popular form of advertising: matchbooks. These matchbooks were distributed to franchised bottlers to be used as promotional advertising and were then distributed to customers in appreciation for their business. The matchbooks were given out to the public by the thousands through drugstore soda fountains, restaurants, and grocery stores as well. Matchbooks were considered exceptional advertising tools because they were so cost efficient—in other words, the cost-to-effect ratio was among the highest of all the forms of advertising.[78]

The degree of success that was attained through these promotional tools is reflected in the general consensus that as a result of their advertising and marketing efforts, Coke has become the most widely recognized commercial product and the best-known trademark in the world.[79]

Warhol's seemingly innocuous images of matchbook covers are therefore very incisive, referring not only to the historically specific competition being waged by these two beverage conglomerates but also to their marketing strategies. This historical situation undoubtedly accounts for the fact that images of Coca-Cola and Pepsi-Cola appear with more regularity than almost any other image in Pop art. In addition to Warhol's paintings of matchbook covers, these products surface in the work of Robert Rauschenberg, Jasper Johns, Tom Wesselmann, and James Rosenquist, as well as George Segal, Edward Kienholz, H. C. Westermann, Marisol, Mel Ramos, Charles Frazier, and Anthony Berlant, other artists associated with the Pop movement.

Many of these images display the incontestable ubiquity of these beverages. Wesselmann's *Great American Nude #39* (1962; fig. 24), *Great American*

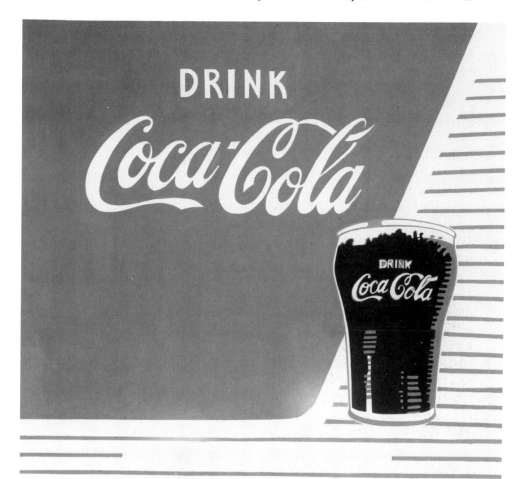

**Figure 22. Andy Warhol,** *Close Cover Before Striking (Coca-Cola),* 1962
Synthetic polymer paint and sandpaper on canvas, 72″ × 54″
© 1990 The Estate and Foundation of Andy Warhol/ARS New York
Courtesy Leo Castelli Gallery, New York
Photo: Geoffrey Clements Inc.

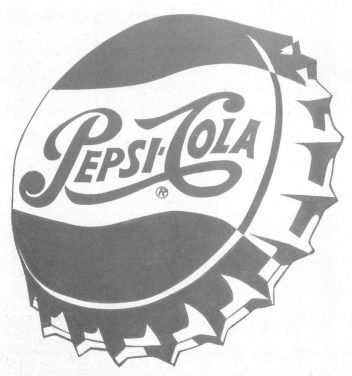

**Figure 23. Andy Warhol,** *Close Cover Before Striking (Pepsi-Cola),* 1962
Synthetic polymer paint and sandpaper on canvas, 72″ × 54″
© 1990 The Estate and Foundation of Andy Warhol/ARS New York
Courtesy Museum Ludwig, Cologne

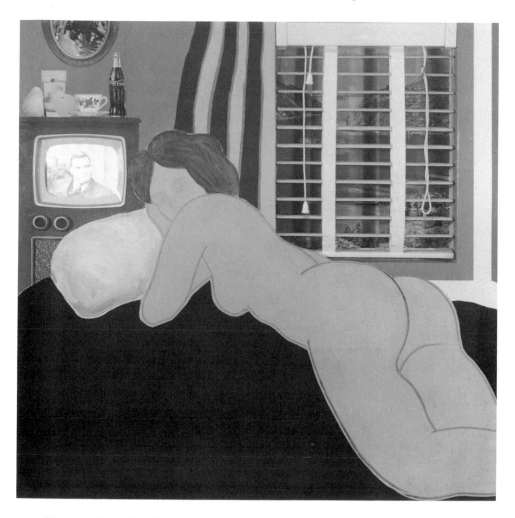

**Figure 24. Tom Wesselmann,** *Great American Nude #39,* **1962**
Charcoal, acrylic, enamel, collage, and assemblage on board, 48″ × 48″ × 2″
© 1989 Tom Wesselmann/VAGA New York
Courtesy Sidney Janis Gallery, New York

*Nude # 40* (1962), *Still Life #20* (1962; fig. 25), and *Still Life #34* (1963; fig. 26) present Coca-Cola bottles and glasses amidst various fruit, flowers, liquor, and food, as a common presence in the standard American household. Wesselman addresses the general theme of "things that are consumed" from food to art to women, and Coke is simply one such product.

Warhol's *Green Coca-Cola Bottles* (1962; fig. 27) and *Coca-Cola Bottles* (1962; fig. 28) illustrate the standardization and mass production of consumer

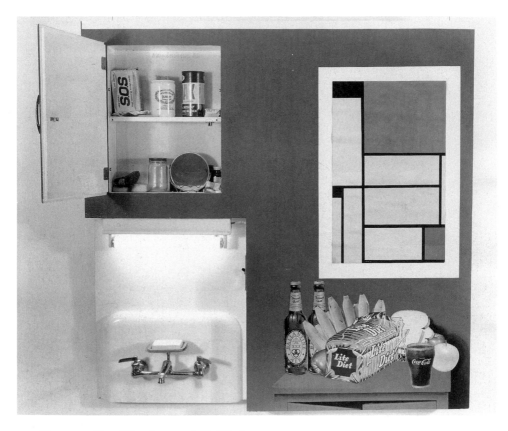

**Figure 25. Tom Wesselmann, *Still Life #20,* 1962**
Mixed media, 48″ × 48″ × 5 1/2″
© 1989 Tom Wesselmann/VAGA New York
Courtesy Albright-Knox Art Gallery, Buffalo, New York; gift of Seymour H. Knox, 1962
Photo: Runco Photo Studios

goods such as Coca-Cola through sterile repetition of the image. In monotonous rows, Warhol depicts the bottles much as they would be found on a supermarket shelf or at the factory. The inclusion of the company's logo in a bright, contrasting color at the bottom of some of the paintings, or the clear rendering of the "Trademark Registered" designation calls attention to the specific product and company identification.

Jasper Johns refers directly to the advertisements in his untitled work of 1963. Rather than simply include the logo or trademark, Johns has utilized the slogan "Coca-Cola refreshes you best"—the comparative theme that was launched in the early 1960s to counter the growing popularity of Pepsi-Cola. The bright red color of the Coke sign contrasts sharply with the relatively

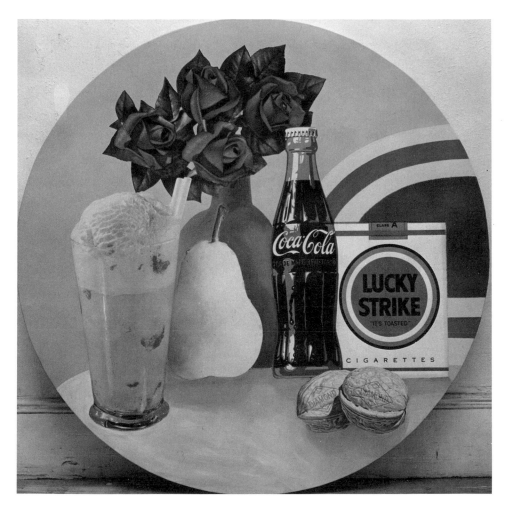

**Figure 26. Tom Wesselmann,** *Still Life #34,* **1963**
Acrylic and collage on board, 48″ diameter
© 1989 Tom Wesselmann/VAGA New York
Courtesy Sidney Janis Gallery, New York
Photo: Eric Pollitzer

empty canvas surrounding it, formally linking the painting to advertising, the goal of which was to set a specific visual image or message apart from the avalanche of advertising with which the public was confronted. By 1968, studies revealed that 84 percent of ads went unnoticed and of the remaining 16 percent, many were considered merely irritating.[80] Against these kinds of odds, corporations were hard-pressed to produce ads that would be remem-

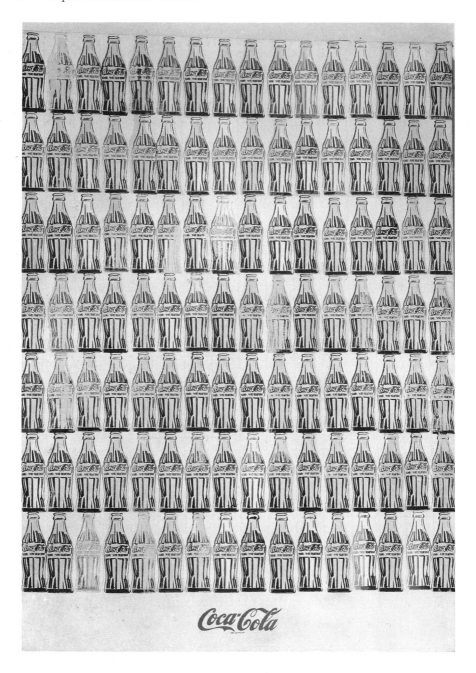

**Figure 27. Andy Warhol, *Green Coca-Cola Bottles,* 1962**
Oil on canvas, 82 1/4″ × 57″
© 1990 The Estate and Foundation of Andy Warhol/ARS New York
Courtesy Leo Castelli Gallery, New York
Photo: Rudolph Burkhardt

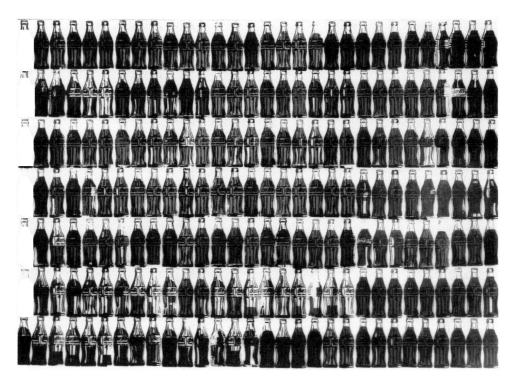

**Figure 28. Andy Warhol,** *Coca-Cola Bottles,* **1962**
Silkscreen ink on synthetic polymer paint on canvas, 82 1/2″ × 105″
© 1990 The Estate and Foundation of Andy Warhol/ARS New York
Courtesy Leo Castelli Gallery, New York

bered by consumers. The visual and thematic impact presented by Johns in his painting parallels Coca-Cola's marketing strategy, which accounted for much of its success.

James Rosenquist also alludes to this immediate recognizability in *Vestigial Appendage* (1962; fig. 29). As in many of his other paintings, *Vestigial Appendage* consists of abbreviated segments of objects and scenes that ostensibly have little relationship to each other. In this particular image, the only clearly legible passage is the fragment of the bottle cap, which, although incomplete, is identifiable as a Pepsi-Cola product. This painting, like the urban environment, bombards the viewer with a myriad of visual images, often fragmentary or momentary, from which selective ones are retained.

The immediate recognizability of the Pepsi-Cola logo is formally challenged by Claes Oldenburg's *Pepsi-Cola Sign* (1961; fig. 30). The unclear application of pigment drips down the rough, textured muslin that covers the

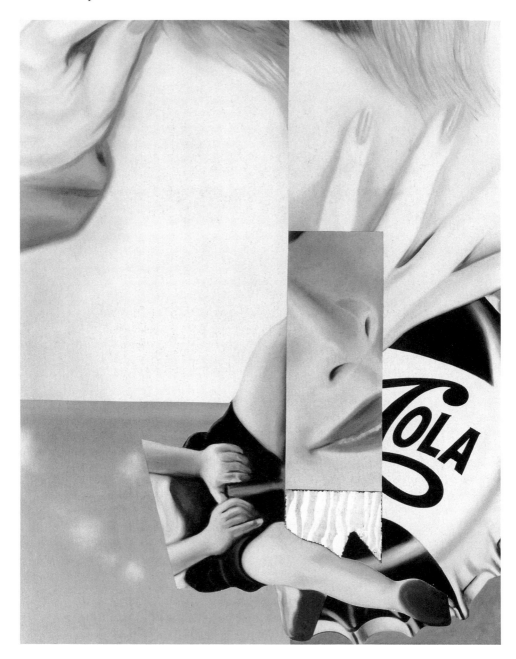

**Figure 29. James Rosenquist,** *Vestigial Appendage,* **1962**
Oil on canvas, 72″ × 93 1/4″
© 1989 James Rosenquist/VAGA New York
Courtesy The Museum of Contemporary Art, Los Angeles: The Panza Collection
Photo: Squidds & Nunns

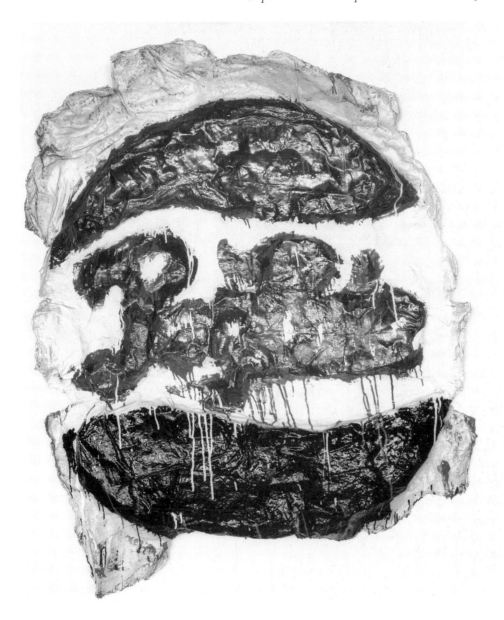

**Figure 30. Claes Oldenburg,** *Pepsi-Cola Sign,* 1961
Plaster-soaked muslin, 58 1/4″ × 46 1/2″ × 7 1/2″
© Claes Oldenburg
Courtesy The Museum of Contemporary Art, Los Angeles: The Panza Collection
Photo: Squidds & Nunns

amorphously shaped wire surface of the sculpture. Yet there is no doubt as to the intended representation. The indistinct lettering does not prevent an identification of the object as the Pepsi-Cola emblem.

Rather than refer to the ubiquity of these soft drinks or their advertisements, Robert Rauschenberg utilizes the actual product in his works, many of which are referred to as combines because they incorporate both painting and sculpture. Two 1958 works, *Curfew* (fig. 31) and *Coca-Cola Plan* (fig. 32) both include empty Coke bottles. In *Curfew,* various seemingly unrelated areas intersect on the canvas, most of which are presented in the painterly, impastoed style of the Abstract Expressionists. Despite the incorporation of photographic images, the only clearly identifiable passage in the painting is the sequence of four Coke bottles, placed on a ledge cut into the upper left-hand corner of the canvas. For this reason, they become the focal point of the work.

In *Coca-Cola Plan* as well, the Coke bottles occupy a predominant position in the work. Placed at the exact center of the piece, they serve as the stabilizing center of the wooden orb below, the construction diagram above, and the wings protruding from each side. The visual images in both *Coca-Cola Plan* and *Curfew* are, in and of themselves, ambiguous in conveying a statement about the soft drink, and the selected titles do not shed any additional light on the matter. This ambiguity was removed, however, when Rauschenberg's work was exhibited at the XXXII Venice Biennale in 1964.

A number of works by Rauschenberg exhibited at the Biennale incorporated Coca-Cola motifs, including *Curfew* and *Buffalo II* (1964; fig. 33). Like *Curfew* and *Coca-Cola Plan, Buffalo II* presents a compendium of disparate images, which, while recognizable, do not combine to reveal any obvious, coherent statement or message.

The American contingent lobbied heavily for Rauschenberg to win the grand prize, which suggests that they saw his art both as an example of the advanced nature of American art and as a suitable ambassador of American culture. Because of the inclusion of patriotic symbols of America, such as the photograph of Kennedy and the bald eagle, along with such institutions as Coca-Cola, *Buffalo II* could be interpreted as a celebration of American culture. *Coca-Cola Plan* can be read in a similarly celebratory way, with its wings reminiscent of those of the Nike of Samothrace, surely a preeminent monument in the history of art. As the Nike of Samothrace represents the apogee of an entire culture, so too could Coca-Cola be considered the legacy of American culture.

After much behind-the-scene politicking, Rauschenberg was awarded the grand prize, the first time in the history of the Biennale that it had gone to an American. While the government, through its commissioner and other

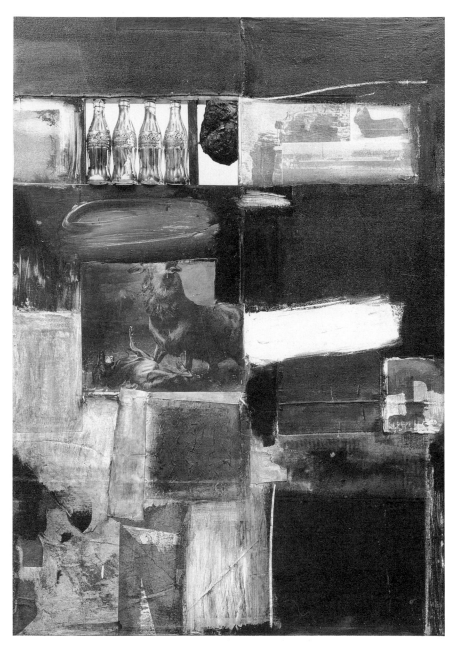

**Figure 31. Robert Rauschenberg,** *Curfew,* **1958**
Oil, paper, fabric on canvas and wood, four Coca-Cola bottles, one bottle cap,
56 1/2″ × 39 1/2″ × 2 5/8″
© 1989 Robert Rauschenberg/VAGA New York
Courtesy Leo Castelli Gallery, New York
Photo: Rudolph Burkhardt

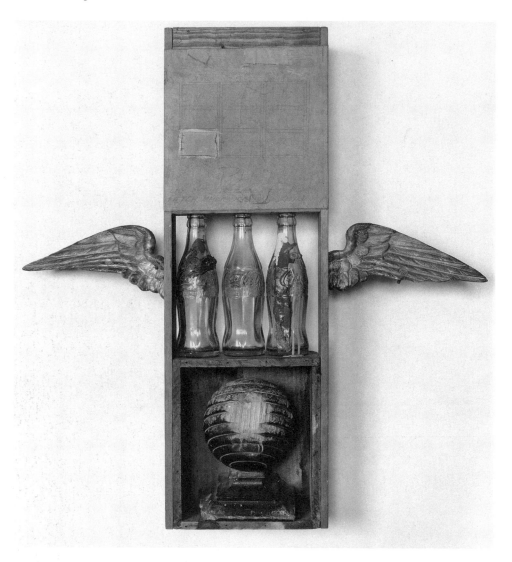

**Figure 32. Robert Rauschenberg, *Coca-Cola Plan*, 1958**
Combine painting, 26 3/4″ × 25 1/4″ × 4 3/4″
© 1989 Robert Rauschenberg/VAGA New York
Courtesy The Museum of Contemporary Art, Los Angeles: The Panza Collection
Photo: Squidds & Nunns

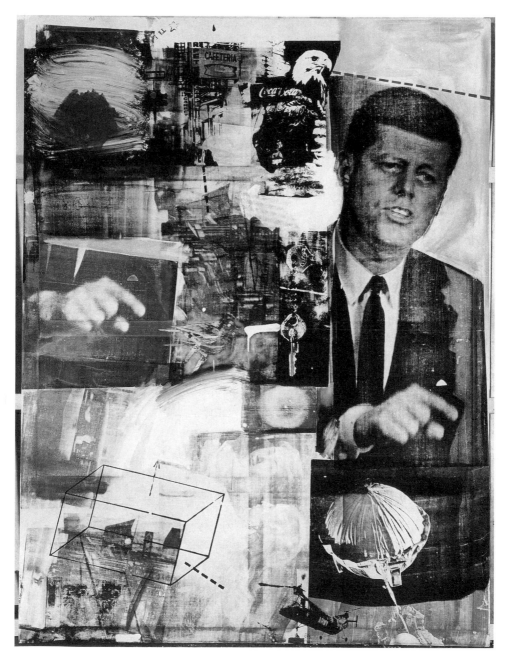

**Figure 33. Robert Rauschenberg, *Buffalo II,* 1964**
Oil on canvas, 96″ × 72″
© 1989 Robert Rauschenberg/VAGA New York
Courtesy Leo Castelli Gallery, New York
Photo: Rudolph Burkhardt

representatives, saw Rauschenberg's work as embodying a positive American spirit, others were not so enthusiastic. The repeated inclusion of references to Coca-Cola and other American products encouraged links between American economic imperialism, represented by the expansion of multinational corporations, and a cultural imperialism now signalled by Rauschenberg's victory. These references also prompted responses that were directed not necessarily at the works themselves but at an American foreign policy, the aim of which was the protection of the investments of its multinational corporations such as Coca-Cola. One such Biennale critic objected: "We [Europeans] are now [in the eyes of the Americans] nothing but poor backward Negroes, good only for being colonized. The first drive is on the spot: it is called Pop Art."[81] Comments such as this demonstrate that even in the international arena these works were read as propaganda for the American way of life, most vividly represented by the consumer ethic. Thus, in the context of the Venice Biennale, Rauschenberg's victory, in light of his incorporation of Coca-Cola and other images of consumer culture into his art, was seen by many as a triumph not just of American art but of the American economic system as well.

Another monolithic corporation that was the subject of Pop art paintings was the Campbell Soup Company. This company, like Del Monte, Coca-Cola, and Pepsi-Cola, dominated its field. In 1961, Campbell Soup Company accounted for close to 85 percent of annual national soup sales.[82] To counter a strong challenge from other soup manufacturers, Campbell Soup undertook a massive advertising campaign in 1961 aimed at cornering the nascent dry soup-mix business. *Dun's Review and Modern Industry,* a journal of business and economics, announced in a feature article that Campbell Soup Company was launching "one of the hottest marketing battles yet to sweep through the already fiercely competitive food industry."[83]

Perhaps the best known of the images of Campbell's soup are the numerous paintings by Andy Warhol. *100 Cans* (1962; fig. 34), among others, invokes the same concepts illustrated by his paintings of Coca-Cola bottles. The neatly stacked cans and redundant labels evoke images of supermarket shelves, and the monotonous repetition suggests the undeviating predictability of the cans' contents.

Wesselmann's *Still Life #32* (1963; fig. 35) presents a pasted-on image of a Campbell's tomato soup can, which starkly contrasts with the rather amorphous shapes of the lemon, orange, and grapes that lie beside it. Using the collage technique, the tangible reality of the advertising image is made all the more striking in juxtaposition to the painted elements in the work.

The actual market battle being waged by Campbell Soup Company at this time is represented by the inclusion of a box of Lipton soup mix in

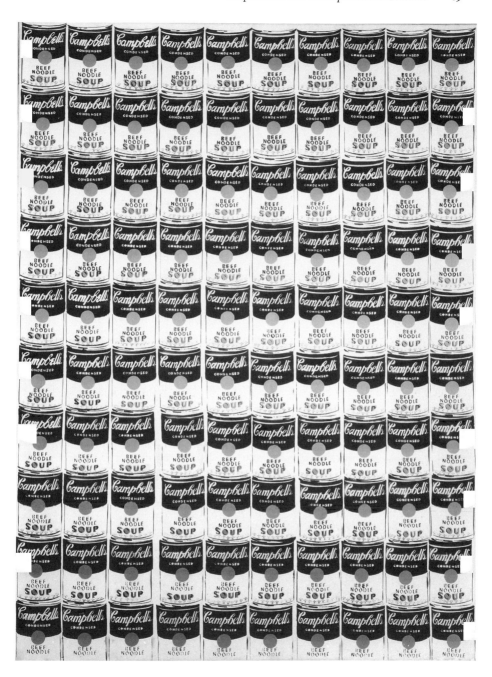

**Figure 34. Andy Warhol,** *100 Cans,* **1962**
Oil on canvas, 72″ × 52″
© 1990 The Estate and Foundation of Andy Warhol/ARS New York
Courtesy Albright-Knox Art Gallery, Buffalo, New York; gift of Seymour H. Knox, 1963

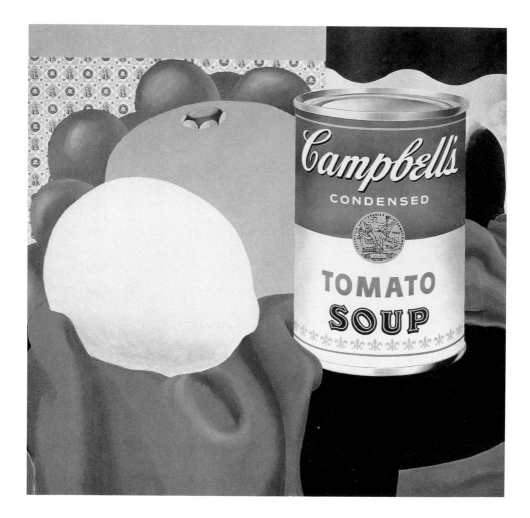

**Figure 35. Tom Wesselmann, *Still Life #32*, 1963**
Acrylic and collage on board, 48″ × 48″
© 1989 Tom Wesselmann/VAGA New York
Courtesy Sidney Janis Gallery, New York
Photo: Rudolph Burkhardt

another one of Wesselmann's works, *Still Life #19* (1962; fig. 19). Lipton dry soup mix had been Campbell Soup Company's major competition, and when Campbell's issued their onslaught of advertising in the early 1960s, Lipton, accordingly, followed suit. Campbell Soup Company invested millions of dollars in the attempt. Their ultimate failure forced them in 1967 to raise the price of their canned soup in order to absorb the losses in the dry-soup-mix division.[84]

As in his other works, Wesselmann utilizes the actual ad, which he carefully attaches to the canvas. In its cheerful domesticity—the consumer items appear grouped on a checkered tablecloth in front of a window with curtains—there is nothing in the visual image that implies a critique of either the manufacturers or the advertisers. In fact, Wesselmann denies any underlying rationale for the selection of specific images. He stated: "Advertising images excite me mainly because of what I can make from them. Also I use real objects because I need to use objects, not because objects need to be used."[85] Despite this disavowal of conscious intent, his use of advertising images directly obtained from advertising agencies links this work inextricably to the historical developments in the industry during this period. It is more than coincidence that Campbell's soup appears in canned form in Pop art while Lipton soup mix appears in boxes. This fact, regardless of how intentional it was on the part of the artists, undoubtedly affected public reception of such an art form.

In its consistent and, indeed, insistent references to images and strategies that had a demonstrable immediacy in the 1960s, Pop art called attention to the rapidly maturing consumer ethic. Although these images of cars and consumer products cannot be considered blatant celebrations of consumptive practices, the reception of Pop art reveals that for the most part they were interpreted as such. That fact aside, the significant point is that Pop art actively entered into the discourse established by consumer culture. The incisive marketing of the Pop movement ensured its success and was a catalyst for the commodification of art. In this manner, Pop art capitalized on the immediacy and recognizability of the imagery of commodity exchange while simultaneously reinforcing that very culture.

# CHAPTER 3

# POP ART AND CONSUMER CULTURE:
## THE MASS MEDIA IN AN AGE OF PUBLICITY

*In the future everybody will be world famous for fifteen minutes.*
—**Andy Warhol**[1]

During the 1960s, the mass media was an undeniably dominant institution in the life of the average American. Correspondingly, images and formats derived from the mass media predominate in Pop art. Before exploring the intersection of Pop art with the various media, it behooves us to examine the relationship between the mass media and advertising, a relationship that is critical to understanding the development of consumer culture during this period, because the two institutions buttress each other, each reinforcing the claims of the other. The relationship is symbiotic—each needs the other. Advertising utilizes the mass media to facilitate the dissemination of its messages; conversely, the mass media (particularly television, radio, newspapers, and magazines) rely on advertising revenues to ensure their economic viability.[2] This connection existed prior to the 1960s but became more pivotal during that era as a result of greatly expanded advertising budgets.

Most people tend to view the mass media as independent entities that, through their format, provide avenues for advertising. However, economically, the media exist because of and for advertising. Although the predominant use of time or space in any particular medium is devoted to articles or shows with ads interspersed throughout, the media would probably cease to exist in this form if the advertisers were to withdraw their ads. In order to increase revenues from advertising fees, the mass media must be able to assure an advertiser of a demographically defined audience. All programming or copy is done with this in mind. Hence, the real product of the mass media is not the show or article, but the audience, which they, in essence, sell to advertisers.

That the entertainment and features are there to deliver an audience for the real message—the advertising—is reflected in the fact that by 1968, the cost of a one-minute commercial ran about $22,000, or five times more than a minute of television entertainment.[3] The television shows serve as mere lead-ins for the real programming—the commercials. The same is true of magazine advertisements. Magazines rarely present a complete article on consecutive pages, since that would allow the reader to focus on the text and ignore the ads.

The dependence of the media on advertising for revenue created a problematic situation in the postwar period because of the unbiased image the media were trying to project, especially in terms of their function as disseminators of news and information. This conflict, as well as its effect on consumer culture, surfaced most vividly in the manner in which the media handled consumer issues.

One example was the media coverage of the Congressional hearings, which resulted in the Fair Packaging and Labeling Act of 1966. During the course of the hearings, G. A. Willis, then president of the Grocery Manufacturers of America, sent letters to a group of sixteen top magazine publishers and the TV Bureau of Advertising reminding them of the "interdependency" between them and "their bread and butter."[4] The results of this pressure were articles in *Reader's Digest, American Weekly, This Week, Saturday Evening Post, Look, Life, Ladies Home Journal,* and regional papers across the country, stressing that food prices were bargains. In addition, many of the television appearances of Senator Philip A. Hart, the major proponent of this bill, were inexplicably canceled, and the "Today" show refused to allow the metropolitan New York Consumer Council to rebut the statements of an opponent of the proposed bill. Despite these obstacles, the bill managed to pass, although not without considerable compromise as a result of the persistent lobbying of the food industry. The final legislation was considered by many observers as "the consumer pyrrhic victory of the decade," not only because of the various deleted clauses but also because there was no carefully implemented plan or mechanism for enforcement.

This one example serves as an illustration of the problematic relationship between the mass media and advertising. Because the food industry accounted for one-sixth of all advertising by U.S. corporations, the national media, particularly the magazines and newspapers, feared retaliation.

Given this dependence on advertising for revenue, the survival of the various forms of mass media was inextricably bound to a reinforcement of an ideology of consumption. The media oriented their programming efforts and articles toward delivering the largest possible audience in the hope of attracting advertising dollars. Although this situation was not exclusive to the late 1950s and 1960s, it was during this period that the relationship became more acute due to the escalating advertising budgets.

Because of the growing corporate need to define and reach larger markets through advertising, as well as the wider availability of the media, the decade of the 1960s was a period in which the media wielded increasing power. One historian noted: "The Kennedy years constituted an important watershed in the national life. In this period, the various arts and businesses of communications, entertainment, and information reached a new level of maturity and power."[5] This interdependence of mass media and advertising lends greater import to discussion of the media and the development of consumer culture. The degree to which the American public relied on the various forms of the mass media for news and entertainment is revealed by statistics: by the mid-1960s, the average American child spent more time in front of a television set than in school, and by 1970, virtually complete television market saturation was reached.[6]

In their insistent references to the mass media in their art works, the Pop artists visually and conceptually integrated the media environment into the realm of high art, often with little transformation and without ostensible critique of their subjects. In so doing, these works reinforced the ideology of consumption, not merely by reproducing the persistent presence of the media in the viewer's surroundings but also by utilizing the very strategies employed by the media both in the works themselves and in the presentation of these works. The formal and presentational mechanisms employed by the Pop artists paralleled those utilized by the media, thereby encouraging the viewers of these art works to "read" them as they would a television screen or newspaper page. Moreover, the aspects of marketing and promotion that were integral to the success of the mass media were equally critical to the success of Pop art.

While all of the mass media experienced rapid growth during the 1960s, the medium that permeated the life of the average American to a greater extent than the others was television. From soap operas to prime-time shows to the evening news, television became the primary source for both information and entertainment. So dominant was the medium of television that Erik Barnouw, author of one of the most comprehensive historical studies of television, refers to the years 1953–1970 as "the image empire." This term is appropriate not only because it acknowledges the predominance of visual images, particularly those transmitted by television, during this period, but also because it speaks to the importance of image, or surface veneer. This manipulative aspect—the ability of the media, especially television, to project a desired, fabricated image of a product, person, or issue—was fully exploited during this period by advertisers, corporations, and politicians alike. The acceptance of Pop art was dependent upon this orientation, for Pop was a movement that succeeded because it cultivated an "image" that could be embraced by its *historical* audience.

Numerous studies have explored the means by which television perpetuates a dominant ideology. Beyond advertising itself, the content and format of television do much to encourage the reinforcement of the ideology of consumption, from the corporate matrix from which programs are generated to the programs themselves. Certainly one must acknowledge that no ideology, no matter how hegemonic or dominant it may seem, is absolute. There will always be alternative or oppositional challenges to that reigning ideology; however, the predominance of the television and its ability to communicate and ensure the perpetuation of consumer culture in the 1960s was overwhelming.

The intersecting relationship between television, the ideological basis of consumer society, and Pop art is revealed by focusing on a key figure of the 1960s—John F. Kennedy. He had an agenda and a personal image to "sell" to the American people, and he realized the critical importance of television in accomplishing his goals. The Pop artists, in their works, acknowledge this capability, and in their presentations, they ultimately perpetuate the images and mechanisms that resulted in the mythification of Kennedy himself.

Throughout his entire career, John F. Kennedy demonstrated a remarkable perspicacity regarding the benefits that could be accrued from proper media handling. These advantages had been recognized by politicians and public figures before him, but Kennedy both "understood the value of media" and "used it more effectively than any public figure since Roosevelt."[7] Although Eisenhower was aware of the power of the media, he never exploited this avenue to the extent that Kennedy did. Conceded a member of Eisenhower's administration: "We all suddenly realized we were busy manufacturing a product down here, but nobody was selling it."[8]

Kennedy, determined not to make the same mistake, worked diligently in the late 1950s to keep his name and face in public view through television, newspaper interviews, and magazine stories. As a result, by the autumn of 1959, even before he announced his candidacy for the presidency, he was recognized by approximately 70 percent of the electorate, a remarkable achievement considering that Kennedy was identified with no major current issue.[9] Kennedy's awareness of the power of television to construct an image appropriate for public consumption was further evidenced by his participation in the 1959 film documentary *Primary,* a record of his campaign for the Democratic presidential nomination. The positive response that Kennedy garnered from that documentary (despite its limited telecast) prompted him to accept immediately the offer to debate his Republican rival, Richard Nixon, in 1960, and to assert during his tenure in office that television could and should help to keep citizens apprised about the activities of government.

Kennedy's skillful utilization of the media did not go unnoticed by the

Pop artists. The image that Kennedy had carefully cultivated during the campaign and throughout his Presidency surfaces in a number of Pop images, such as *Buffalo II* (1964; fig. 33) and *Retroactive I* (1964; fig. 36) by Robert Rauschenberg, and *President Elect* (1960–1961; fig. 37) by James Rosenquist. These paintings incorporated images of Kennedy that were extracted from the mass media, an acknowledgement that the American public's familiarity with Kennedy was media derived. The Pop artists produced these works specifically in response to Kennedy's election in 1960 and assassination in 1963. They had, therefore, a historical immediacy that increased their impact and contributed to the process of Kennedy's mythification. Each of these Pop images addresses both Kennedy's specific usage of the television medium and wider issues of how this medium is able to communicate a coherent ideology despite its fragmented and predetermined format.

The image of Kennedy appears as an integral part of the works of Robert Rauschenberg more frequently than that of any other public figure. *Buffalo II* and *Retrospective I* are just two of at least ten other works in which Kennedy's image appears. In each case, the artist employed an image of Kennedy that was derived directly from the television screen or newspaper photograph. Well dressed and impeccably groomed, the President gestures while forcefully making a point during a speech, as he did during the televised campaign debates.

Rauschenberg utilized the silkscreen technique, which allowed him to transfer photomechanically a press photograph onto the canvas, resulting in a representation of greater immediacy and recognizability that belies the intervention of the artist. The poor registration of pigment in these images echoes the often blurry transmission of images via television (or via newspapers), thereby linking the image visually to its source.

This same photograph was used in the large, mural-sized painting that Rauschenberg created for the New York World's Fair in 1964. Placed on the exterior of the New York State Pavilion, Kennedy's image greeted visitors from all over the world. In this manner, Rauschenberg was contributing to the mythologizing of the recently assassinated President for international audiences. The inclusion of works such as *Buffalo II* in the Venice Biennale of that same year underscored this process. Given that the Biennale, like the World's Fair, was directed at an international audience and that these works were exhibited in the American pavilion, it is not surprising that they were interpreted, as were Rauschenberg's Coca-Cola images, as statements in support of American foreign policy as developed by Kennedy and continued by Johnson.

Rauschenberg's initial use of this photograph reveals his recognition of the decisive impact of the media coverage that Kennedy received and the

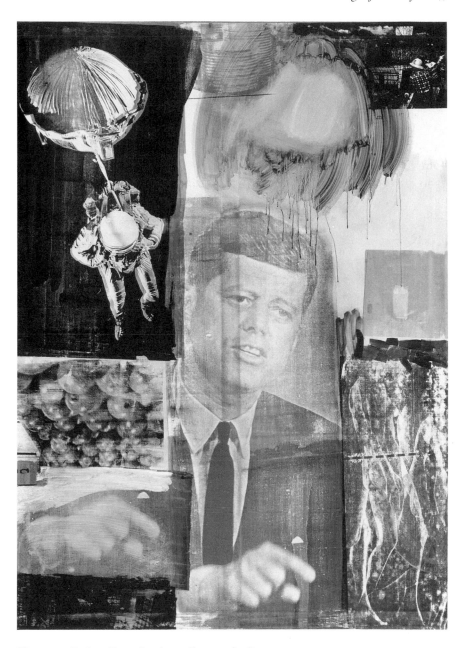

**Figure 36. Robert Rauschenberg,** *Retroactive I,* **1964**
Oil on canvas, 84″ × 60″
© 1989 Robert Rauschenberg/VAGA New York
Courtesy Wadsworth Atheneum, Hartford; gift of Susan Morse Hilles
Photo: Wadsworth Atheneum

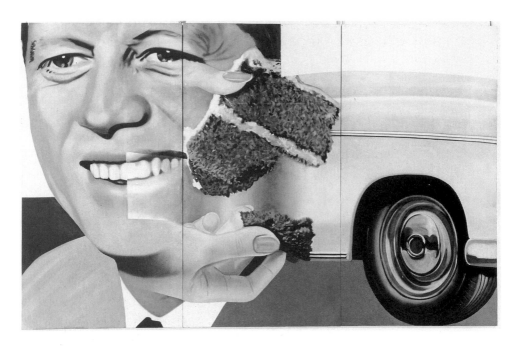

**Figure 37. James Rosenquist, *President Elect*, 1960–1961**
Oil on masonite, 84″ × 144″
© 1989 James Rosenquist/VAGA New York
Courtesy Musée national d'art moderne, Centre Georges Pompidou, Paris

incisiveness of this image. Although excerpted from the print media, Rauschenberg got the idea of focusing on Kennedy while watching the 1960 election returns on television. During the course of that evening, he produced a drawing composed of various images from Kennedy's campaign. As clear evidence of the interrelationship between Pop art and the contemporary events, Rauschenberg arranged to have the drawing sent to Kennedy because he felt that this drawing was part of the electoral spectacle. Unfortunately, the current whereabouts of the work is unknown.[10]

The November 1960 victory of this young, handsome president and his role as a symbol of a new era in American history also served as the impetus for a work by James Rosenquist. Titled *President Elect*, the painting was executed in 1960–1961, immediately after the election. As in Rauschenberg's works, an immediately recognizable image of Kennedy is just one of the myriad passages in the work. Flanked by a slice of cake and an automobile, Kennedy can be seen as merchandise, as simply another product to be marketed. Other formal attributes of the painting reinforce the interpretation of this work as analogous to advertising. *President Elect* is of billboard scale— 7' x 12'—and Rosenquist used oil paint on masonite, the same material he had used as a sign painter.

In addition to the issue of content, these works by Rauschenberg and Rosenquist duplicate the format of television. These Pop artists achieve this by presenting the image of Kennedy as one of many diverse elements, and there often seems to be no clear relationship or connection between the various passages in each work. This fragmentation was, and continues to be, characteristic of the television medium. Television programming is organized around entertainment or news features with interspersed advertisements, and as a result, the viewer rarely gets an uninterrupted stretch of any single show or genre. This constant intermingling has the effect of authenticating the entire realm of experience with little differentiation, so that an ad has the same impact as news of an international crisis or an amusing sitcom. The Pop artists appropriated this technique of leveling the wide range of experience in visual terms, as seen in these images of Kennedy. The viewer is prevented from arriving at any concrete reading of the relationship between all of the various parts because of the fragmentation and patchwork-quilt quality of these works. Unlike traditional academic art works, these Pop paintings have no clearly designated focus, creating a certain degree of ambiguity. The Pop artists selected a format that, like television, blurs distinctions between actual events and staged recreations, direct statement and innuendo, fact and fiction, and denotation and connotation.

An interpretation of these Pop paintings as critical of Kennedy's media-manufactured image is neutralized by the lack of visible transformation from news photo to canvas. Rather, these works are better described as a form of homage. This homage is less a statement about Kennedy's politics than it is unabashed admiration of the President's understanding and use of the media—an understanding on which the Pop artists themselves capitalized. Interestingly enough, Lyndon B. Johnson went virtually unrecognized by the Pop artists during his tenure in office, despite the fact that he was described by one historian as a "television impresario," and his interest in television was described as a "fixation."[11] This was no doubt due to the fact that Johnson was far less telegenic than his predecessor and thus never generated the mass appeal that Kennedy had enjoyed.

The great faith that these political leaders placed in the ability of television to reinforce specific images or agendas was not misplaced. Television of the 1960s can be seen as a vehicle for the personalization and validation of many of the policies and proposals set forth by both Kennedy and Johnson. Television programs were able to "translate" complex economic and technical ideas and present them in an entertaining and simplistic manner. For example, it can be argued that popular support for Kennedy's space program increased as a result of shows during the 1960s such as "Star Trek," "The Outer Limits," and "The Invaders," which made the pressing need for further scientific study to learn about and eventually control interplanetary activity dramatically clear, and which filtered intimidating space technology through the more comfortable realm of the domestic arena. This message was conveyed even to the youngest of Americans; cartoons such as "Astroboy" and "The Jetsons" introduced the concept of life on other planets, making space travel seem not only possible, but fun.

In addition, Johnson's escalating expenditures for and increased commitment to the Vietnam conflict coincided with an unusually high number of war programs on television. While there is no evidence that these programs, such as "McHale's Navy," "Hogan's Heroes," "F Troop," "Combat," "Rat Patrol," "Gomer Pyle, U.S.M.C.," "Jericho," "Wackiest Ship in the Navy," "Mr. Roberts," and "Twelve O'Clock High," were consciously produced to encourage support for the Vietnam War, they had the effect of reinforcing the patriotic imperative to demonstrate military strength whenever deemed necessary.[12]

In a number of assemblages, Tom Wesselmann addresses the position that television had achieved by the 1960s as a dominant and pervasive institution. Wesselmann places an operable television in works such as *Great American Nude #39* (1962; fig. 24) and *Still Life #28* (1963; fig. 38), among others, creating an environment that simulates a typical American home. The television appears surrounded by various food items—fruit, bottles of beer or Coca-Cola—and is presented in a clearly delineated interior space.

As works of art, these assemblages speak to the homogenization of television programming. Ads, newscasts, and entertainment are all treated in the same fragmented manner, utilizing similar camera techniques and formats. The images that appear on the TV sets in Wesselmann's works do not disrupt the tableaux, despite the logical expectation that changing such a major image would affect the rest of the assemblage. To a great extent, regardless of what appears on the television, the impact of an entire tableau is the same. Because Wesselmann presents the television amidst the panoply of consumer goods, the scenario that is transmitted simply fits into that context, both visually and conceptually, as yet another product to be consumed. Wesselmann's explanation for his inclusion of the television suggests that he did not perceive the changing image on the screen as having a significant effect. He asserted that he included the television "not only for the television image—who cares about the television images?—but because I cared about the dimension it gave to painting, something that moved, and gave off light and sound."[13]

Wesselmann's assemblages parallel the tendency of television to homoge-

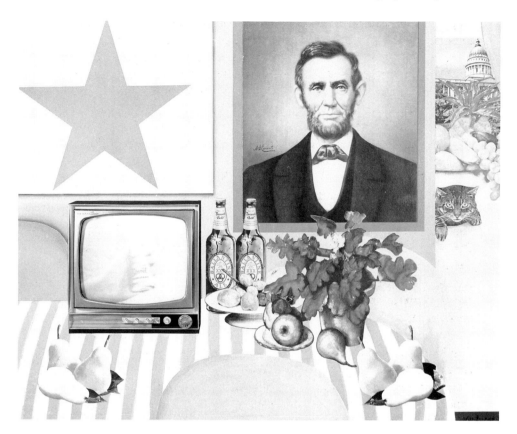

**Figure 38. Tom Wesselmann, *Still Life #28*, 1963**
Acrylic, collage, and assemblage on board, 48″ × 60″
© 1989 Tom Wesselmann/VAGA New York
Courtesy Sidney Janis Gallery, New York

nize events, visual images, and, ultimately, all human experience through its format. The leveling effect that television promotes makes the actual image on the TV screen almost irrelevant as a visual factor in Wesselmann's work. The artist presents a compendium of formal styles, from passages that are extremely flat and nonrepresentational, to trompe l'oeil areas, very illusionistically painted, to sections that include collaged photographic images. Then, of course, there are the televisions themselves, tangible and immediate. There is no apparent hierarchy to these various formal presentations, and this ambiguity bestows equal weight on each mode of representation. Like the homogeneity of television, Wesselmann offers us a spectrum of equally viable styles.

Many of the collaged photographs in Wesselmann's assemblages were taken from actual advertisements. Like the other Pop artists, Wesselmann drew inspiration from another form of mass media—newspapers and magazines. The print media were major sources of Pop art imagery not only because of the ease with which such illustrations could be incorporated into Pop representations of the contemporary environment but also because the Pop sensibility paralleled the conceptual underpinnings that accounted for the success of the print media as a vehicle for the dissemination of information.

Sensational journalism was a popular press genre in the 1960s. The superficial coverage of tragic or heartwrenching events was compelling to a middle-class audience, and editors saw this strategy as a means of counteracting the challenge posed by television. Warhol's *129 Die in Jet (Plane Crash)* (1962; fig. 39) and *A Boy for Meg* (1961; fig. 40) address this type of sensational journalism. Taken from actual front-page editions of the *New York Post* and the *New York Mirror,* these images reflect the degree to which violent death and the activities of celebrities took precedence over topical political, social, or economic issues in much of the print media. Warhol's faithful reproduction of the front page of these newspapers calls attention to the strategies that were utilized to attract an often fickle readership. The visual impact of both the front pages and Warhol's works are derived from the juxtaposition of gripping headlines and graphic or eye-catching photographs. The actual written accounts of the events appeared on the inside pages, necessitating purchase of the newspaper. This was marketing strategy at its best. Pop artists like Warhol understood this.

One feature that was a mainstay of most American newspapers due to its public popularity was the comic-strip section. So pervasive were comic strips that as early as 1948, British anthropologist Geoffrey Gorer noted in his publication *The American People: A Study in National Character:* "With the notable exception of the New York *Times,* almost every American newspaper carries comic strips. They are one of the few important bonds . . . uniting nearly all Americans in a common experience. . . . As one travels about the country one may be unable to learn what is happening in Congress or at the United Nations meetings; but there is no excuse for ignorance of the latest adventures of Superman, Li'l Abner, Joe Palooka, Skeezix Wallet, and the numerous other protagonists of these synthetic fantasies."[14]

Despite the fact that the history of comic strips extends back centuries and is international in scope, by the 1960s comic strips had come to be seen as peculiarly American. Most of the best-known syndicated strips were exported to foreign countries, where, rather than having an international application, they were viewed as "portrait[s] of the American people."[15] Indeed,

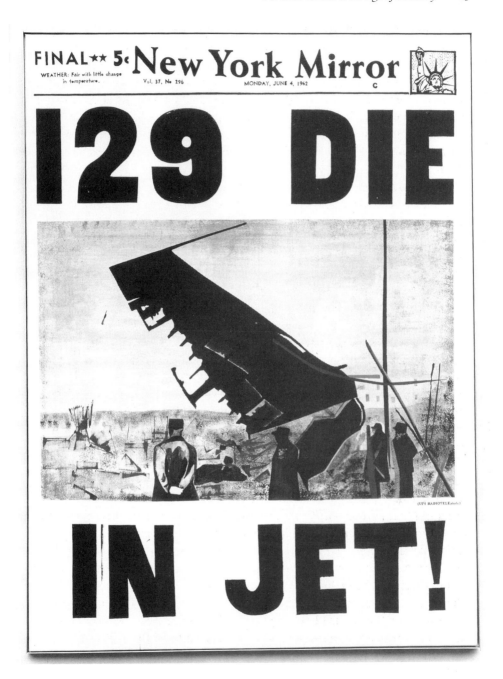

**Figure 39. Andy Warhol,** *129 Die in Jet (Plane Crash),* **1962**
Synthetic polymer paint on canvas, 100″ × 72″
© 1990 The Estate and Foundation of Andy Warhol/ARS New York
Courtesy Museum Ludwig, Cologne

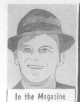

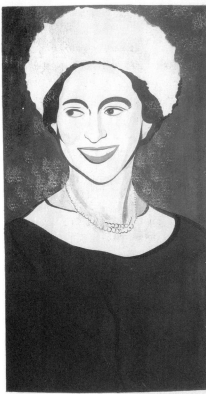

**Figure 40. Andy Warhol, *A Boy for Meg,* 1961**
Synthetic polymer paint on canvas, 72″ × 52″
© 1990 The Estate and Foundation of Andy Warhol/ARS New York
Courtesy National Gallery of Art, Washington, D.C.; gift of Mr. and Mrs. Burton Tremaine

the U.S. Information Agency (USIA) recognized the effectiveness of the comic strip in communicating an image of American culture. This agency capitalized upon this capability by circulating a comic titled *Visit to America*, which related the adventures of a young Asian journeying around the United States. This comic strip was printed in 2,700 newspapers in eighty-six countries with a total circulation of 100 million.[16] In addition, in 1961, the USIA distributed 800,000 copies of a comic-strip booklet explaining the Alliance for Progress throughout Latin America. The request of a superintendent of schools near Bogotá, who wanted additional copies for the schools in his district, and the fact that the government of Guatemala was using the booklet as a reading exercise in its rural schools, are indications that these booklets reached their intended targets.[17]

For the American audience, comic strips were clearly an entertainment rather than news feature and played an important role not only in contributing to the economic viability of the newspaper but also to the development of middle-class morals, values, and lifestyles. As such, they functioned in a manner very similar to advertising in reinforcing certain codes and norms of behavior. In simplistic terms (given the abbreviated format), comic strips defined good and evil, virtue and corruption, familial relationships, and appropriate social and business conduct. Through its standardized format, the comic strip or book was able to encode ideological claims and address a large public. This form of entertainment can arguably be considered a ritual—it was so popular and its structure so codified not only in terms of style but also of narrative. Anthropologists studying the practice of ritual have demonstrated that rituals develop from defined belief systems and function to reinforce and perpetuate such beliefs. In order to accomplish this, rituals involve a high degree of prescription, extensive repetition, and widespread participation, all of which are fundamental to the comic strip. Thus, while studies of comic strips have tended to regard them as entertaining reflections of American life and culture, their much more significant role in actively constructing ideologies must be acknowledged.

Images of comic strips and their more extensive version, the comic book, provided inspiration for the Pop artists. Jasper Johns' painting *Alley Oop* (1958; fig. 41) is one such work. While it is identified by the title, it is presented in a painterly, undefined manner so that the narrative is neither legible nor visually discernable. Yet it is obviously a comic strip—the standard format is immediately recognizable. Utilizing loose brushstrokes common to the works of the Abstract Expressionists, Johns presents a formal examination of this American institution.

Some of the comic strips considered most representative of American culture (and hence heavily exported) were the products of Walt Disney Pro-

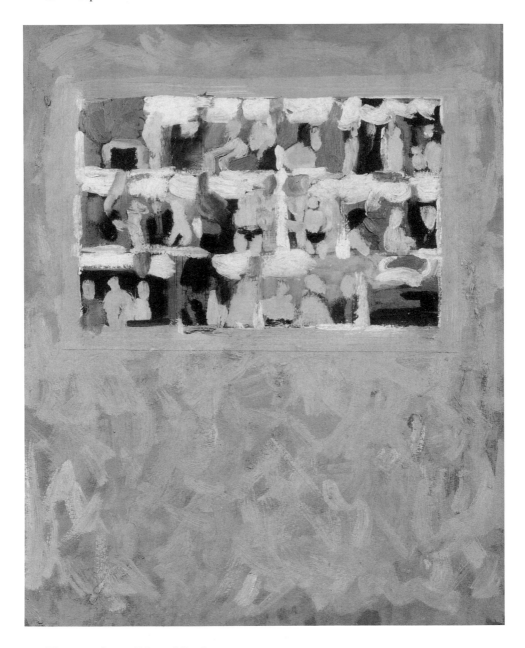

**Figure 41. Jasper Johns, *Alley Oop,* 1958**
Oil and collage on cardboard, 23 5/16″ × 18″
© 1989 Jasper Johns/VAGA New York
Courtesy Collection of Mr. and Mrs. S. I. Newhouse, Jr.
Photo: Jim Strong

ductions.[18] Walt Disney Productions was fast becoming one of the most profitable corporations in the United States. While it had been in the film and animation industry for decades, it was not until the 1960s that it secured its legacy in America.[19] Disneyland was opened in 1955, and by 1960, it was a cultural landmark. In addition, it was during the 1960s that Walt Disney Productions began to aggressively exploit and market the licensing and production of Disney products.

It is, therefore, no accident that Roy Lichtenstein's *Look Mickey* (1961; fig. 42) depicts the two most famous stars in the Disney stable, Mickey Mouse and Donald Duck.[20] Lichtenstein produced this painting in response to a request from his sons, whose choice was undoubtedly influenced by the ubiquity of these cartoon characters in their environment. These characters were particularly appealing because they were not human but were anthropomorphized animals. Despite their appearance, the story lines involved narratives that were easily digested and comprehended by a mass audience. Lichtenstein's image focuses on a typical scenario. Donald Duck, the more clumsy and bumbling of the two, expresses his excitement over his fishing catch, not realizing that he has, in fact, hooked himself. Mickey Mouse stands behind him, snickering at Donald's ineptness at fishing. The scrapes in which these cartoon characters repeatedly found themselves were always resolved by the end of the comic strip, book, or cartoon and emphasized traditional American values of ingenuity, hard work, and comradery.

Lichtenstein, like Johns, was intrigued by the formal qualities of the medium. In particular, Lichtenstein was interested in the calculated simplicity and clarity of form that was dictated by the requirements of the mass printing process. Stated the artist: "This [comic strip] technique is a perfect example of an industrial process that developed as a direct result of the need for inexpensive and quick color-printing. These printed symbols attain perfection in the hands of commercial artists through the continuing idealization of the image made compatible with commercial considerations. Each generation of illustrators makes modifications and reinforcements of these symbols, which then become part of the vocabulary of all. The result is an impersonal form."[21]

As is evident from this statement, Lichtenstein was impressed with the resolution of the formal problems through industrial techniques. He demonstrates his awareness of the codification of the format and the way in which the format of comic strips controls how the public "reads" them. In *Look Mickey,* Lichtenstein has emphasized this "impersonal form" by eliminating all evidence of artistic touch (unlike Johns' *Alley Oop*), leaving a sanitized, clearly legible image for mass consumption.

Lichtenstein also explored other representative forms of comic books:

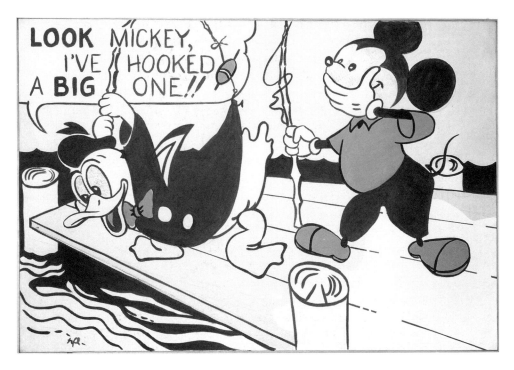

**Figure 42. Roy Lichtenstein, *Look Mickey*, 1961**
Oil on canvas, 48″ × 69″
© 1989 Roy Lichtenstein/VAGA New York
Courtesy National Gallery of Art, Washington, D.C.

romance and war comics. In each case, he selected stereotypical images that characterized the genre both in terms of content and form. *Hopeless* (1963) depicts a young woman in the throes of an emotional crisis. Her head rests on a pillow, and as tears stream from her eyes, she thinks: "That's the way—it *should* have *begun*! But it's hopeless!" Romance comic books centered on the ups and downs of the love lives of young men and women. Roughly equivalent to the soap operas on television, they provided vicarious romance for thousands of (mostly female) readers.

While Lichtenstein's choice of subject matter ostensibly refers solely to a mass form of printed entertainment, it also addresses the significant social role of romance comics. Like television soap operas, these comic-book narratives served as the equivalent, in the realm of personal relationships, to the "how-to" and self-help books that were proliferating during this period. Due to the upheaval brought about by the changing nature of the American family and workplace—rising divorce rates, increasing numbers of single-parent families, and influx of women into the corporate workplace—traditional courtship patterns and interpersonal relationships no longer seemed appropriate. These comics, soap operas, and books outlined various contemporary situations that were then resolved and provided viewers with guidelines for acceptable behavior in this new era.

Lichtenstein's paintings illustrate scenarios in which the stereotypical emotionalism of the depicted female is only the superficial manifestation of an internal challenge to traditional mores and behavior patterns. In *Drowning Girl* (1963; fig. 43), a young woman in tears is in danger of drowning as treacherous waves crash around her head. Yet she staunchly asserts her independence in the caption that floats in the thought bubble over her head: "I don't care! I'd rather sink—than call Brad for help!" Too proud to ask a man for help, this woman would rather lose her life.

The upheaval in societal roles is the subject of *Engagement Ring* (1961; fig. 44) as well. In this painting, a well-dressed woman in the foreground apprehensively asks the professional-looking man in the background: "It's . . . It's not an *engagement ring,* is it?" Clearly distressed and anxiety ridden at the possibility of marriage, this comic-strip frame attacks the conventional expectation that women should welcome marriage and that it should be the sole goal of their lives.

This notion that the life of the modern woman was far more inclusive and liberated and revolved around more than simply attracting and keeping a male, surfaces in *Oh, Jeff . . . I Love You Too, But,* (1964). A young woman, her brow furrowed in serious concentration, speaks on the phone she holds to her ear: "Oh, Jeff . . . I love you too, but . . ." In this case, the "but" says it all. She has acknowledged her love for Jeff, but there are other considerations in her life.

These comic books were instrumental in helping a mass audience deal with the constant changes that resulted from the upheaval in the social fabric of the American lifestyle, and Lichtenstein's depictions reinforce the ideas presented by monumentalizing them in painting. Lichtenstein's war comic-book images function similarly, albeit in a different social arena.

Given the United States' involvement in the Korean War and subsequently the Vietnam conflict in the years shortly after the cessation of World War II, the predominance of war comic books was not simply expected, but to a great degree, a necessity. There was a demonstrable need for a mechanism or apparatus that "translated" this constant militarism and its underlying ideological basis into terms the average American could understand. Children (especially males) who had grown up with the legacy of world war would be called upon to fight in Vietnam, and aside from the footage and reports on the evening news, channels for the dissemination of information

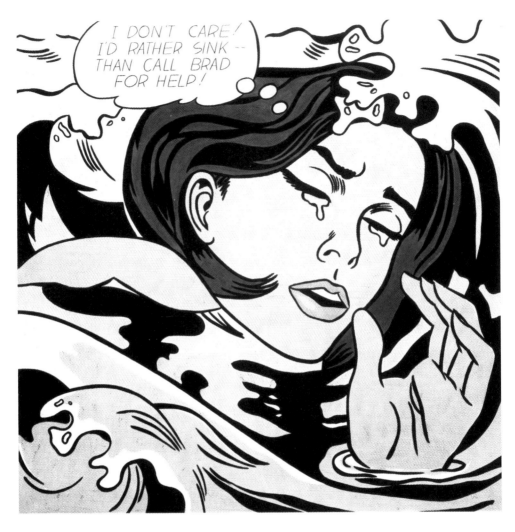

**Figure 43. Roy Lichtenstein, *Drowning Girl,* 1963**
Oil and magna on canvas, 67 5/8″ × 66 3/4″
© 1990 Roy Lichtenstein/VAGA New York
Courtesy Leo Castelli Gallery, New York

on this level were limited. War comic books fulfilled this need. In a clear, narrative format, such comics provided a continual supply (since they were produced in serials) of military action. The heroes (always identified with the United States) invariably triumphed, and the enemies (usually presented as ethnically distinct) were always defeated. Through the reiteration of this standard plot line, the certitude of America's military position was reinforced,

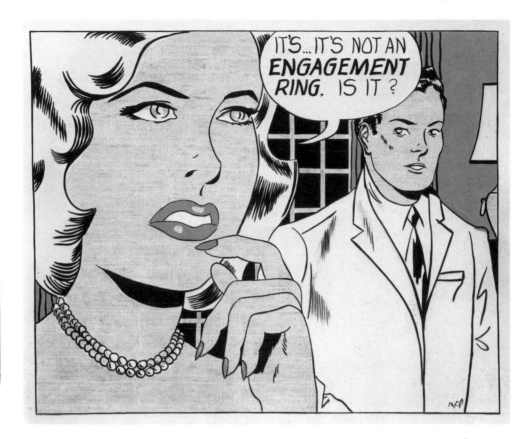

**Figure 44. Roy Lichtenstein, *Engagement Ring*, 1961**
Oil on canvas, 67 3/4" × 79 1/2"
© 1990 Roy Lichtenstein/VAGA New York
Courtesy Leo Castelli Gallery, New York

and the image of the country's opponents as evil, corrupt, and inferior was ingrained.

Lichtenstein's images reiterate this formulaic approach. His painting *Whaam!* (1963; fig. 45) depicts a pilot firing his weapons and hitting his intended target, another plane that explodes into a fiery burst of metal fragments and flames. The caption, relatively small in size, conveys the pilot's thoughts and provides a psychological study of the military mindset. States the caption: "I pressed the fire control . . . and ahead of me rockets blazed through the sky . . ." The victorious fighter is identified as American by the large insignia on the side of the jet—the same insignia that appears in Rosenquist's *Pad* (1964; fig. 4) and *F-III* (1965; fig. 61).

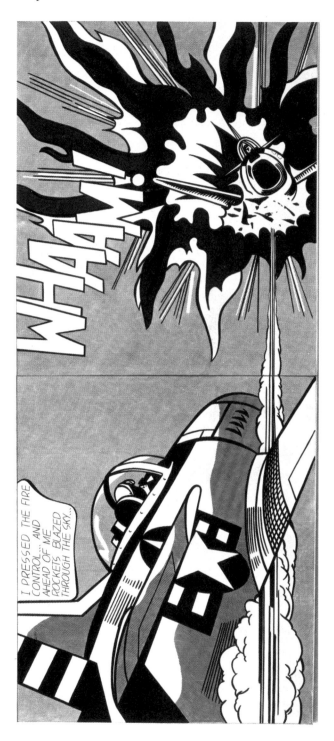

**Figure 45. Roy Lichtenstein,** *Whaam!,* 1963
Magna on canvas, two panels, 68″ × 160″
© 1990 Roy Lichtenstein/VAGA New York
Courtesy Leo Castelli Gallery, New York
Photo: Rudolph Burkhardt

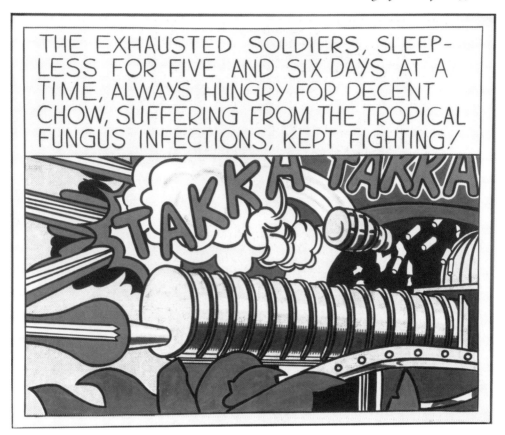

THE EXHAUSTED SOLDIERS, SLEEP-
LESS FOR FIVE AND SIX DAYS AT A
TIME, ALWAYS HUNGRY FOR DECENT
CHOW, SUFFERING FROM THE TROPICAL
FUNGUS INFECTIONS, KEPT FIGHTING!

**Figure 46. Roy Lichtenstein,** *Takka Takka,* **1962**
Oil on canvas, 56″ × 68″
© 1989 Roy Lichtenstein/VAGA New York
Courtesy Museum Ludwig, Cologne

*Takka Takka* (1962; fig. 46) also focuses on dynamic, aggressive military action and depicts the heat of battle. Here, the blazing machine guns and flying grenades dominate the scene, and the presence of the soldiers is implied by the caption. Lichtenstein excerpted this frame from a World War II comic but has chosen to make the references less specific through alterations to the caption. The caption that accompanied the original frame was: "On Guadalcanal, the exhausted Marines, sleepless for five and six days at a time, always hungry for decent chow, suffering from the tropical fungus infections, kept on fighting!"[22] Lichtenstein's version reads: "The exhausted soldiers, sleepless for five and six days at a time, always hungry for decent chow, suffering from the tropical fungus infections, kept fighting!" By excising the reference to Guadalcanal and by changing the specific "Marines" to the more general "soldiers," Lichtenstein extends the relevance of the message. Rather than stand simply as a historical reference, the image could be read by viewers of the 1960s as pertaining to the contemporary conflicts. In so doing, Lichtenstein adopts the didactic strategy that made this whole genre of comics so popular.

Lichtenstein reinforced the function of romance and war comics as vehicles for the dissemination of acceptable behaviors and values not only through his choice of content but also of style. Visually, his work mimics the format of such comics. Lichtenstein retains the bright primary colors and stark black outlines that were characteristic of comic strips and that made them easily legible. In addition, his compositions are faithful to the original frames from which he excerpted the images. Lichtenstein even went so far as to remain true to the dimensions of the comic-strip frame in his versions. Ultimately, except for the medium of oil or magna on canvas and the larger scale, there is very little visible artistic transformation.

Lichtenstein's choice of production techniques indicates that his attempts to reproduce comic-strip images were conscious and not simply the result of casual happenstance. Lichtenstein uses BenDay dots, a process utilized by newspapers to achieve shades and tones. Named after its developer, Benjamin Day, the process involves varying the size and spacing of dots to create color areas. Lichtenstein's decision to use this stencil technique was, like his other choices, based on his desire to keep as closely as possible to the original images and to emphasize the existence of comic books as commodity items. In an interview, Lichtenstein admitted that he used BenDay dots in order to "stay as close to an expedient commercial reproduction as possible."[23] In keeping with the mass-produced nature of comic strips, Lichtenstein soon relegated most of the stenciling to assistants, which he claims increased his productivity.[24] Lichtenstein's delegation of segments of the production process reveals his concern with quantity and a mentality very much in line with the pervasive corporate sensibility. Clearly, Lichtenstein's interest in comic strips extended beyond mere formal considerations to the very nature of comic strips—their manufactured quality and function in American society.

Andy Warhol, like Lichtenstein, produced a number of paintings of comic-strip images that addressed the content, form, and dissemination of this mass medium. *Dick Tracy* (1960; fig. 47) and *Popeye* (1961; fig. 48) are examples of this. During the early 1960s, Dick Tracy was one of the American public's favorite comic strips. Heavily moralistic, Dick Tracy combined melodrama with an in-depth view into the world of criminology. The strip had a didactic tone and was often accompanied with authentic "tips for crime-stop-

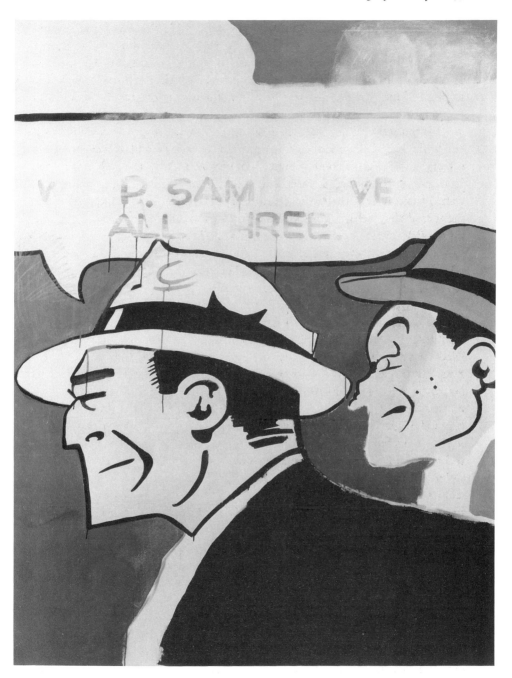

**Figure 47. Andy Warhol,** *Dick Tracy,* **1960**
Synthetic polymer paint on canvas, 79″ × 45″
© 1990 The Estate and Foundation of Andy Warhol/ARS New York
Courtesy Collection of Mr. and Mrs. S. I. Newhouse, Jr.
Photo: Jim Strong

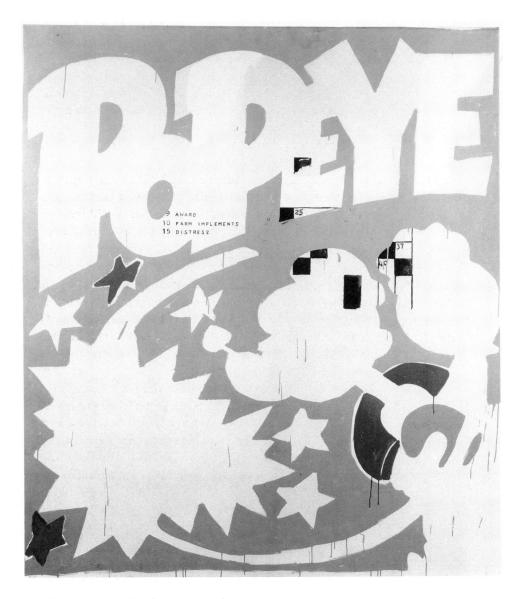

**Figure 48. Andy Warhol,** *Popeye,* **1961**
Synthetic polymer paint on canvas, 68 1/4″ × 58 1/2″
© 1990 The Estate and Foundation of Andy Warhol/ARS New York
Courtesy Collection of Mr. and Mrs. S. I. Newhouse, Jr.
Photo: Jim Strong

pers." Dick Tracy's imaginary world was centered on the challenges of American urban living. Like the romance and war comic books, Dick Tracy provided proof that the difficulties of contemporary American life could be resolved in an acceptable and quick manner (the brevity of comic strips demanded conciseness) while providing the American public with a modern hero. In analyzing the appeal of this comic strip, one scholar concluded: "It provides the audience with a legitimate scapegoat, the criminal, who is relentlessly pursued. . . . Readers . . . know that the detective will triumph over crime in the end."[25]

Warhol presents a typical frame from the comic strip. Dick Tracy appears in the foreground, the focus of all attention. The narrative is unclear—the caption is illegible, and there is little action in the scene that would indicate the unfolding story line. Yet it is not difficult to derive a sense of Tracy's forceful personality. The harsh angularity with which Tracy is portrayed and the stark contrasts of dark and light convey a sense of strength and moral fiber. In contrast, Tracy's foil, who appears at the right of the painting, is composed of curvilinear lines and muted gray tones. Moreover, his chin is incompletely rendered, suggesting a certain lack of substance, and it contrasts sharply with Tracy's resolutely right-angled, darkly outlined chin. The caption, most of which Warhol has chosen to obliterate, is almost incidental to the scene—much of the message is conveyed by Dick Tracy's firmly set jaw.

Popeye, like Dick Tracy, was immensely popular during the late 1950s and 1960s. One of the reasons for the enduring appeal of such a character was that Popeye (like Superman, another "hero" portrayed by Warhol) presented a positive, upbeat image of American national character in the aftermath of World War II. These figures never courted conflict and resorted to force only out of necessity. Their expected triumph at the end of each episode reaffirmed the power of virtue and right. These fictitious narratives, although less direct than the war comics, were nevertheless valuable in justifying the lingering Cold War ideology that demanded persistent military action.

This perception of Popeye as reluctant fighter, but forceful victor when the situation demanded, is addressed in Warhol's 1961 painting. Despite the simplicity of the outlines and forms and lack of detail, the image is unmistakable; Popeye, with his massive forearms, is shown punching his unseen opponent. As in the typical plot, Popeye must resort to physical violence in order to triumph. Warhol also reminds the viewer of the newspaper source of the comic strip by revealing part of a crossword puzzle beneath the image and lettering. That this particular image is representative of this comic strip is suggested further by Roy Lichtenstein's version of *Popeye* (1961), done without knowledge of Warhol's painting. In Lichtenstein's work, Popeye engages in precisely the same action as in Warhol's painting, albeit with a visible target for his wrath. Even the formal elements, such as the stars and curvilinear lines that indicate the force of Popeye's blows, are exactly the same in both works, revealing the extent to which all of these elements had become codified and served as potent signs for the mass readership.

The Popeye comic also provides incisive illustration of the intersection of comic strips with the ideology of consumption. Comic strips were originally conceived as circulation builders, and in the 1960s, they continued to be regarded as features whose purpose was to help sell papers. Warhol's inclusion of the crossword puzzle in his *Popeye* is a direct reference to this function. However, by this time, the value of the comic strips in the marketing of other products had been established, so that the importance of the "funnies" went far beyond their daily printing. An author of a 1960 study of the business aspect of comic strips noted: "Enterprising manufacturers have found the veritable gold mine in the comic strips. Merchandise, particularly in the form of dolls and toys, inspired by comic strip characters have had nothing but success."[26] This marketing strategy could not have escaped the grasp of the Pop artists, all of whom were well versed in advertising practices.

By depicting images from a variety of comic strips in art works that then sold for substantial amounts of money, the Pop artists reinforced the marketability of such images. Concomitantly, by passively mimicking both the form and content of such comic strips, these artists increased the dissemination of the myths that this influential form of mass media represented.

The celebrity status that these comic-strip characters acquired was not unique to these fictitious personages but was a growing phenomenon of the 1960s. As an institution whose very existence depended on the mass media, the celebrity apparatus provides a more incisive illustration of the manner in which the media not only create myths but also inform behavior and construct a reality. It also demonstrates how important the mechanisms of publicity had become—a mechanism that was integral to the maturation of consumer culture and to the success of Pop art.

This system was most visible in Hollywood. The pervading sense of loneliness and anxiety that was a result of the imposition of corporate bureaucracy and mentality was combatted in Hollywood with an unequaled display of excess and surface glitter. The lifestyle in "Tinseltown," as Hollywood appropriately came to be known, emphasized high visibility and extravagant conspicuous consumption.

The American public embraced Hollywood and all it represented, perceiving it as a "dream factory," not only because of the escape it provided through the movies it produced but also because of the glamourous image projected by the community itself.[27] So engrossed was the average American in delving into the lives of Hollywood celebrities that sociologist Bernard

Rosenberg asserted in 1957 that "the 'average' American's knowledge about the lives, loves and neuroses of the demi-gods and goddesses who live in the Olympian heights of Beverly Hills far surpasses his knowledge of civic affairs (local, state and national combined)."[28] This contention is substantiated by the fact that the circulation of tabloids and magazines dealing with Hollywood celebrities and their lives surpassed that of national news magazines.[29]

Perhaps the epitome of the Hollywood creation was Marilyn Monroe. While the extent of her thespian abilities remains debatable, the degree to which she was a product of the "Hollywood myth machine" goes unquestioned. During her lifetime, she was the object of national adulation, and her suicide in August 1962 only served to crystallize the myth of the unattainable goddess. While critics and reporters academically discussed Monroe's career and compared her life with those of Byron, Baudelaire, Rimbaud, van Gogh, Nijinsky, Dylan Thomas, and James Dean, the public saw only the victimized beauty whose tragic death pushed her into the realm of martyrdom.[30] By January of 1963, five months after her death, articles were being published on "the cult of Marilyn."[31] Marilyn's stature and popularity reflect the effectiveness with which she had been marketed. Ironically, rather than end her objectification, her sensational death served only to amplify and perpetuate that process.

The Pop artists reacted to the overwhelming sentiment then associated with Marilyn's image. Andy Warhol silkscreened a number of canvases immediately following her passing. Their exhibition at the Stable Gallery in the fall of 1962 coincided with and undoubtedly garnered additional attention because of the mystique and sensational atmosphere surrounding her death. *Marilyn Diptych* (1962; fig. 49) typifies these paintings. The instantaneous recognition experienced by the viewer stems from Warhol's utilization of a publicity photograph that reveals no private or idiosyncratic information about the actress. By cropping the portrait so that no clothing, accessories, or background are visible, all information must be extracted from the face alone, thereby forcing the viewer to focus on Marilyn's haunting visage. The utilization of garish colors not only serves to mask Marilyn's true character but also alludes to the painted faces of Hollywood. Warhol applies the inks in such a way as to make it obvious that the area covered by the ink does not exactly match the area with which we would associate that color (e.g., the eyeshadow or lipstick). This exaggerates to a pathetic degree the idea of Marilyn as manufactured construction.

Works by Tom Wesselmann and Claes Oldenburg also refer to this cosmetic, superficially fabricated creation. In Wesselmann's *Mouth #14 (Marilyn)* (1967) the viewer is confronted with a pair of red lacquered lips that part slightly in a smile to reveal a set of perfect white teeth. Identified by the title

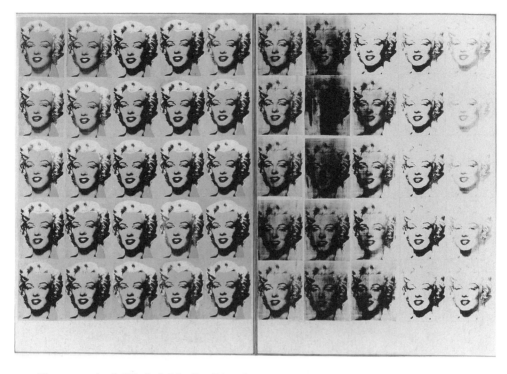

**Figure 49. Andy Warhol, *Marilyn Diptych,* 1962**
Silkscreen ink on synthetic polymer paint on canvas, two panels, each panel 82″ × 57″
© 1990 The Estate and Foundation of Andy Warhol/ARS New York
Courtesy The Tate Gallery, London

as being those of Marilyn Monroe, they could just as easily belong to any other starlet created by the Hollywood studio system. The scale of the work, 5' x 9', relates the lips to a billboard, on which Marilyn's movies were advertised. Marilyn herself was, in any case, larger than life.

Oldenburg takes this conceptualization one step further. In a work titled *Lipstick with Stroke Attached (for M.M.)* (1967–1971; fig. 50), created for a special exhibition "Homage to Marilyn Monroe" at the Sidney Janis Gallery in 1967, Oldenburg presents neither a recognizable portrait of Marilyn nor even an excerpted feature, but just the lipstick—one of the myriad of cosmetic products upon which Hollywood depended for the creation of illusions and the manufacture of images and personas.

A Pop art work that, like Warhol's carefully timed production of *Marilyn,* derived much of its impact from its incisiveness, was James Rosenquist's *Marilyn Monroe I* (1962; fig. 51), which he painted in the final year of her life. The painting is composed of fractured images of an inverted, anonymous

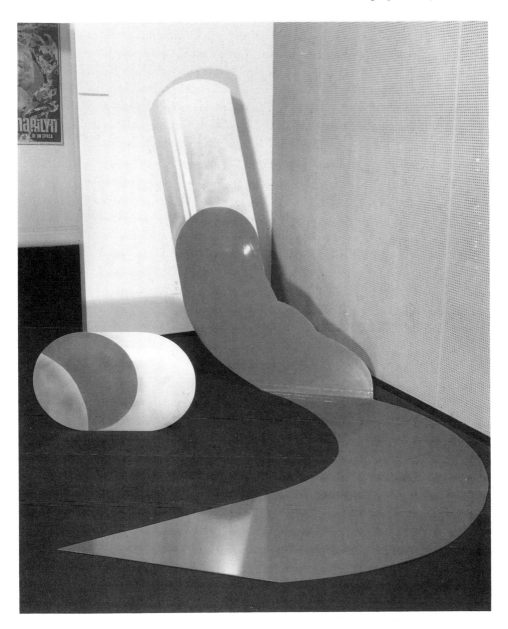

**Figure 50. Claes Oldenburg,** *Lipstick with Stroke Attached (for M.M.)*, **1967–1971**
Metal, hinged, 72″ × 72″ × 36″
© Claes Oldenburg
Courtesy Claes Oldenburg

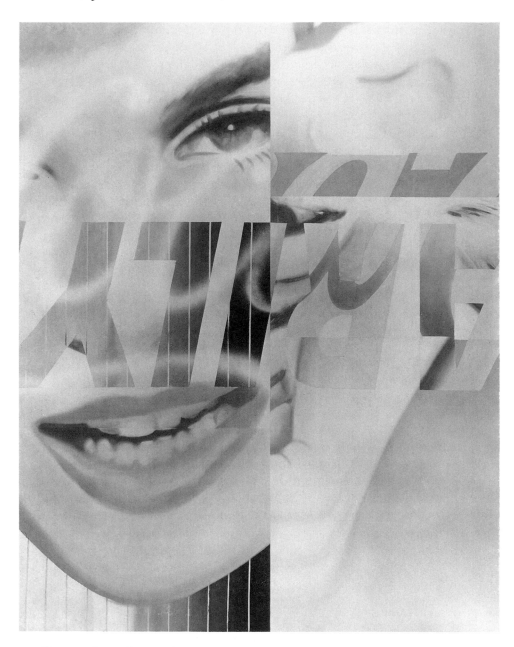

**Figure 51. James Rosenquist, *Marilyn Monroe I*, 1962**
Oil and spray enamel on canvas, 93″ × 72 1/4″
© 1989 James Rosenquist/VAGA New York
Courtesy Collection, The Museum of Modern Art, New York;
The Sidney and Harriet Janis Collection

female face, not necessarily recognizable as that of Marilyn. The identification of the woman depicted is revealed by the large block letters spelling "Marilyn," which are emblazoned across the canvas and face. The manner in which the media and Hollywood were able to take a person and transform her into a persona through cosmetics and the carefully controlled mechanisms of publicity is on review here.

As a more cryptic image, Rosenquist's painting does not have the immediacy of Warhol's version. Yet, the degree to which both of these representations emphasize Marilyn Monroe as manufactured product can be demonstrated by contrasting them with the depiction of Marilyn by the Abstract Expressionist Willem de Kooning, painted eight years earlier (fig. 52). In de Kooning's version, Marilyn possesses none of her easily recognizable traits, nor is she portrayed in one of her roles. Seemingly an apparition that materializes out of the furious brushstrokes that comprise the background, she is clearly the product of the artist's personal vision rather than the calculated product of the Hollywood myth machine.

Another prototypical celebrity during the 1960s who became a subject for many Pop art paintings was Elizabeth Taylor. Although she had been in the spotlight since her early acting years, it was not until she starred in *Cleopatra* in 1963 that her popularity reached its zenith. Her private life made the front page of major newspapers, and her marriage to Eddie Fisher, subsequent divorce, near-fatal bout with pneumonia, and marriage to Richard Burton (her costar in *Cleopatra*) were all reported in great detail. Articles were not restricted to tabloid journalism but also extended to discussions on the technical legal problems involved with her frequent change of marital status.[32] *Business Week* and *U.S. News & World Report* published articles on Taylor's financial status; one such article compared Taylor's salary ($7.1 million) for *Cleopatra* to that of the highest paid U.S. business executive ($650,000) and of the president of the United States ($150,000).[33] By 1964, reports were circulating on "the fastest, flashiest show around," the "encounter between man and myth"—namely, the nightly spectacle of the crowds, literally thousands in number, who waited in the streets to get a glimpse of Elizabeth Taylor emerging from the Broadway theater where Richard Burton was starring in *Hamlet*.[34]

Warhol's interest in Taylor can be compared to that of an avid fan, as is evidenced by the range and number of his works in which she is the subject. In 1962, he produced *Daily News*, which was a reproduction of an actual front page with the headlines "Eddie Fisher Breaks Down: In Hospital Here; Liz in Rome" and a photograph of the two celebrities. Warhol also produced *The Men in Her Life (Mike Todd and Eddie Fisher)* and *Eddie and Liz*, paintings

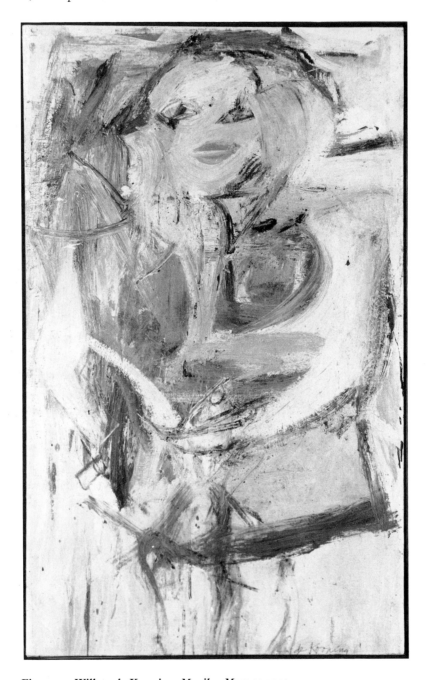

**Figure 52. Willem de Kooning, *Marilyn Monroe*, 1954**
Oil on canvas, 50″ × 30″
© Willem de Kooning
Courtesy Collection of Neuberger Museum, State University of New York
at Purchase; gift of Roy R. Neuberger
Photo: Jim Frank

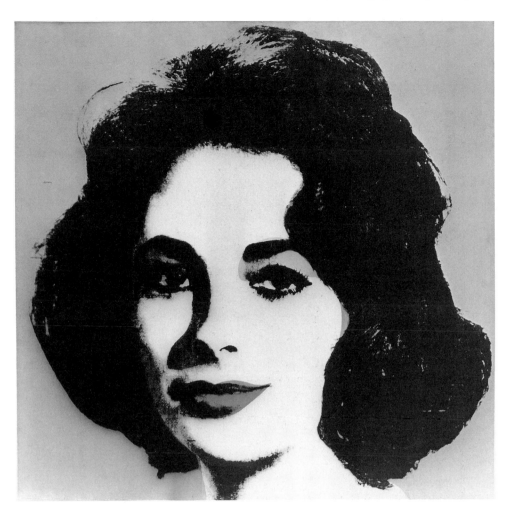

**Figure 53. Andy Warhol,** *Liz #6,* **1963**
Silkscreen ink on synthetic polymer paint on canvas, 40″ × 40″
© 1990 The Estate and Foundation of Andy Warhol/ARS New York
Courtesy Leo Castelli Gallery, New York
Photo: Dorothy Zeidman

that chronicled Taylor's complex and constantly changing love interests through silkscreened images based on news photographs.

In 1963, he silkscreened a number of canvases of *Liz #6* (fig. 53) and *Liz as Cleopatra* (fig. 54). *Liz #6,* like *Marilyn,* offers an impersonal, contrived portrait derived from a publicity photo. Like most publicity images, this representation conveys a physical attractiveness, but little more. As in his other

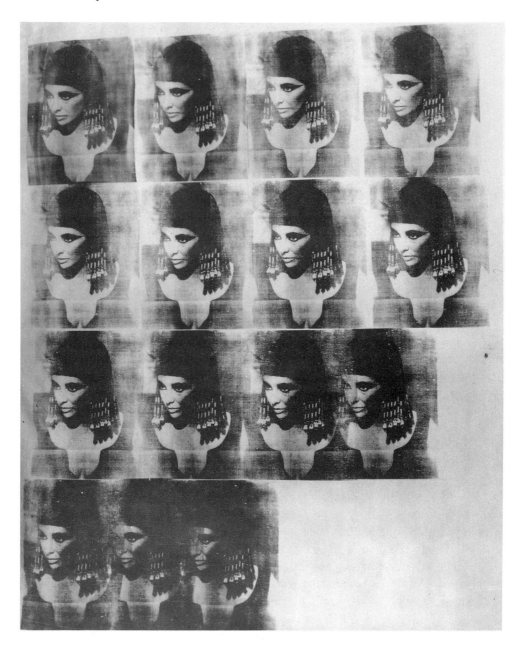

**Figure 54. Andy Warhol,** *Liz as Cleopatra,* **1963**
Silkscreen ink on synthetic polymer paint on canvas, 82″ × 65″
© 1990 The Estate and Foundation of Andy Warhol/ARS New York
Courtesy Leo Castelli Gallery, New York

celebrity portraits, Liz's make up is applied in an excessive and unrestrained manner, and the colors selected are garish and shrill.

In *Liz as Cleopatra,* the distinction between Liz Taylor the person and Liz Taylor as character no longer exists. The glamour and exoticism of Liz Taylor, star, is communicated through the depiction of Liz in her role as the regal, exalted, and ultimately, mythic personage. Like Cleopatra, Liz Taylor has transcended into the realm of legendary status. The creation of larger-than-life personas both on and off the screen was instrumental in the film industry's strategy to maintain its audience, which was being enticed away by the growing panoply of television shows. The abundance of large-scale epic movies in the late 1950s and early 1960s, such as *Ben Hur* (1959), *Lawrence of Arabia* (1962), *Cleopatra* (1963), *The Fall of the Roman Empire* (1964), *The Greatest Story Ever Told* (1965), and *The Bible* (1966), attests to this strategy. Visually, the redundancy of Liz's image not only mimics the film stills from the movie but also refers to the plethora of media photos that were instrumental in creating and maintaining Taylor's celebrity status.

The Hollywood system that produced these revered celebrities missed no opportunity to utilize these media creations to market yet other products. The practice of employing celebrities as spokespeople had proven effective, and most corporations were quick to jump on the endorsement bandwagon. James Rosenquist's untitled work ("Joan Crawford Says . . .") of 1964 (fig. 55) illustrates this strategy. In the work, the perfectly coiffed and assiduously made-up star cheerfully extols some product. As is evident from Rosenquist's carefully cropped image, the product is inconsequential and does not even appear in the painting. What was crucial in ensuring the success of this marketing strategy was the validation and approval from a credible star, regardless of whether or not the celebrity actually used the product.

The Hollywood industry that sustained this contrived celebrity system was symptomatic of the instability of the surrounding society. Corporate culture had produced bureaucratic, faceless, impersonal masses, and Hollywood offered salvation and escape from this alienating environment in the form of larger-than-life personas. Yet the celebrities that were created by the mass media for public consumption on the silver screen, television set, or over the airwaves only truly existed as long as they could sell themselves to an audience that was often fickle and demanding. Like any obsolete product, as soon as interest in a particular celebrity dwindled, he or she simply faded into obscurity, becoming a nonentity. The extent to which the Pop artists recognized this is evident not only from their work but also from their utilization of the media to publicize their production.

The most graphic illustration of the intersection between the mass media, the cult of celebrity, consumer culture, and Pop art is provided by the assas-

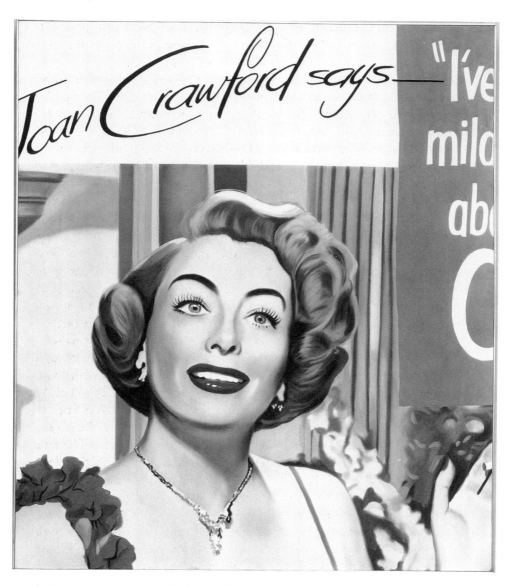

**Figure 55. James Rosenquist, Untitled ("Joan Crawford Says . . . "), 1964**
Oil on canvas, 92″ × 78″
© 1989 James Rosenquist/VAGA New York
Courtesy Museum Ludwig, Cologne

sination of John F. Kennedy in 1963. Perhaps never has there been an episode to rival the dominance of the mass media as was seen on 22 November 1963 and the subsequent days. Not only did the media devote all coverage to the assassination, but the audience it reached was also unparalleled. The public witnessed the assassination "live," increasing the impact of the event. The incessant media coverage of the events through the funeral, which included the shocking murder of suspect Lee Harvey Oswald by Jack Ruby, the swearing in of Lyndon B. Johnson as the nation's next president, and the poignant farewells of Kennedy's widow and children to the fallen leader, burned into the American memory a media construction of the event. Collective memory of this event is composed of footage seen on television, the somber voice of the newscaster, and the compelling photos in the print media. The extraordinary power of the media is demonstrated by statistics: by 6 P.M. that day, 99.8 percent of the American public had heard that Kennedy had been killed.[35] This unprecedented media saturation assured the crystallization of Kennedy's mythic status. In a sense, Kennedy became the ultimate celebrity. Moreover, this extensive coverage cemented the media's powers of coercion and legitimated the image of integrity that the media wanted to cultivate.

Andy Warhol produced *Sixteen Jackies* (1964; fig. 56) in response to Kennedy's death, illustrating this process of mythification and marketing through the media. Warhol selected specific photographs of Jackie Kennedy that have since become icons due to their wide dissemination in the period following the assassination and their constant reproduction since then. Taken from issues of *Life* magazine specially devoted to coverage of Kennedy, the photographs are immediately recognizable despite their cropped format. The four photographs depict Jackie during this fateful week: stepping off the plane upon arrival in Dallas, at the side of Johnson as he was sworn into office, waiting to join the funeral procession to the Capitol, and smiling in the motorcade as it drove through Dallas.

The serial presentation of the images recalls the haunting ubiquity of these photographs in the media in the weeks following the assassination. As in Rauschenberg's paintings, the grainy quality of the silkscreen registration is reminiscent of print reproductions of these photographs. And reproduced they were. *Life* magazine changed its planned issues of 29 November and 6 December in order to be able to incorporate photos and articles about Kennedy and the assassination and even went so far as to scrap 300,000 previously printed copies at a replacement cost of $1.2 million.[36] The strategy paid off; both of these issues sold out immediately. The demand for more copies was overwhelming, and bootleggers were getting up to $20 for the regularly priced twenty-five-cent issues.[37] People avidly consumed not just the event but also the products associated with the event.

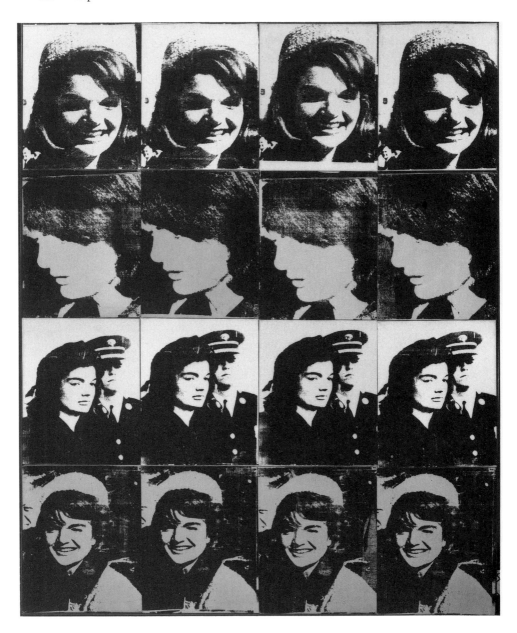

**Figure 56. Andy Warhol,** *Sixteen Jackies,* **1964**
Silkscreen ink on synthetic polymer paint on canvas, each panel 20″ × 16″, overall 80″ × 64″
© 1990 The Estate and Foundation of Andy Warhol/ARS New York
Courtesy Collection of the Walker Art Center, Minneapolis; Art Center Acquisition Fund, 1968

These paintings (there were a number of variations of *Jackie*) do not just comment upon but are also themselves part and parcel of this incessant consumption. These recognizable and undiluted representations did more than provide a statement about the important role of the media in creating a public perception of these people and events. Given their immediacy, they ultimately participated in the very construction of that reality.

The mass media in the 1960s were logical vehicles for the marketing of objects, people, and ideas due to their pervasiveness and influential presence. Pop art contributed to the perpetuation of the power and authority of the media, for rather than laying bare the various premises and characteristics of each medium that functioned to create a unique "reality," the works merely echoed that construct in their content, form, and presentation.

# CHAPTER 4
# POP ART AND CONSUMER CULTURE:
## THE CULT OF DOMESTICITY AND CONSUMPTION IN THE HOME

*My kind of art involves coming to grips with . . . the fact . . . that in everything you do there's something technological being done to you and how you can personalize that or relate to it.*

—Claes Oldenburg [1]

The intersection of Pop art with consumer culture is revealed by exploring not only the macroeconomic, corporate aspects of this culture but also the microeconomic, personal aspects. By the 1950s, consumption had become a way of life in the average middle-class American household. Most Americans were avid consumers and participated fully in the growth of such a system, and many Pop art works address the issue of consumption in the home.

While discussions of advertising, the media, and corporate interests might suggest that these institutions were imposing a singular ideology on an unsuspecting public, that was far from true. Consumer culture of the 1960s flourished in an accepting social and moral climate that centered on an ethos of self-fulfillment. In other words, although advertisers, corporations, and the mass media were insistently attempting to sell their products to the public, there was a prevalent attitude amongst middle-class Americans that not only allowed them to deem acceptable the ideology of consumption but that even further facilitated its maturation. In cyclical fashion, advertisers lost no chance to exploit this attitude in their ad campaigns, thereby expanding and reinforcing this ethos of self-fulfillment.

Americans came to believe that self-fulfillment was a necessary and admirable goal in an increasingly impersonal society and that participation in the process of consumption would lead to such self-realization. Interest in self-fulfillment had its roots in the transition from a rural-agricultural society to an urban-industrial one. [2] Up until the turn of the twentieth century, Americans emphasized continual hard work, sacrifice, civic duty, and strict moral standards. This Protestant ethic was appropriate for the small-scale, agriculturally oriented businesses. With the growth of the large, bureaucratic corporate organization, however, social relationships began to change. Rather than engender a close-knit, familial attitude amongst the employees, these organizations encouraged competition between co-workers, resulting in alienation and lack of strong social ties. In addition, the ever-increasing scale of these corporations created an impersonal and often sterile environment. As early as the 1950s, publications such as David Riesman's *The Lonely Crowd* (1950) and William H. Whyte's *The Organization Man* (1956) focused on this development. Whyte noted that while a great deal of attention had been paid to "the economic and political consequences of big organization—the concentration of power in large corporations, for example, . . . no less important is the principal impact that organization life has had on the individuals within it."[3] Whyte pointed out that despite the fact that many Americans claimed to adhere to the Protestant ethic, "the harsh facts of organization life simply do not jibe with these precepts."[4] Sociologist David Riesman concurred and noted that the successful man or woman in the corporate structure had "no clear core of self."[5] Indeed, this was Whyte's definition of an "Organization Man"—someone who not only worked for the Organization but also *belonged* to it.

The increasing geographical and social mobility of the populace also heightened the sense of alienation and impersonality, making the search for self-realization and identity more urgent and imperative.[6] Before the rapid urbanization of the country, people tended to live and die in the same community. This community provided confirmation of their identity and continuity or tradition in their lives, and therefore their sense of self was derived from a solid foundation. The mobility that accompanied urbanization produced severe psychological dislocation, since the individual became separated from the traditional channels of socialization and became dependent upon associates, social acquaintances, and mechanisms such as the media for the establishment of an identity.

Another factor in this change was the rapidly developing technology associated with urban life. The wider availability of indoor plumbing, central heating, and canned food, for example, made life seem somewhat artificial and sterile compared to the rigor and immediacy of farm life. Social observers shortly after the turn of the century were already lamenting the "Era of Predigestion," an appropriate description for a world of mediated or secondhand experience.[7]

The growth of an interdependent national market economy also made the ideals of autonomous selfhood increasingly difficult to sustain. Historian T. J. Jackson Lears points out that for entrepreneurs as well as wageworkers, financial success or ruin came to depend upon policies formulated far away and upon situations beyond the individual's control.[8] For these reasons, maintaining a sense of self became more and more problematic.

All of these factors—the development of the corporate organization, the increased social and geographical mobility, the technological developments, and the growth of a national market economy—combined to make the Protestant ethic untenable and inappropriate. This ethic, which had dominated the nineteenth century, gave way to an attitude that functioned to counteract the hierarchical and impersonal nature of corporate life by emphasizing self-indulgence and gratification through consumption. As sociologists Peter Berger and Thomas Luckmann explained: "Conspicuous patterns of consumption take the place of continuous interpersonal contacts within an individual's biography. . . . Material objects rather than human beings must be called upon to testify to the individual's worth."[9] Another observer defined such a consumer culture as "delineation of a self by acquisition."[10]

The postwar period was one of affluence, dominated by corporate culture, and the pursuit of self-fulfillment became more entrenched as an integral part of the American lifestyle. As such, the home became a particularly critical arena in which much of the upheaval wrought by maturing consumer society was played out. Corporate strategies, government strategies, and personal interests all coalesced during the 1960s to create a nation of consumers.

The government saw the growing interest in self-fulfillment through consumption as something to be nurtured, and it worked to encourage increased consumption in the American home. While corporations could utilize advertising to induce additional purchases, government officials had to be more creative in finding ways to convince the public to buy more to support their Keynesian programs. These officials most easily accomplished this by persuading American citizens that consumption was a national imperative, thereby equating consumptive practices with patriotism. In the light of the lingering Cold War and the concern over the potential devastation from nuclear warfare, the nation was receptive to this idea.

This connection was firmly established during the Eisenhower administration, at the height of the Cold War. In 1959, for example, the American National Exhibition was constructed in Moscow. The large-scale exhibition was intended as a "portrait of America" and consisted of numerous buildings, each of which housed exhibitions relating to some aspect of life for a "typical American family."[11] The show, which was "crammed with the fruits of American prosperity," was, according to the director of the fair, intended to "show the Soviet people how we live. . . . There will be nothing political or military. We are trying to keep propaganda out of it."[12]

Despite such claims, the real purpose of the exhibition was obvious, reinforced as it was by the presence of Vice President Richard Nixon and Soviet Premier Nikita Khrushchev at its opening. Each of the leaders took this opportunity to trumpet the superiority of life in his respective country. Leading Khrushchev through an exhibition of a model American home, Nixon spoke of conditions in the United States as being "closest to the ideal of prosperity for all in a classless society."[13] While in the kitchen, Nixon and Khrushchev entered into a debate about washing machines. Said Nixon: "We hope to show our diversity and our right to choose. We do not wish to have decisions made at the top by government officials. . . . Would it not be better to compete in the merits of washing machines than in the strength of rockets?"[14]

Known as the famous "kitchen debate," this exchange was extensively reported in the press to the American public. Accompanied in the news media by numerous photographs, this was a particularly powerful scenario for the American public, because it made the distinction between the American way of life and that of the Soviet Union clear both through rhetoric and the locale (a typical American suburban home). In a review of the historic meeting, *Newsweek* proclaimed: "Finally, it was a contest of two diverse ways of life—of modern capitalism with its ideology of political and economic freedom; and of Communism."[15] It also strengthened the belief that national security could be ensured by escalated consumption—that competing with the Soviet Union in terms of appliances such as washing machines would make an arms race unnecessary. With the Berlin crisis in 1962 and the Cuban missile crisis of the same year providing the American public with an illustration of the ever-present threat of Communism, both the Kennedy and, later, the Johnson administrations had ample opportunity to perpetuate this association. Kennedy himself expressed his concern in his January 1963 Economic Report that the nation was "still falling substantially short of its economic potential—a potential we must fulfill both to raise our standards of well-being at home and to serve the cause of freedom abroad."[16] During the late 1950s and 1960s, the ideological nature of consumption was intensified by the insistent linking of consumption with patriotic and military concerns, and it became eminently clear to the average American that national strength was inextricably bound to a healthy consumer economy.

The confluence between governmental political imperatives, increased consumption, and the individual American household surfaced in the characterization of this period as the "push-button age." As a result of increasingly sophisticated scientific technology, the push button came to be associated in the public mind with the ultimate power—that of nuclear annihilation. The popular public perception was that the president had a push button on his desk that could wipe out entire geographical areas as easily as a housewife could turn on a vacuum cleaner. This belief was enhanced by articles with titles such as "Pushbutton Defense for Air War" and by statements in publications such as *U.S. News & World Report:* "Push a button today, and more than 200 missiles with nuclear warheads would go speeding to specific cities in Russia."[17]

The characterization "push-button age" was not limited to military or scientific usage alone, however. Concurrently, the push button proliferated on appliances and products for the home. In this manner, however subliminal, the connection was made between the advanced military technology and the individual American household.[18] During this period, the appliance industry focused its efforts on marketing rather than on engineering research to improve its products, demonstrating that this connection existed primarily on the level of symbolism. Indeed, there were few technological advances in appliances and housewares during the 1960s, and the push button simply replaced dials and levers and performed the same function.[19]

The association was beneficial both for the sales of these household products and for public acceptance of military equipment. If the military and government trusted major defense contractors such as General Electric, Westinghouse, and Goodyear to make their weapons, then a consumer could surely rely on the same companies for their televisions, automobiles, and housewares.[20] Conversely, associations with household goods made military and scientific hardware seem more down to earth and less remote. Capitalizing on this connection, General Electric produced ads in 1955 for a new push-button electric range that depicted a homemaker cooking hamburgers on this range with America's first operational nuclear power plant in the background. The message about the positive value of atomic energy as well as the advanced nature of General Electric's appliances would not have escaped any viewer.

Besides the subtle association with nuclear warfare, the fascination with the push button was due to changing dynamics of the typical American household. Labor-saving devices had strong appeal to the increasing number of women entering the work force. Companies capitalized on this, marketing appliances with push buttons as labor-saving devices. This accounts for the rapidly rising sales of such products in the 1960s.

It is impossible to evade these issues in discussing James Rosenquist's *Pushbutton* (1960–1961; fig. 57). In both the visual presentation and the title, Rosenquist alludes to developments in 1960s housewares. A row of push buttons lines the bottom of the painting, while a hand on the right reaches down toward them. While Rosenquist depicts the buttons in isolation, thereby rendering the exact appliance unidentifiable, they are visually very similar in format to those found on electric blenders.

Although the electric blender had been around since 1937, the introduction of the multiple push-button switch in the late 1950s set off "the greatest competition" that evolved into the "Battle of the Buttons."[21] The proliferation of push buttons on the blender can be seen as an embodiment of the sensibility of the era—a fascination with technology and the corporations'

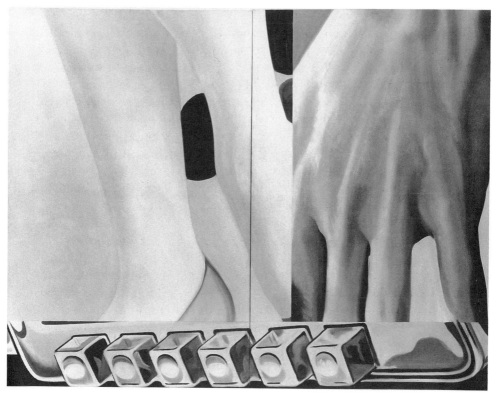

**Figure 57. James Rosenquist,** *Pushbutton,* **1960–1961**
Oil on canvas, 82 3/4″ × 105 1/2″
© 1989 James Rosenquist/VAGA New York
Courtesy The Museum of Contemporary Art, Los Angeles: The Panza Collection
Photo: Squidds & Nunns

ability to capitalize on it. After the relatively limited capabilities of the high and low controls, Oster introduced a four-speed blender in 1964. By 1966, these blenders were accompanied by eight buttons, and, not to be outdone, Waring introduced a nine-button machine the following year.[22] The utilization of dual-control circuitry doubled the capability of such an appliance, allowing a nine-button blender to be marketed as an eighteen-speed appliance. Despite the confusing profusion of buttons and speeds (few homemakers could explain the difference between liquefy and puree), the allure was irresistible, and the late 1960s represents the peak period in the history of blender sales.[23]

Considering the fact that the four-speed blender was not introduced until 1964, Rosenquist's painting can be viewed as prophetic (if in fact the object depicted is a blender) in his understanding of the direction in which product marketing was headed, since he portrays an appliance with six push buttons. This illustrates his keen understanding of the strong consumer current and the direction in which American society was headed. It also demonstrates that Pop did venture beyond mere reflection of consumer culture and participated in its very construction.

The fascination on the part of the American public and the obsessive marketing efforts of large corporations extended to all types of housewares. For example, the postwar years saw a rapid growth in the cookware business, especially pots and pans, such as that presented in Andy Warhol's *Cooking Pot* (1962; fig. 58). Warhol reproduces an advertisement for an enamel cooking pot that is illustrated in the fragmentary notice. Porcelain enamelware was immensely popular in the 1960s. Descoware, Copco, and Dansk Designs were among the most successful lines produced. Warhol faithfully duplicates the ad, complete with accompanying consumer information—the size, color, price, and features of this cooking pot. As indicated by the size of the lettering, it is clearly the price that is the appeal of this pot. Manufacturers sold one-quart porcelain enameled cookware for $1.95 in the early 1950s, so seventy-seven cents for a four-quart pot in 1961 was quite a bargain.[24]

This kind of cookware was being marketed with a new urgency due to the growing popularity of fast foods and canned goods. These technological advances, along with the hectic schedules of working women, were making traditional cooking less practical and less appealing.

The fast-food field experienced massive growth during the late 1950s and 1960s. The development of the McDonald's fast-food chain epitomizes this tremendous expansion. McDonald's began its growth in the mid-1950s and experienced "boom years" in the early 1960s. So explosive was the growth of this field, and of McDonald's in particular, that by 1961, economic analysts were declaring, "Thriving drive-ins are the hottest thing in the restaurant business today," and a few years later, they were asking, "Doesn't anyone cook at home any more?"[25] By the early 1970s, McDonald's had surpassed both the army and the U.S. Department of Agriculture (with its school-lunch program) as the highest-volume distributor of prepared food in the country.[26]

With its emphasis on speed of service, organizations like McDonald's catered to the new lifestyle, which, as evidenced by the popularity of other convenience foods and appliances, was very fast paced. The price of this speed was the homogenization of taste. Yet this standardization was also a factor in the success of these companies, for it offered a comfortable predictability from which it did not deviate regardless of geographic location. In discussing

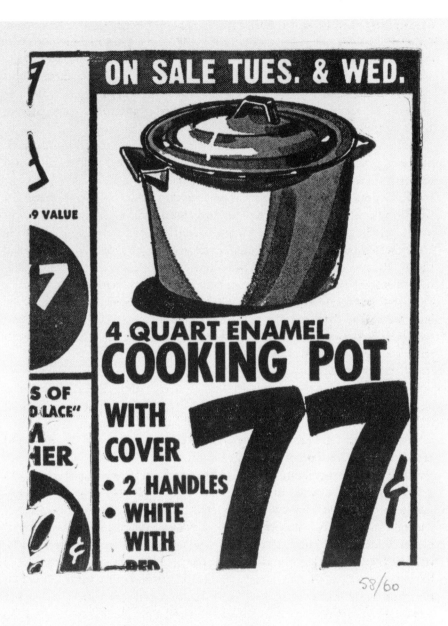

**Figure 58. Andy Warhol, *Cooking Pot*, 1964**
Photoengraved newspaper mat, 5 7/8″ × 4 5/8″
© 1990 The Estate and Foundation of Andy Warhol/ARS New York
Courtesy Collection, The Museum of Modern Art, New York; gift of Peter Deitsch Gallery

McDonald's success, one social observer noted: "Order, predictability, stability—all lend an aura of certainty and a feel of an eternal nature amidst the rapid flux of changes which traumatize people and nations with 'Future shock'."[27]

The development of the fast-food industry corresponds well to the ideology of consumption of the late 1950s and 1960s. The emphasis on maximum efficiency, limited personal interaction, and codified behavior (for both employee and customer) at these fast-food diners paralleled the bureaucratic mentality so prized in corporate America. As expected, advertising played an important role in the predominance of certain companies. McDonald's hamburgers were among the most heavily advertised products in America, thereby contributing to its current status as a "cultural institution."[28]

Claes Oldenburg's *Giant Hamburger* (1962; fig. 59) and *Falling Shoestring Potatoes* (1966; fig. 60) present, in monstrous scale, the prototypical fast-food meal. The size of these items can be interpreted as a reflection of the insatiability of the American consumer's appetite for such products, or alternatively, as a representation of the degree to which fast-food outlets dominate the national landscape. While the gargantuan, garishly painted hamburger and fries are, arguably, unappetizing, at the same time their construction as soft, stuffed sculptures renders them appealing, like the seductive consumer culture they symbolize.

The previously discussed expansion of corporations like the Campbell Soup Company and Del Monte can be attributed in part to the accelerated pace of life. These companies capitalized upon this pace by advertising their products as time and labor saving, thereby creating a market. The repeated inclusions of canned, bottled, and processed goods in the works of Andy Warhol, Tom Wesselmann, James Rosenquist, Robert Rauschenberg, Jasper Johns, Claes Oldenburg, and Roy Lichtenstein, as a corpus, mirror the incessant presence of such products in the consumer environment. Even further and more importantly, they set forth this presence as natural and unproblematic. Like Wesselmann's inclusion of television sets in his assemblages, canned and processed food surfaces in Pop as one element among many. Very rarely do the Pop artists designate any hierarchy among the depicted objects. This has the effect of levelling all elements and experiences, rendering the presence of processed foods as natural as that of people and landscapes. In this manner, these works validate the ideological claims of consumption.

Like the push button, processed foods were also linked to the national military interest. The expanding sales of prepared, particularly canned, goods was partly due to the threat of nuclear war. In a televised speech, President Kennedy appealed for a national effort on the part of individual families to build fallout shelters.[29] This directive from the president helped sell canned

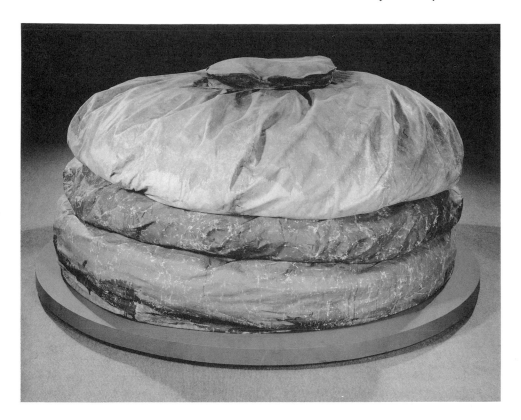

**Figure 59. Claes Oldenburg, *Giant Hamburger*, 1962**
Painted sailcloth stuffed with foam, 52″ × 84″
© Claes Oldenburg
Courtesy Art Gallery of Ontario, Toronto; Purchase, 1967

goods and other household items as people stocked up for the potential apocalyptic event. As with the "kitchen debate" and the proliferation of push buttons, the ideology of consumption was linked to the nation's strength; in this instance, however, the connection was made on a much more personal and direct level. The construction of fallout shelters and the purchase and hoarding of canned goods promised to ensure the perpetuation of the ideal family structure and traditional American values, making the need for consumption all the more real and urgent.

While the persistent references to canned goods and processed foods in the work of the Pop artists did not refer specifically to their use in fallout shelters, they did serve to reinforce the presence of such products in the home as natural and necessary. In Wesselmann's works, for example, the cans sit

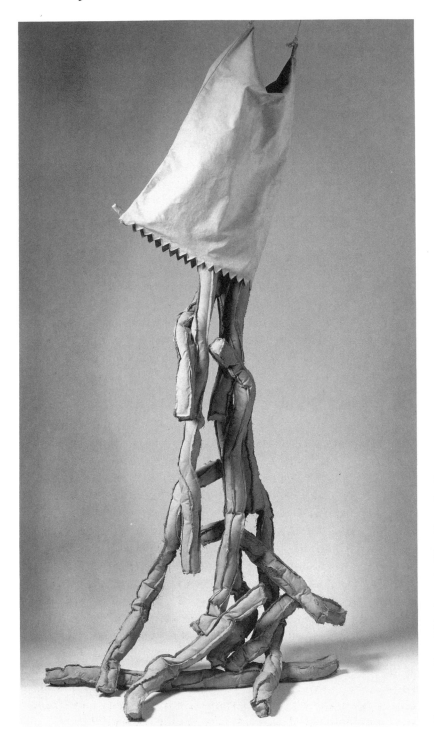

**Figure 60. Claes Oldenburg, *Falling Shoestring Potatoes*, 1965**
Painted canvas, kapok, 108″ × 46″ × 42″
© Claes Oldenburg
Courtesy Collection of the Walker Art Center, Minneapolis,

unproblematically amidst the cheery dining-room settings, on homey check-ered tablecloths, surrounded by arrays of plants, fruits, and paintings on the back walls. Outside the windows, which are framed with ostensibly home-made drapes or curtains, appear illusionistic landscape scenes—nature at its finest.

In order to facilitate this constantly increasing consumption, both the Kennedy and Johnson administrations realized that they would have to pass legislation to encourage spending. Kennedy's proposed tax cut, which he struggled to enact from 1961 until his death in 1963, served this purpose. Kennedy's Council of Economic Advisers believed that the "key instrument of policy for meeting our responsibilities for high employment and faster economic growth" was a major program of tax reduction and reform.[30] Kennedy concurred and asserted that "no more important domestic economic legislation has come before the Congress in some 15 years," revealing the significance he attached to this congressional bill.[31] Johnson held similar sentiments; he was, in fact, responsible for the eventual enactment of this tax-cut proposal in 1964.

The principle of a tax reduction fits well into the established Keynesian program of the 1960s because, theoretically, reducing the tax an individual renders to the government increases the amount of available capital that the individual has to invest or spend. Keynes strongly believed that changes in consumer spending were directly related to changes in income and formulated what is referred to as the "multiplier concept." Not only would higher after-tax personal incomes stimulate consumer spending but such spending, along with lower tax rates for businesses, would also result in higher profit levels and more available cash for businesses. They, in turn, would invest more. Thus, the spending of one person or firm becomes income for another and is again respent. Clearly, based on this theoretical model, a tax-reduction program would facilitate increased consumption. Indeed, statistics kept during the years 1954–1964 demonstrated the validity of such a theory: 93 percent of all additions to people's disposable income was spent, and the effect of each new dollar of disposable income on consumption reached 94.9 cents.[32] This led one economic historian who analyzed the economic development during this period to conclude that "the Kennedy-Johnson tax cut of 1964 represented the culmination of the Keynesian revolution."[33]

Increased spending was also encouraged by the greater availability and more extensive use of credit. Alvin Hansen, a professor of political economy at Harvard during the postwar era, expressed the view of many Keynesian economists when he stated in 1960: "In a growing society an expansion of credit, public and private, is not only permissible but necessary. In such a society investment must exceed saving. Credit must fill the gap."[34]

Despite the coherent orchestration of increased consumption by corporations and the government and the responsiveness of the American public as evidenced by the growth of the economy at an annual average rate of 4.6 percent during the decade 1959–1969, there was a dimension of this development that extended beyond economics. While advertising and industry spokespersons presented this maturing consumer culture as a natural and inevitable development of the free enterprise system (and therefore to be celebrated as a symbol of American democracy and capitalism), the urgency and the strident tone of the marketing efforts suggests that this magnitude of consumption was in fact far from natural. Further exploration of consumption in the home and its image in Pop art reveals that the drive to consume was a strategy that served in part to negotiate the problematic role of women in American society and the changing dynamics of the traditional family structure. To that extent, it fulfilled an ideological function.

The social construct of the nuclear family underwent significant changes in the 1960s. During the decade, the number of "traditional families" in which the father was the breadwinner and the mother was a full-time home-maker fell dramatically, while single-parent, female-headed households, or households in which both parents worked, increased.[35] These social transformations—rising divorce rates, influx of women into the work force, increased mobility—resulted in widespread and substantial social disruption in the fabric of domestic life. Although this process was not exclusive to the 1960s, the transformation did accelerate during these years. While all members of the nuclear family were affected by these shifting attitudes and practices, the effects of these changes are best illustrated by focusing on the role of women, since they had traditionally been considered the centrifugal force in the domestic arena.

The role of women as homemakers and keepers of the hearth came under greater attack in the 1960s. The challenges to this position were the result of a number of factors. The ethos of self-fulfillment, the burgeoning counter-culture and New Left values as espoused by Herbert Marcuse and Norman O. Brown, and the women's liberation movement all contributed to bringing about a measurable shift in women's attitudes toward their role.[36] Women were less willing to subordinate their personal freedom and desires to perpetuate the traditional ideals of domesticity.

The upheaval in the domestic realm was reflected and exacerbated by the producers of consumer culture, who sought to capitalize on the situation. This social disruption became a focal point of corporate marketing strategies. Women had long been acknowledged as primary consumers in the typical household, and corporations and advertisers oriented their promotional campaigns toward women.

Ads of this period sought to convince consumers (i.e., women) that purchasing the proffered goods and services would enhance their lives. For example, in an attempt to be as all-encompassing as possible, most appliances were marketed as labor-saving devices, which allowed more-liberated women to see these products as providing additional time for themselves, while use of such products by more-traditional women would free them up to spend extra time with their families. But neither relinquishing nor tenaciously adhering to traditional values and roles came easily. Many women who saw themselves as feminists were reluctant to abrogate totally their responsibilities as homemakers, while those who still staunchly believed in the traditional role of women could not deny the need for increased recognition and independence. Because these conflicts had not been, indeed, could not be, fully resolved, the constant inundation of ads for high-tech household products or convenience foods that women encountered only heightened the feelings of confusion and guilt that were common during this period.

Advertisers viewed women not just as consumers but as objects of consumption as well. Advertisers had long since developed the strategy of incorporating images of attractive females in the ads as a means of drawing attention to the ads and helping sell the products.

Wesselmann's *Great American Nude* series (e.g., *#39* [1962; fig. 24], and *#40* [1962]) stands as an overtly self-conscious reference to a traditional art form. Yet it also addresses the uses to which images of women were being put by the advertising industry. In each, Wesselmann depicts a flatly rendered female nude sprawled across the foreground of the painting. Because the figure is painted in unmodulated pink with little detail, she quite literally becomes an object, since the lack of articulation with which she is described makes it impossible for the viewer to endow her with identity or personality. Moreover, because she appears surrounded by consumer goods, one might well conclude that she is, like everything around her, a commodity. This analysis is corroborated by the popularity of sexual innuendo in advertising of the period, from cars to liquor, clothing to real estate.[37]

Thus, women during the 1960s functioned within a matrix of institutions, values, and morals that were undergoing significant change. As a result, the home became a particularly contested arena for the resolution of these conflicts. The Pop artists were well aware of these developments and of the issues associated with women's roles (both as consumer and as object), the domestic impact of national political and military agendas, the ideology of consumption, and the changing dynamics of the typical American family, all of which surface in their work.

Perhaps the one Pop art painting that best illustrates the intersection of these various issues is James Rosenquist's 1965 painting, *F-III* (fig. 61). In this

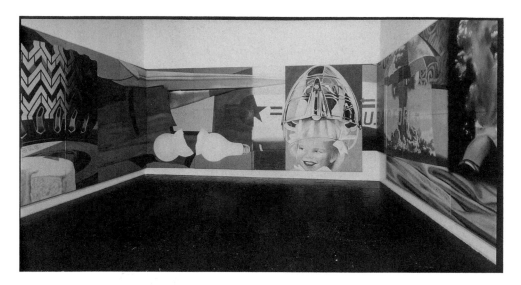

**Figure 61. James Rosenquist, *F-III*, 1965**
Oil on canvas with aluminum, 10′ × 86′
© 1989 James Rosenquist/VAGA New York
Courtesy Jeffrey Deitch

panoramic (86-foot-long) mural, Rosenquist reveals a compendium of images that can be read as a comment upon the incursion of public (governmental, corporate) concerns into the private realm of the home and the way in which the disintegrating ideal of the American nuclear family provided advertisers with an opportunity to encourage increased consumption.

The central image that spans virtually the entire length of the painting and that is acknowledged by the title is the jet fighter F-III. The F-III was the result of the need by both the navy and air force for a more sophisticated fighter-bomber and interceptor.[38] The lingering Cold War ideology led government officials to adhere to a doctrine of Massive Retaliation that had been established in the 1950s.[39] It was this doctrine that provided the justification for the F-III proposal. In 1959 both military branches instituted official proceedings to gain government approval for the design and production of such a jet. The first F-III prototype was tested in December 1964, and in April 1965, the Defense Department made a formal commitment to production of the F-III.[40] Rosenquist could not have been more up-to-date or incisive in his selection of military hardware.

Beyond the Cold War rhetoric and national defense interests, the F-III also represented a substantial financial expenditure and a boost to the economy. Originally budgeted at $7 billion, such a program was welcomed

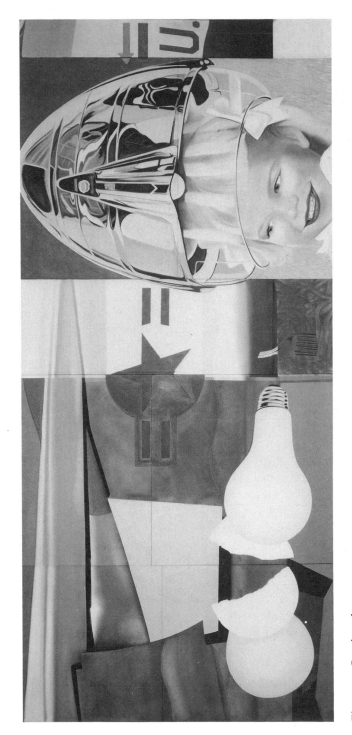

Figure 61. Continued

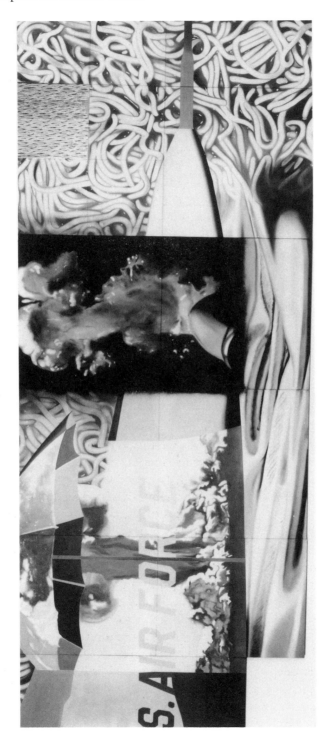

Figure 61. Continued

by Keynesian economists.[41] Rosenquist revealed his awareness of this facet and the immediacy of his subject matter when he responded to the question, "What is the F-111?" with the reply: "It is the newest, latest fighter-bomber at this time, 1965. . . . The prime force of this thing has been to keep people working, an economic tool; but behind it, this is a war machine."[42] The military aspect of this painting is enhanced by the presence of an atomic blast that appears as a mushroom cloud near the front nose of the jet. Viewers of *F-111* would have made these same connections. Although the details of the F-111 program remained undisclosed, the public was certainly aware of the technological, military, and economic issues that construction of this fighter represented as a result of articles in mass-circulation periodicals such as *Time, Newsweek, U.S. News & World Report,* and *Business Week.*[43]

As Nixon had done verbally in the "kitchen debate," Rosenquist utilizes visual rhetoric to convey the symbiotic relationship between national defense aims and consumption in the home. Consumption was necessary to promote a healthy economy and therefore a strong nation, and conversely, a military commitment would ensure the free enterprise system. Rosenquist visualizes this connection in the various elements that comprise *F-111*. On the far left panel, the jet fighter's tail is overlaid with wallpaper as a connection to the domestic arena. As in his earlier painting *Pad*, Rosenquist here juxtaposes light bulbs with the Air Force emblem. This placement is logical considering that companies such as General Electric and Westinghouse not only produced light bulbs but also were major defense contractors.

Other consumer goods appear across the length of the *F-111*. In one of the left panels, near the bottom of the painting, Rosenquist has included an angel food cake. Cake mixes presented one of the most problematic challenges for those involved in marketing processed foods, and the angel food cake in *F-111* alludes to the obstacles it faced. Cake baking not only was an activity closely associated with homemaking but also, as market researchers found, had symbolic associations. One market researcher concluded that "baking a cake traditionally is acting out the birth of a child."[44] While many women welcomed the convenience that cake mixes offered, a considerable number of consumers were disturbed by the total appropriation of the cook's role that these mixes represented. This would seem to explain the strong resistance to prepared cake mixes that corporations encountered when these products were first introduced on the market. As a result of market studies, corporations changed the mixes so that certain fresh ingredients (e.g., eggs, milk) had to be added by the cook. The earlier mixes had, in a sense, made one of the functions of the homemaker obsolete. This one example amply illustrates the conflicts that surfaced in an age in which the role of women was undergoing drastic transformation.

Resistance to processed food can also be attributed to a concern for reduced nutritional value. Many women claimed that they added milk to the earlier cake mixes to ensure adequate calcium content. Rosenquist's angel food cake addresses this through the small flags that are planted in the surface. As if to overtly combat the perception that prepared foods were lacking in nutrients, the lettering on the flags reads: niacin, iron, riboflavin, protein, vitamin-B, and food energy.

Processed foods also appear in *F-III* in the form of broad areas of spaghetti. Although the can itself is absent, the spaghetti is bright orange in color and clearly refers to canned rather than homemade spaghetti. By displaying this array of processed food intermingled with fighter-bombers and atomic blasts, Rosenquist makes visible the ideological claims that underlay the "kitchen debate" and the directives to construct fallout shelters—that increased consumption would ensure national strength.

One of the most completely articulated and detailed sections of *F-III* is the depiction of a young girl under the hair dryer, which appears near the center of the painting. This image not only stands out visually but also most succinctly addresses the complex corpus of issues revolving around consumption, national military interest, self-fulfillment, and women's roles in the home.

Rosenquist's choice of a hair dryer is incisive as a representative product of the developing technology, particularly home appliances. While numerous variations of hair dryers, both hand held and wall mounted, had been marketed over the years, it was not until 1963, after extensive research, that the Rayette division of Faberge Incorporated produced the first hard-hat dryer especially designed for home use.[45] As a result of the extraordinary success of this model, the field was soon deluged with competitors, and by the end of the decade, the hard-hat home model dryer was a staple in the product line of any major business specializing in personal care.

Although this was a home appliance, it was one that was used almost exclusively by women and that appealed to the increasingly recognized need for self-fulfillment. Corporations were quick to encourage and capitalize on the growing ethos of self-fulfillment by manufacturing products that satisfied the urge for self-improvement or self-indulgence. Yet, as Rosenquist presents it in *F-III,* it also serves as a reminder of the changing role of women in America. Rather than a mature woman, a smiling, cherubic girl sits under the dryer. This image can be interpreted as a reference to the socialization processes that were disrupted by the new morality and lifestyles. Instead of trying on her mother's dresses or shoes, this young girl is learning to use the new appliances that will become a mainstay of her generation's lifestyle.

Rosenquist reveals the connections between the economic imperatives of consumption, new technology, and military action through the visual parallels between the conically shaped, shiny metal hair dryer and the F-III. In this manner, the use of military imagery links a conceptualization of national strength with technology in the home and serves to reinforce an ideology of consumption as a political imperative. Rosenquist's placement of the girl and hair dryer right over the location of the jet cockpit suggests that such technology and consumption were driving forces during this period.

Overall, *F-III* provides a visualization of the intersecting issues that consumption in the home involved and demonstrates that these issues were far from simplistic or easily resolved. The connections that were made between consumption, political ideological agendas, developing technology, and changing women's roles ultimately had a profound and lasting effect on the structure and dynamics of the American family.

The critical importance of the domestic arena as a proving ground for the ideology of consumption is evidenced by the strident and insistent efforts of government officials and corporate executives to induce ever-escalating purchases. The linking of consumption with the national interest helped justify these efforts. Pop art reinforces these connections and directives by presenting visual descriptions of complex ideological claims. As primary consumers and as the pivotal figures in the domestic arena, women played a critical role in this negotiation of intersecting interests. The Pop artists addressed the changing role of women in the 1960s and the growing climate of self-fulfillment as well as the pervasive objectification of women in advertisements. The eventual absorption of these works into the consumer matrix mitigated their potential to provide insightful critique about the burgeoning consumer culture.

# CHAPTER 5
# THE POP MOVEMENT AND THE INSTITUTIONAL MATRIX:
## THE ARTISTS

*Being good in business is the most fascinating kind of art. . . . Making money is art and working is art and good business is the best art.*

—*Andy Warhol* [1]

In 1965, the Jerrold Morris Gallery in Toronto planned a Warhol retrospective, in which they intended to include Warhol's previously discussed sculptural replicas of Brillo pad and Campbell's tomato juice cartons. However, when they applied for a certificate from the National Gallery of Canada to certify that the boxes were in fact works of art and therefore exempt from duty under item 695C of the Tariff Act, they were turned down. The National Gallery of Canada referred the organizers of the exhibition to the Dominion Customs Appraisers' Branch of the Department of Revenue, which subsequently decided that the boxes were subject to duty, which would have amounted to $4,000. Because they could not afford this unforeseen cost, the Morris Gallery deleted the boxes from the exhibition. [2]

The following year, Roy Lichtenstein produced dinnerware that was made available to the public through mail order and that was nationally advertised. Despite the fact that the ads appeared in art periodicals and that the copy emphasized the relative exclusivity of such an offer—"Certainly not open stock!" and "The dishes cost a great deal"—this dinnerware obviously was being marketed to a larger public. [3] The sale of high art has rarely been so blatantly advertised.

Both of these examples highlight the disappearing delineation between art and consumer products that Pop art encouraged. This blurred distinction was due not solely to the content and form of Pop art works but to their presentation as well. The development and establishment of any art movement is contingent on factors independent of the art works themselves, and Pop was certainly no exception. The success of Pop can, in part, be attributed to the fact that the avenues for the presentation of this art form were increasingly dominated by the principles of promotion and publicity, and Pop art fit nicely into this established construct. Thus, the connection of Pop art to consumer culture extends beyond the images themselves to the way in which this movement was marketed. For this reason, an exploration of the institutional apparatuses and individuals who worked within that matrix—artists, dealers, collectors, and critics—is critical to a study such as this.

While art has functioned as a commodity for centuries, fine or high art had always retained a certain aura or value that set it apart from the world of mundane consumer goods. The advent of Pop art, however, brought about a blurring of that distinction and, in fact, heightened a perception of art as commodity, as Warhol's Brillo boxes and Lichtenstein's dinnerware indicate.

Pop art further enhanced the explicit role of art as commodity because it represented a significant historical shift from an emphasis on the creation of the art work (the concept of art as the result of a creative act) to the presentation of art. This pronounced concern for the presentation and marketing of art as opposed to the creation of art was particularly noteworthy, coming as it did on the heels of Abstract Expressionism and other art movements in which a premium was placed on art as an individualistic, personal interaction between the artist and the medium. The Pop artists soundly renounced the emphasis on artistic touch and the character of pigment application that had been a hallmark of so many of the modernist movements of the late nineteenth and early twentieth centuries. This growing importance of presentational strategies parallelled the shift in emphasis from production to consumption that was characteristic of the popular Keynesian doctrine. Pop thus not only reflected important developments of its time but also correspondingly validated that shift to consumption in the realm of cultural discourse.

The Pop artists themselves played a pivotal role in the immersion of art into the matrix of publicity, advertising, and promotion. In order to understand the significance of this historically specific development, the predominance of modernist doctrine in art of the postwar period must be acknowledged. Although definitions of modernism and avant-gardism have varied since the application of the terms to art in the late nineteenth century, one characteristic that became more pronounced over the years was the hostile, antagonistic attitude that avant-garde artists maintained toward their public. Particularly in the 1950s, artists evinced a growing disregard for the general public. Although Abstract Expressionists like Barnett Newman did write extensively about the conceptual underpinnings of their art, one still gets the sense that their audience was restricted to an elite coterie of knowledgeable art-world participants.

In contrast, the Pop artists courted the public's attention. These artists gave numerous interviews that appeared in a wide range of publications, from art journals to mass-circulation periodicals. In addition, artists such as

Andy Warhol were highly visible public figures. This was quite a change from the much more hermetic stance of the Abstract Expressionist artists.

The facility with which the Pop artists utilized the media and understood the need for and benefits of promotion and public relations can largely be attributed to their backgrounds. Each of the Pop artists had significant experience in the commercial art world. As such, these artists were imbued with a solid understanding of the dynamics and principles underlying marketing strategy and advertising.

The Pop artists engaged in commercial art that ranged from producing advertising illustrations and creating window displays to painting billboards. These artists, rather than simply dabbling in commercial art, were immersed in it, and their employment in these fields during the 1950s was considerable. Significantly, these artists were extremely successful at this work, and their services were in great demand.

Andy Warhol was introduced to the fashion and advertising industries while still in college at the Carnegie Institute of Technology in Pittsburgh. He was employed during the summer at the Joseph Horne department store, where his job included arranging window displays and thumbing through *Vogue* and *Harper's Bazaar* looking for "ideas."[4] After moving to New York in 1949, Warhol received a number of diverse assignments that included an advertisement illustration for CBS Radio's report on crime, a drawing for an RCA Victor record album, book-jacket designs for New Directions Press, and illustrations for a Doubleday Press publication of *Amy Vanderbilt's Complete Book of Etiquette*. In addition, he designed stationery for Bergdorf Goodman and Christmas cards for Tiffany's. He received numerous accolades from art directors for his shoe advertisements for I. Miller. These advertisements eventually won Warhol major awards. Warhol also utilized his earlier experience in designing window displays, and he worked for Gene Moore, the well-known display director for Bonwit Teller and Tiffany's.

Like Warhol, Robert Rauschenberg and Jasper Johns found employment in the commercial art field in the early years of their careers. They collaborated under a single pseudonym, Matson Jones, while working for Gene Moore. Rauschenberg and Johns designed numerous window displays, which were so impressive that they were paid $500 a job, the highest price possible.[5] These windows were usually characterized by whimsy and wit and were very eye-catching (figs. 62 and 63). As a result of their efforts, other job offers followed. A cover they designed for a medical journal received an advertising design award, and Reynolds Metal offered them a contract to design the windows of the company's New York showroom. Rauschenberg and Johns definitely had captured the sensibility that was so crucial to effective advertising.

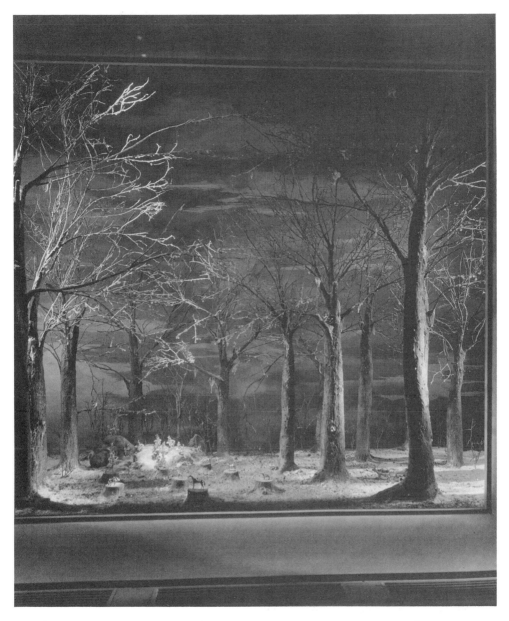

**Figure 62. Matson Jones (Robert Rauschenberg and Jasper Johns), window display for Tiffany & Co., 1956**
© 1989 Robert Rauschenberg and Jasper Johns/VAGA New York
Courtesy Robert Rauschenberg and Jasper Johns for Gene Moore for Tiffany & Co.

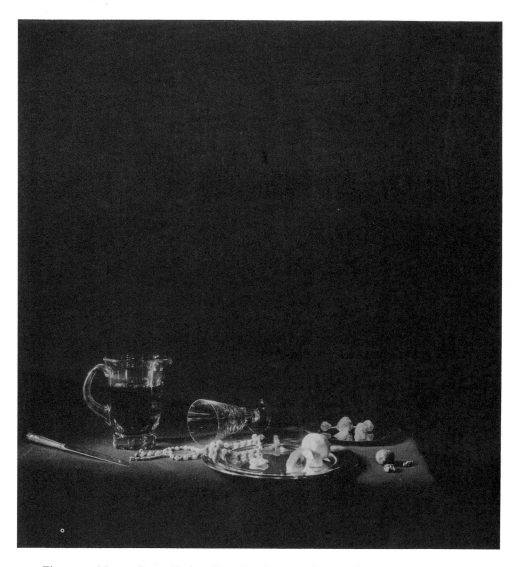

**Figure 63. Matson Jones (Robert Rauschenberg and Jasper Johns), window display for Tiffany & Co., 1956**
© 1989 Robert Rauschenberg and Jasper Johns/VAGA New York
Courtesy Robert Rauschenberg and Jasper Johns for Gene Moore for Tiffany & Co.

Gene Moore hired James Rosenquist as well to design window displays for both Tiffany's and Bonwit Teller. Rosenquist had been introduced to Moore by Rauschenberg but did not limit his work with windows to those stores. His designs also appeared in the windows of Bloomingdale's in the late 1950s. Rosenquist is perhaps best known for his experience in billboard painting, and in many of his window designs, Rosenquist transferred the style and scale of billboards to the smaller spaces. Behind the mannequins appeared large, flatly-painted close-up images that suggested fragmented billboards.

Billboards were, like store windows, effective as highly visible public advertisements. Most of the billboards painted by Rosenquist served to publicize movies, but he also created billboard ads for products such as Hebrew National salami and Man Tan. After some months of experience, Rosenquist acquired a reputation as one of the best billboard artists in the business; like the other Pop artists, he met with great success in his commercial art endeavors.

The experiences of Tom Wesselmann and Claes Oldenburg in commercial art were more circumscribed in both scope and duration than those of the other Pop artists. Wesselmann, originally hoping to be a cartoonist, managed to sell a few cartoons to magazines, but he never got the extensive public exposure that the other artists received with window displays or billboards. He did execute later some advertisements that were published in the *New Yorker*.

Oldenburg's foray into commercial art focused on advertising as well. His apprenticeship at an advertising agency during the early stages of his career furnished the necessary exposure to marketing techniques and advertising images that was to condition his later art.

The Pop artists also gained insight into the intersection between art and commerce through the "exhibitions" of their art work in department store windows—a practice that reinforced both the commodity status of art and the value of advertising. Even before he hired Rauschenberg to design windows, Moore placed some of Rauschenberg's early work in Bonwit Teller's windows. The publicity from this event was sufficient that *Life* magazine ran a story about Rauschenberg and his art along with photographs of the Bonwit Teller windows. "Moore noticed me before Leo Castelli [Rauschenberg's dealer] did," Rauschenberg once noted, laughing.[6]

Throughout the 1950s, Moore occasionally displayed paintings by Johns and Rauschenberg in Bonwit Teller's windows, and in 1962, Moore exhibited Warhol's Campbell's soup paintings, concurrently with the Ferus Gallery exhibition in Los Angeles of other paintings from the same series.

This background experience in the realm of advertising and commercial art sheds light on the Pop artists' unique grasp and comprehension of the dynamics of the corporate world, a world in which success depended on good promotion and effective utilization of publicity. The Pop artists did not merely mine commercial imagery for the content of their art but also used the techniques associated with advertising to "market" their work. Toward this end, the artists functioned as publicists, as explicators of their work, and as entrepreneurs. While the presentation of their work may not have been calculated on the part of all the Pop artists, they all understood the benefits that could be gained by such exposure. It is no accident that the artist who is considered the most prototypical Pop artist is Andy Warhol, the most accomplished publicist and promoter of this movement.

The Pop artists were far more accessible and gave more interviews than had their much more introspective and often reclusive predecessors, the Abstract Expressionists.[7] The prominence of the artists provided a wealth of information about the art works. This allowed the Pop artists to explicate their own production and define the parameters of the art movement. The public got a great deal of information "straight from the horse's mouth." Perhaps the most frequently quoted material on Pop art is the series of interviews organized by Gene R. Swenson for *Artnews* magazine in 1963. In response to the question "What is Pop art?," each artist presented his opinion in great depth. These interviews have since become a definitive source of information on Pop. The importance accorded interviews by scholars and public alike is indicated by the fact that the vast majority of the many monographs on Pop art include statements by the artists themselves.

Most notable for his utilization of the mass media for publicity purposes was Andy Warhol. Warhol acknowledged the value of projecting a recognizable public image through the many interviews that he granted. These interviews reveal the scrupulously alert mind of a promoter. Yet the statements made by the artist are far from unproblematic and straightforward. Scholars have often noted that Warhol's comments are notoriously unreliable and that Warhol often gave incorrect factual information that would cast doubt on the veracity of the rest of his statements. Hence, most critics concluded that Warhol was "a notably untrustworthy witness."[8] Warhol occasionally looked to others for responses to questions; "Just tell me what to say," he directed a bystander at one of his television interviews.[9] While this does call into question the value of his statements in elucidating various aspects of his art, it reveals a comprehension of considerably greater significance—Warhol realized that it was the act of publicity, rather than the information divulged, that was of prime concern. What was important was generating interest and sustaining that interest so that one's audience would keep coming back for more.

Warhol demonstrated his appreciation of this concept when he scheduled an extensive college lecture circuit in 1967. Not content to restrict himself to press interviews, Warhol arranged (through a lecture bureau) to give a series of lectures on various college campuses. Rather than appear in person, Warhol sent actor-dancer Allen Midgette in his place, with his hair sprayed silver to duplicate Warhol's look. The fact that he was an imposter was not discovered until some months later, at which time many of the schools demanded that the real Warhol return and "redo the lectures."[10] Through the attendant publicity that this debacle received, Warhol increased his audience and name recognition.

Warhol pursued the dissemination of information about himself through a series of books as well. In these books, *The Philosophy of Andy Warhol (From A to B and Back Again)* and *POPism: The Warhol '60s,* Warhol expounded upon his views about art and life.

Given the importance that Warhol attached to publicity of both himself and his work, it was no coincidence that his own continuing monthly publication, which he established in 1972, is entitled *Interview* and consists of interviews with famous people from the entertainment industry and high society.

Warhol was not the only Pop artist who realized that public perception of the art works was inextricably linked to the perception of the artist. James Rosenquist, like Warhol, was an active participant in social events around town. Reportedly, he drank every night, danced, and "called attention to himself."[11] Rosenquist himself claimed that he spent every night out during the 1960s.[12]

Activities such as those in which Warhol and Rosenquist were engaged gave the Pop movement a higher public visibility than had been enjoyed by previous art movements. Not only did their interviews provide the public with more information, accurate or not, but also they underscored the extent to which promotion and advertising dominated the 1960s, even in the realm of art. This has led some critics to conclude, as Calvin Tomkins stated, that "Warhol's art was the art of publicity."[13]

Ultimately, this incessant publicity pushed Warhol, as representative of the Pop movement, into the realm of celebrity. In light of the Pop artists' interest in Hollywood and the celebrity system as displayed in their art, this transition was most appropriate. The sensibility that allowed celebrities to serve as spokespeople and sell products regardless of whether or not they actually used the product was transferred to the art world. It mattered little what these artists were saying; what was important was the fact that they were saying it. The Pop artists were the beneficiaries of a new authority of the artist; however, that authority rested not on the concept of artistic genius, but on the notion of celebrity. The mechanisms of a consumer society, which were the subject of Pop art paintings and sculptures, were being used by the Pop artists themselves, particularly Warhol, to present their work to a larger audience. In this manner, the presentation of the art took precedence over the production of the work.

Like many of those figures whose portraits he had painted, Warhol had become a creation of the media. People who had never seen a Warhol painting knew who he was. It is not too farfetched to suggest that the artist had become the artistic product, and ultimately, a commodity. This status was confirmed in 1965, at the opening of an exhibition of Warhol's work at the Institute of Contemporary Art in Philadelphia. Four thousand people showed up, far exceeding the expectation, and fearing for the safety of the art works, the staff decided to remove all of the art from the walls. This delighted Warhol: "It was fabulous: an art opening with no art!"[14] Despite attempts by guards to control the crowds, Warhol and his companion, Edie Sedgwick, were mobbed for autographs and eventually had to be escorted out of the building via the roof and a fire escape. Later, Warhol expressed his delight with the crowd reaction: "I'd seen kids scream over . . . rock idols and movie stars—but it was incredible to think of it happening at an *art* opening. . . . But then, we weren't just *at* the art exhibit—we *were* the art exhibit, we were the art incarnate and the sixties were really about people, not about what they did. . . . Nobody had even cared that the paintings were all off the walls."[15] Clearly the myth of Andy Warhol had transcended the art objects themselves. Warhol reveled in his high visibility; when asked by dealer Ivan Karp what he wanted since he ostensibly "had it all," Warhol responded, "I want more fame."[16]

Warhol's celebrity status continued to expand despite the ascent of numerous other art movements and artists in the 1970s and 1980s. In 1985, Warhol appeared in an episode of "The Love Boat," a prime-time television show whose constantly changing cast was composed of guest stars selected solely on the basis of their celebrity status. Appropriately enough, Warhol played himself. He was also hired as a celebrity spokesperson for Amiga computers and Vidal Sassoon hair-care products. Perhaps the ultimate proof not merely of Warhol's status as a celebrity but also of his absorption into the institutional consumer matrix was his service in the 1980s as a spokesperson for diet Coke and a package designer for Campbell Soup Company. Having used their products as the subject of his earlier art, Warhol eventually became a conduit in the advertising operations of these monolithic corporations, who exploited his celebrity status and established association with their products.

Not all of the Pop artists courted the spotlight to the degree that Andy Warhol did, but as the prototypical Pop artist, Warhol became representative of an entire movement. The cult of personality and the emphasis on celebrity informed not just the art works but the presentation of those works as well. Indicative of this orientation was the growing practice by galleries during the 1960s of advertising exhibitions in the print media with photographs of the artists rather than of the art works.[17] This publicity helped bring Pop art to the attention of the wider public and explains the references to this movement outside of established art-world channels. For example, one episode of the groundbreaking and controversial television show "All in the Family" was focused on modern art. Oriented toward a middle-class viewing audience, "All in the Family" centered around a "typical" lower-class family and explored various issues from that perspective. In this particular episode, an artist mistakenly acquires Archie Bunker's favorite chair and incorporates it into an assemblage, not unlike Rauschenberg's combines—part sculpture and part painting. Rather than utilize a randomly selected name for the artist, the show's writers and producers bestowed on their fictitious artist the name "Lichtenrausch."

Beyond their roles as explicators and publicists, the Pop artists also expanded the role of artist as entrepreneur and acknowledged that like any corporation, they were involved in a business. Although they all had gallery dealers to represent them and deal with the purchases of their art, the Pop artists were intimately engaged in the financial aspects of the art world.

Warhol's desire to be "an Art Businessman" was a fundamental goal of his entire career. Even during the early years, financial success was a major preoccupation. When asked what impressed him about an early Jasper Johns drawing of a light bulb, rather than point to any formal qualities, Warhol said that it was the price: "I couldn't understand how he could get five hundred dollars for a drawing."[18] Another often repeated anecdote about Warhol's choice of subject matter reinforces this perception of the artist, despite the skepticism with which this anecdote must be received. In 1962, Warhol was searching for new ideas for his paintings and asked Muriel Latow, a gallery dealer, for advice. She suggested that he paint what he loved more than anything else, and the result was the series of "money" paintings.[19] In another version of this story, Warhol recounts that Eleanor Ward, owner of the Stable Gallery, was bluntly asked in 1962 whether she planned to give Warhol a show. According to Warhol, Ward pulled a two-dollar bill out of her wallet and said, "Andy, if you paint me this, I'll give you a show."[20] Both anecdotes, however apocryphal, blatantly expose the financial mindset of those associated with Pop.

Robert Rauschenberg shared such financial concerns and chose a public forum in which to make a statement about the inequities of the art market. At the Sotheby's auction of the Robert C. and Ethel Scull collection in 1973, which was extensively covered by the press and television, Rauschenberg approached Scull after the sale had grossed $2,242,900, shoved the collector in the chest, and accused him of infidelity and the auction house of "profiteering."[21] Protested Rauschenberg: "I've been working my ass off just for you to make that profit."[22] When Scull argued that Rauschenberg would benefit from increased sales of his future work at higher prices as a result of the auction, the artist responded: "You buy the next one [painting], OK?—at these prices."[23] This exchange prompted Rauschenberg to lobby on behalf of the campaign for artist's royalties on resales of works.

Roy Lichtenstein, like Rauschenberg, had given serious thought to the problem of the resale of art works. He discussed it at some length in an interview published in *Partisan Review* entitled "Pop Art, Money, and the Present Scene." Although he concluded that developing a coherent resale system was not feasible, he did suggest that the artist, if interested in the appreciation of his art works, should retain a number of paintings from each period of his career, so that the artist would also reap the financial benefits of events that affect the prices of his works, such as the Scull auction.[24]

The entrepreneurial attitude of James Rosenquist surfaced at a recent Sotheby's auction of another portion of the Scull collection on 10 and 11 November 1986. *F-III*, which originally had trouble finding a buyer when Rosenquist painted it in 1965, was sold for $2.9 million, the second-highest price paid to date for a contemporary work of art. Rosenquist's response to this sale was: "I never signed the painting. It's unsigned. Maybe I'll charge a million to sign it."[25] While it is probable that this comment was made in jest, it is revealing because it suggests that Rosenquist was more concerned with financial security than with his artistic legacy.

Claes Oldenburg made his understanding of marketing issues clear when he produced *Soft Version of Maquette for a Monument Donated to the City of Chicago by Pablo Picasso* in 1969. Most discussions about this sculpture have focused on the translation of Picasso's well-known Chicago monument into Oldenburg's idiomatic soft sculpture. However, the motivation for Oldenburg's work revolved around the issue of the marketing of a work of art. Incited by the fact that the city of Chicago had copyrighted the Picasso monument (located in the Civic Center) and was selling reproductions of it, attorneys William N. Copley and Barnet Hodes commissioned Oldenburg to create another version of the monument, to be used in a lawsuit challenging the city's copyright of the sculpture.[26] Oldenburg considers the relevant legal documents as part of his sculpture, indicating that the legal challenge and marketing issues are as important, if not more important, than the aesthetic statement of the work.[27]

Through their active participation in the interpretation and promotion of their works, as well as through their involvement in the financial aspects of the art world, the Pop artists took on an expanded role that demonstrated a keen awareness of and appreciation for corporate culture. Their backgrounds in commercial art and their insistence on mining advertising and popular culture for images that surfaced in their art contributed to their comprehension of the structure and strategies of the corporate world.

In their utilization of the very strategies and techniques that had proven so spectacularly successful for the large multinational corporations, the Pop artists were inextricably drawn into an institutional matrix that reinforced an ideology of consumption. By accepting and actively exploiting these strategies, the Pop movement ultimately denied the possibility of effective critique of this system. As such, the artists, through their statements and actions, did not merely reflect consumer culture but also actively absorbed or deflected criticism about such a system.

# CHAPTER 6
# THE POP MOVEMENT AND THE INSTITUTIONAL MATRIX:
## THE DEALERS AND COLLECTORS

*So you need a good gallery so the "ruling class" will notice you and spread enough confidence in your future so collectors will buy you. . . . No matter how good you are, if you're not promoted right, you won't be one of those remembered names.*

—*Andy Warhol*[1]

The economic structure of the art world is based on a network of dealers and collectors (along with auction houses). One might assert that because these institutions are primarily involved in the buying and selling of art work, the connection to consumer culture is obvious and therefore needs no elaboration. This is far from true. The success of Pop art was due in part to dealers who aggressively promoted both the specific artists and the movement in general and to collectors whose professions made them part of the corporate environment that provided the content and context for Pop works. Both of these parties were, arguably, more receptive to Pop because they understood the complex of issues that the blatant images of processed foods, celebrities, and comic strips represented. In a sense, by marketing and purchasing Pop works, the dealers and collectors were completing the works.

This is not to suggest that this relationship of dealers and collectors to consumer culture represented a radical change. The role of dealers has always been, by definition, business oriented, and there are numerous examples in preceding centuries of dealers who actively and successfully promoted their artists. Likewise, collectors have tended to emerge from the ranks of those who control production in society, because they are able to accrue the vast amounts of money that serious collecting demands. Yet in the 1960s, these participants began to wield greater influence in determining the direction of art. Closer examination of the players involved in the establishment of Pop art provides us with a better understanding of the marketing and commodification processes that contributed to the success of this movement.

It is difficult to document with great accuracy the actual economic development of the various galleries during this period, since financial records are not readily available. Nevertheless, it is clear that the most successful dealers were those who understood the mechanisms of publicity, price management, and advertising. That earlier art dealers were also successful businessmen cannot be denied. In the postwar years, however, dealers had to respond to the growing demands of the maturing consumer society. Their awareness of corporate business practices reveals the pervasiveness and effectiveness of corporate models and strategies and places the business of art dealing squarely in the intensifying current of consumer culture. Among the dealers involved with the establishment of Pop were Richard Bellamy, Leo Castelli, Sidney Janis, Ivan Karp, and Eleanor Ward. By focusing on Leo Castelli, the one gallery dealer who became most closely associated with the Pop movement and who is representative of the dealers as Warhol is representative of the artists, the contribution and role of the dealer can be illustrated.

The success of the Leo Castelli Gallery, founded in 1957, demonstrates that the market for Pop art was immense and that proper handling of that market could be profitable. Castelli realized the potential marketability of Pop art, and by the mid-1960s represented Robert Rauschenberg, Jasper Johns, Roy Lichtenstein, Claes Oldenburg, James Rosenquist, and Andy Warhol. Established concurrently with the initial experiments in Pop, Castelli Gallery currently enjoys the distinction of being "the most influential purveyor of contemporary art in the world."[2] Leo Castelli's success in promoting Pop art provided him with the stature and financial stability to influence the direction of subsequent art movements.

Castelli was well aware of the importance of placing artists' work in visible and influential collections. For example, according to one account, Castelli reduced the price of a certain painting so that Alfred Barr, director of the Museum of Modern Art, could buy it out of special funds, thereby avoiding having to seek the board's approval.[3] This suggests that Castelli realized the obstacles with which the acceptance of the painting was faced, and he found a viable solution to the problem. It also reveals that he understood the impact that representation in the Museum of Modern Art's permanent collection would have on subsequent sales of that artist's work.

Such placement was a problem during the early years of the Pop movement, when the hostility from established critics was particularly virulent. Castelli made every effort to counteract and undermine that reaction through promotion and price management. A good example of this savvy maneuvering by Castelli was his lobbying on behalf of Robert Rauschenberg at the 1964 Venice Biennale. When Rauschenberg was awarded the grand prize, many people accused Castelli of "fixing" the Biennale. It was no secret that Alan Solomon, the commissioner of the American pavilion, was Castelli's good friend, nor that four of the eight American artists being shown were represented by Castelli. The dealer orchestrated Rauschenberg's arrival in

Venice to coincide with the official opening and spent the week entertaining and holding receptions for various groups of people. Rumor had it that Castelli utilized his considerable linguistic skills (he speaks five languages fluently) to lobby the international panel of judges who would select the prize winners; others deny that this contact ever took place.[4] Given the dealer's high visibility during the Biennale, the accusations of a conspiracy masterminded by Castelli to ensure Rauschenberg's victory were not surprising. Indeed, the financial results were staggering. In the period between 1963, the year before the Biennale, and 1965, the year after, the prices of Rauschenberg's works quintupled.[5]

Although Castelli dislikes being portrayed as a shrewd manipulator of prices who orchestrates art developments, it cannot be denied that he is an astute businessman. He was instrumental in arranging sales of the Pop artists' works that benefitted all involved. When James Rosenquist finished *F-III* in 1965, Castelli realized that it was "virtually unsalable."[6] Because Castelli felt that "at the time, it was important to sell something," and he was "rather desperate about selling the picture," Castelli and Rosenquist finally settled on selling the 86-foot-long painting in fragments.[7] On the last day of the exhibition, collector Robert Scull purchased the work for a reported $60,000. A story about the sale of the painting appeared on the front page of the *New York Times,* and was reported in *Time* magazine as well, providing extensive publicity for Rosenquist, Scull, and Castelli.[8] When it was discovered later that Scull had paid considerably less than $60,000, Castelli was accused of seeking to inflate Rosenquist's prices artificially.[9] So adept was Castelli at such financial arrangements that Jasper Johns reportedly created his bronze *Ballantine Ale Cans* (1960) in specific response to Abstract Expressionist Willem de Kooning's remark about Castelli that "you could give that son of a bitch two beer cans and he could sell them."[10] Appropriately, Castelli sold Johns' sculpture for $960; in 1973, it brought $90,000 at auction.[11]

The success of Castelli and other dealers depended upon the availability of collectors willing to purchase these works of art. Such individuals were numerous, and one observer went so far as to assert that Pop art "was and is a collectors' movement. Collectors were the principal champions of the group, and they are responsible for the success of the school."[12] Castelli himself attributes a great deal of his achievement to the perspicacity of the collectors.[13]

One example of the importance of collectors that reveals the symbiotic relationship of collectors and dealers was the financing of the Green Gallery. Collector Robert Scull agreed to purchase at least $18,000 annually from the gallery, which had been founded in 1960 by Richard Bellamy. This financial backing helped sustain the gallery during its initial rocky period. Bellamy started exhibiting some of the Pop artists' work in 1962, and in an interview conducted in the early 1980s, he made statements that suggest that he understood the ramifications of Pop's intersection with consumer culture and the gallery system's participation in that process. Bellamy recalled: "A lot of attention was being thrown upon galleries and artists, due to the Pop Art phenomenon, and we certainly participated in that. We had some important shows, and several artists from the original roster were offended and left for reasons of conscience after I began to show Pop Art. Several artists protested that I hadn't sold any of their work, and they might have felt that I was disloyal to what they stood for by showing work [i.e., Pop art] that seemed to subvert their careers." [14] This statement reveals that Bellamy was cognizant of the antagonistic relationship with established art that Pop had engendered. The exhibition of Pop in the Green Gallery represented an affirmation of an ideological position vis-à-vis consumer culture, and the decision to show the works of artists such as Oldenburg and Rosenquist suggests that Bellamy willingly acquiesced. In addition, this statement reveals the pervasiveness and dominance of consumer culture. While some of the non-Pop artists represented by Bellamy objected to Pop, ostensibly on stylistic grounds, Bellamy's statement suggests that the underlying reason for their concern was economic—that their careers would be subverted and that their works would no longer sell due to the popularity of Pop art.

All of the major Pop art collectors were people who had benefitted from the rampant consumption of the postwar years; they were industrialists (e.g., Peter Ludwig, Giuseppe Panza) and corporate executives (e.g., Leon Kraushar, Robert Scull). The attraction of Pop art for these collectors can be attributed in large part to its imagery derived from the consumer environment. Many of these collectors saw Pop art as an affirmation of a society based on commodity exchange, but even for those who viewed Pop as a critique of such a system, the art still served to deflect criticism from their own business activity. Ultimately, Pop art provided both visual and conceptual illustration of the validity of the established imperative to consume.

The largest Pop art collection was amassed during the 1960s by Leon Kraushar, an insurance broker from New York. He was not involved in the early developmental stage of the movement and only started collecting Pop after it had become fairly well established. So enthralled was Kraushar by the Pop images that he rapidly purchased numerous examples, transforming his home "into a kind of temple of pop art." [15]

Pop art appealed to Kraushar because it "spoke directly to me about things I understood." [16] Kraushar did not have a background in art and seemingly responded to the paintings on a direct, visual level, rather than in terms of their contribution to the historical continuum of art. The references made by Pop art to the consumer environment and strategies were probably comforting because they corresponded to Kraushar's own experiences. Beyond any visual or conceptual empathy he may have had for Pop, Kraushar was acutely aware of the role of art as commodity and as sound investment. He insisted that "these pictures are like IBM stock, don't forget that, and this is the time to buy, because pop is never going to die. I'm not planning to sell my IBM stock either."[17] Kraushar loved to sit in the midst of the works, reveling in his acquisitions. "I don't even look at the pictures," he explained. "I just know they're there—and that I have the best and biggest collection in the world."[18]

In late 1967, Leon Kraushar died of a heart attack, and his collection was sold as a unit the following year to Karl Ströher, a West German collector. Ströher sold a few pieces and added others, but the bulk of the collection was kept intact. The collection, now known as the Ströher collection, remains one of the two largest collections of Pop art in the world.

The other Pop collection that ranks with the Ströher collection in size and scope is the Peter Ludwig collection in Cologne. Peter Ludwig is an industrialist who owns a candy manufacturing company in Germany. Unlike Leon Kraushar, however, Ludwig holds a doctorate in art history and had been involved in the art field for years prior to the ascent of Pop art.

The fact that the two largest collections of Pop art are located in West Germany provides further confirmation of the assertion that Pop's success was due to its immersion in consumer culture. In the postwar era, the United States was instrumental in the redevelopment and restructuring of the German economy. As a result, the West German economic system, compared to those of other European countries, most closely resembles that of the United States.[19] This historical situation makes the appeal of Pop art to the West Germans logical. The validation of consumer culture that Pop represented would be particularly applicable in their country as well. Peter Ludwig explained that his motivation for buying Pop art was due to his "conviction that the American way of life was becoming universal and that American artists drew their power from being closest to the source."[20]

Despite the size of the Ludwig and Kraushar-Ströher collections, the collector most closely identified with the Pop movement was Robert Scull.[21] Scull was an entrepreneur who began as a sign painter and eventually organized his own industrial design firm.[22] He soon expanded into the taxicab business, real estate, and insurance.[23] His background in commercial art and as a corporate executive made him receptive to Pop. Scull was one of the first collectors of Pop art, and his collection, parts of which were auctioned off in 1973 and 1986, comprised a definitive history of the movement.

Scull himself was very much part of the Pop sensibility, and as a self-made financial success, he undoubtedly saw Pop works as reassuring images of the consumer environment. Moreover, Scull valued these works for non-aesthetic reasons that reveal to a greater extent the manner in which the marketability of Pop art was instrumental in reinforcing an ideology of consumption.

Scull's aggressive acquisition of Pop art led critics to suggest that his major concern was financial in nature and that he bought art primarily for investment purposes. Ivan Karp, Leo Castelli's associate during the 1960s, stated: "Leo was always affable with Scull, but I don't believe he ever felt comfortable with him for one minute. . . . He behaved toward art the same way he behaved toward his taxi business. There was always a contest about the price."[24] Many critics viewed Scull as a speculator, and the sale in 1973 of many of Scull's Pop art acquisitions prompted articles such as that by critic Barbara Rose, entitled "Profit without Honor."[25] This perception of Scull seemed to be corroborated by Scull's own statements. For example, Scull's reaction to his first art purchase was: "I felt as though I had bought all of AT & T."[26]

In addition, Scull, the son of Russian immigrants who worked his way up the corporate ladder, saw art as a means to social status. When asked about accusations that he purchased art for "social climbing," Scull replied: "It's all true. I'd rather use art to climb than anything else."[27] This blatant admission, which was obviously tinged with self-deprecating irony, did not endear him to much of the art world. Scull saw the advantages of association not only with the art works but also with the artists. Enamoured by the cult of celebrity, Scull insisted on meeting all of the Pop artists personally.

The fierce competition amongst the various collectors for Pop works reveals the pivotal position occupied by collectors in the establishment of Pop. As early as 1960, Emily and Burton Tremaine, Frederick Weisman, Ben Heller, and Robert Scull were all fighting over paintings by Jasper Johns. They even began to negotiate with Johns and Castelli, Johns' dealer, to purchase paintings before Johns had even started them.[28] Despite the attestations of these collectors that they purchased art for its aesthetic merits, the fact that they were buying works before they were even painted suggests otherwise.

The efforts of dealers such as Leo Castelli and the interest of collectors such as Robert Scull were critical to the establishment of Pop art. The immersion of Pop into this nexus of promotional strategies, commodification of art, and corporate mentalities anchored the movement firmly in the force field of consumer culture. The marketability of this movement ensured its phenomenal ascent, and together with the paintings and sculptures themselves, exposes the pervasive and dominant character of the consumer ethic in the 1960s.

# CHAPTER 7
# THE POP MOVEMENT AND THE INSTITUTIONAL MATRIX:
## THE CRITICS

*Unquestionably, American criticism is in a transitional stage that is sinking ever deeper into crisis.*

—*Max Kozloff (1964)* [1]

Although it was primarily the artists, dealers, and collectors who were instrumental in ensuring the success of the Pop movement, a complete understanding of the dynamics of the art world necessitates scrutiny of the critical establishment. When Pop first surfaced in the late 1950s, the critical establishment was an entrenched and important institution. However, the appearance of Pop was problematic for many critics, since it seemed to reject so many of the ideas, attitudes, and elements that had been extolled in earlier abstract art. Critics were thus placed in a position of either renouncing their support of the earlier movements and changing the criteria by which they evaluated art, or dismissing Pop as an inconsequential aberration in the historical continuum of art by declaring that Pop's formal and conceptual contributions were minimal. While there were those critics who promoted Pop art, most of the established corps of critics chose the latter course of action and responded to Pop with caustic, often vitriolic prose.

This hostility can be traced to a variety of factors. First and foremost, critics were distressed by the diminishing importance of formal considerations in relation to content in Pop art. The ascendancy of art criticism in the United States in the twentieth century had been closely tied to the development of the avant-garde. The historical continuum of avant-garde art had moved toward increasing abstraction, and criticism, correspondingly, gravitated toward a preoccupation with formal issues. This was manifested in a critical approach that revolved around a steadfast involvement with exposing the plastic capabilities of artistic media as opposed to an involvement with illusionism or content. Not only did critics respond favorably to the trend toward greater abstraction but conversely their interest in formal issues and positive response toward this development no doubt encouraged artists to pursue it diligently.

Critics were hard-pressed to deal with Pop in terms of what had, by then, become the accepted critical canon, because the content of Pop was so obvious as to overshadow formal considerations. When they did attempt to analyze the art, Pop failed to fulfill their expectations of what serious art (i.e., art engaged in the discourse about formal issues) should look like. By the early 1960s, Clement Greenberg was the most influential critic and was closely linked to the establishment of Abstract Expressionism. In 1965, he published his essay "After Abstract Expressionism," in which he discussed the development of Abstract Expressionism. He perceived that movement as emerging out of the rigid strictures of synthetic Cubism toward a looser, more painterly style that was more analytical in its approach. In closing, Greenberg addressed the artists involved in Pop (which he refers to as "neo-dada"). He concluded: "Whatever novel objects they represent or insert in their works, not one of them has taken a chance with colour or design that the Cubists or Abstract Expressionists did not take before them. . . . Nor has any one of them . . . yet dared to arrange these things outside the directional lines of the 'all-over' Cubist grid. . . . Not that I do not find the clear and straightforward academic handling of their pictures refreshing after the turgidities of Abstract Expressionism; yet the effect is only momentary, since novelty, as distinct from originality, has no staying power."[2] Greenberg's assessment of Pop art is clearly based on the artists' treatment of the traditional visual elements, which he finds unnoteworthy.

Herbert Read, another well-established art critic, appraised Pop in a 1965 article. The title, "Disintegration of Form in Modern Art," indicates both his evaluation of Pop and the affinity of his approach to that of Greenberg. Read accused the Pop artists of sacrificing formal rigor—what he referred to as "esthetic discipline." Due to the lack of this "esthetic conscience," Read concluded that Pop art retreated into incoherence.[3]

A review of the art criticism of the 1960s reveals this insistence on applying the established critical canon to Pop. Peter Plagens presented a determined attempt to uncover the formal contributions of Pop in his 1966 article "Present-Day Styles and Ready-Made Criticism." He believed that "the question of Pop's formalism involves the deepest elements of style," and he traced the development of the concept of style from "the first of the modernisms" through Action Painting.[4] He remarked that with Action Painting, style receded to the *act* of picture-making. "The great art-historical phenomenon of Pop," he declared, "is that it has managed . . . to nudge style back another notch—to social and esthetic attitudes existing in full form within the artist *before* the act of picture-making."[5] In coming to this conclusion, Plagens broadened the definition of style beyond the actual visual elements to incorporate the often nebulous, nonspecific mindset of the artist. This suggests that intentionality, and even subconscious input, should be considered in discussions of style. This shift allowed Plagens to accommodate Pop within the strictures of the established critical canon.

While Plagens was more inclusive in his deliberation, Harold Rosenberg narrowed the parameters of his critique. Like Plagens and other critics, Rosenberg addressed formal issues in his essay "The Art World: Marilyn Mondrian." He noted in the introduction that "now, . . . the underlying abstractness or formalism of Pop is being passionately urged upon the attention of the art world" and proceeded to explore the aesthetic contribution of Pop.[6] Rosenberg, however, rather than simply focus on form and ignore content, went so far as to assert that content ceased to exist in Pop art. In discussing Lichtenstein's work (Rosenberg considered Lichtenstein to be "the artist who best represents the basic motives of Pop Art"), the critic stated that Lichtenstein's "aesthetic reprocessing, which homogenizes 'vulgar' art with high-art forms and high art with formal derivatives from the mass media, cancels the content of both and leaves only design."[7] This logic allowed Rosenberg to expose what he considered the contribution of Pop: "The extinction of content in Pop Art enabled it to . . . serve as a bridge between the art of latecomers to Action painting . . . and the varieties of abstract modes that emphasize areas of color disposed on materials of a given size and shape."[8] Denying the presence of content permitted Rosenberg to fit Pop into the prevailing critical canon and to view the paintings as steps in the progression toward a greater assertion of the picture plane and of surface integrity. In so doing, Rosenberg could continue to maintain the viability of his evaluative criteria and judgment despite the rapidly changing styles and sensibilities in art with which he was being confronted.

There were other critics who realized that Pop called into question some of the fundamental underpinnings of codified critical criteria. Barbara Rose described the traditional critical approach as mired in "idealist esthetics," which she defined as an outlook that holds "that the work of art is a timeless Absolute, whose value transcends any specific social and historical context, and is measureable by a changeless standard of quality."[9] She believed that much of the new art was based on pragmatic values, in which the aesthetic was extended "beyond the unique object into the life and environment of everyman."[10] She used this polemical situation to critique the state of criticism and its methodological dogmatism and concluded that the predominance of idealist absolutes and standards made formalist-oriented criticism inappropriate for art of the 1960s.

Max Kozloff also castigated his fellow critics for adhering to an absolute, anachronistic approach. Even as early as 1964, he exhorted: "The critical record on the two liveliest areas of the moment [one of which he identifies as

Pop art] . . . is inadequate, not because it often disapproves, but because it has not adjusted to a changing climate of inquiry, and to the evolving pictorial language which is its result. If ambitious work is becoming increasingly controversial and undigested, it is because the professional critics, those daily committed to judgment, are ever more loath to move out from their fixed positions."[11] This is not to suggest that Kozloff supported Pop; in fact, he labeled the Pop artists "the new Vulgarians" and could not decide whether Pop art was pathological or merely dull.[12]

It was not just on formal grounds that Pop art was derided by critics. A second source of agitation was the Pop artists' apparent disregard for the notion of art as a lofty, moral enterprise.[13] To these critics, Pop art lacked the heroic and mythic dimension that had come to be equated with serious intent and artistic integrity. Because the Pop artists ostensibly refused to place their art within, or even acknowledge, the strict and limiting aesthetic guidelines along which art had been developing in the previous decades, critics decried their art and were alarmed that it was accepted by dealers and collectors, as well as by a substantial segment of the public at large. "The truth is," Kozloff declared, "the art galleries are being invaded by the pinheaded and contemptible style of gum chewers, bobby soxers, and worse, delinquents."[14] Critic and artist Sidney Tillim concurred. He concluded that "pop art and this 'new' object art [the work of Jim Dine, Robert Rauschenberg, and Jasper Johns] . . . constitute the decadence and destitution . . . of modern art."[15]

This perception of Pop art as decadent, and therefore somehow immoral, was also due to the way in which Pop seemed to challenge the notion of authenticity, a cornerstone of artistic production and critical theory. Walter Benjamin addressed this issue in his seminal 1936 essay "The Work of Art in the Age of Mechanical Reproduction." Benjamin asserted that the reproduction of works of art (such as that afforded by the silkscreen and stencil techniques used by the Pop artists) resulted in a loss of aura, or authority. Benjamin claimed that what any reproduction lacked was authenticity, upon which rests historical testimony, and, ultimately, the authority of the object. But does this still hold true in an era whose fundamental characteristic is mass production? In Pop art works, the historicity of the object lies precisely in its reproduceability.

As a result of Pop art's immersion in a culture of consumption and mass production, critics who viewed Pop art as lacking the heroic and mythic dimension they deemed crucial to serious art labeled Pop as kitsch, rather than as avant-garde. The tenets of avant-gardism, especially vis-à-vis art's formal internal progression, had evolved into the predominant determinant of artistic value. The dialectical process and rejection of tradition that were fundamental to avant-gardism had led to the growing predominance of abstraction and non-narrative art. In the 1940s and 1950s, the avant-garde found its champion in Clement Greenberg, whose previously cited statements elucidate his position. Due to his pronouncements, avant-garde art became increasingly formulaic, exclusionary, and dogmatic. In referring disparagingly to Pop as kitsch, critics were utilizing Greenberg's definition of the term as codified in his 1939 essay "Avant-Garde and Kitsch." To these critics, Pop art seemed to fulfill Greenberg's criteria for kitsch: "To fill the demand of the new market a new commodity was devised: ersatz culture, kitsch. . . . Kitsch, using for raw material the debased and academicized simulacra of genuine culture, welcomes and cultivates this insensibility. It is the source of its profits. . . . Kitsch is the epitome of all that is spurious in the life of our times. Kitsch pretends to demand nothing of its customers except their money."[16] Because Pop could be categorized as kitsch with such ease, one could just as easily conclude that Pop therefore had no redeeming value, formal or otherwise.

The lack of any evident transformation in the translation from ad or mass-media image to art work was another source of virulent criticism. In contrast to Abstract Expressionism, in which the emotions of the artist were prominently displayed on the canvas' surface in the form of slashing brushstrokes or ethereal fields of color, the visual evidence of the Pop artists' engagement was minimal. Critics such as Erle Loran were led to ask, "Pop artists or copy cats?"[17] Peter Selz, then curator at the Museum of Modern Art, concurred. He declared: "The interpretation or transformation of reality achieved by the Pop Artist, insofar as it exists at all, is limp and unconvincing. It is this want of imagination, this passive acceptance of things as they are that make these pictures so unsatisfactory at second or third look. They are hardly worth the kind of contemplation a real work of art demands."[18]

For most critics, Abstract Expressionism (as the culmination of decades of progressive abstraction) had become a standard against which all subsequent art was evaluated. The resoluteness with which Pop art embraced representation was objectionable to many critics on those grounds. These critics perceived postwar art as developing in a primarily linear progression toward greater abstraction, and figuration and illusionism were seen as a regression—a retreat to easy solutions by artists who were incapable of dealing with difficult formal questions.

This return to representation had political ramifications as well. Many of the proponents of Abstract Expressionism, both artists and critics, had been partisans of left-wing politics during the 1930s but grew increasingly disillusioned about the possibility of fundamental social change. As art historian Serge Guilbaut has emphatically demonstrated in *How New York Stole the Idea of Modern Art: Abstract Expressionism, Freedom, and the Cold War* (1983), this connection between the American avant-garde, as embodied by Abstract Expressionism, and a disenchantment with the state of leftist politics had much to do with the success of Abstract Expressionism. In "Abstract Expressionism, Weapon of the Cold War" (1974), art historian Eva Cockcroft asserts that Abstract Expressionism, precisely because of its emphasis on abstraction, was presented by influential figures in the realms of politics and art as a demonstration of the virtues of "freedom of expression" in an "open and free society."[19] Figurative painting, on the other hand, was reminiscent of the "regimented, traditional, and narrow" orientation of socialist realism.[20] For this reason, many of the established critics, who had been instrumental in orchestrating the ascendancy of Abstract Expressionism, found Pop art to be the antithesis of the ideas they championed.

Certainly not all critics presented opinions that grew out of leftist sympathies. Hilton Kramer, known for his staunch conservatism, joined in the vocal chorus of disdain over the rise of Pop art but claimed that the development of this movement was in fact a godsend for critics. He asserted that "this work is interesting for what is said *about* it rather than for what it, intrinsically, is."[21] Kramer further stated that "Pop art is, indeed, a kind of emancipation proclamation for the art critic, and . . . it may just conceivably be possible that *some*, though surely not all, of the interest this movement has generated among critics . . . is traceable to the sense they have of being placed by this new development in a more advantageous position vis-à-vis the work of art than they have heretofore enjoyed."[22] Despite Kramer's declaration of independence, critics did not gain a position of predominance in relation to the art works; indeed, their importance in the establishment of future movements was significantly diminished.

Although this litany of factors helps to explain the hostility on the part of most established critics toward Pop art, it does not explain the success of the movement. The obvious question then, is why, given the dominant role of critics such as Clement Greenberg in the establishment of previous movements (particularly Abstract Expressionism), did the critics' derisive pronouncements have so little effect in sounding the death knell for Pop? Why did Pop succeed in spite of the critics?

In order to answer this, we must scrutinize the nature of critical practice as an apparatus that functioned in concert with other art-world institutions. This entire institutional matrix existed in dynamic equilibrium, and while the sphere of influence of the artists, dealers, and collectors expanded, that of the critics correspondingly diminished. In addition, we must acknowledge that criticism is itself a historically defined and determined practice. The answer to these questions can therefore only be found by studying critical practice in the postwar years.

The dismal situation in which the critical establishment found itself in the 1960s, and which is alluded to by Max Kozloff in the statement that opens this chapter, was due at least in part to the fact that others were assuming the traditional roles of the critic, such as that of explicator. Since the development of modernist doctrine in the late nineteenth century, the fortunes of the critic had been tied to the growing predominance of abstraction, which required extensive "translation" for a lay public. This development culminated in the 1940s and 1950s with Abstract Expressionism, a movement whose ultimate acceptance was dependant upon the support and explanations of critics. Curator and critic Henry Geldzahler, an influential figure in the Pop movement, explained how he saw the relationship: "The critic speaks to the audience out front and points to the paintings behind him. He is an unfortunately necessary link in the communication between the artist and the public."[23]

The advent of Pop art, ostensibly the antithesis of Abstract Expressionism, challenged critics' traditional dominance as interpreters. From the public perspective, Pop art, in contrast with Abstract Expressionism, was admirably simple and contained immediately recognizable subject matter. Although much of the public did not consider this to be "art," the images themselves did not seem to require much dissection.

In addition, the critic's function as a "necessary link in the communication between the artist and the public" was rendered obsolete by the willingness of the Pop artists to discuss their work. The role of critic as explicator and "translator" was further diminished by the expansion of the media, an appropriate development given the media orientation of Pop. Critic Barbara Rose explained it: "Media coverage made art public once more. . . . [It] allows the artist to speak directly to the mass public without recourse to the screening process of critics or cultural institutions."[24] Many critics felt that the expanding use of the media was a means of circumventing conventional criticism.

The finality of many of the critics' pronouncements severely weakened their positions as arbiters of taste with the power to ensure the success or failure of a movement. In an attempt to impress upon their readers the depth of their opposition to Pop, many critics encouraged the total rejection of Pop. In some cases, they predicted the end of art as the dire consequence should Pop not be suppressed. Max Kozloff ended his article on Pop with the plea: "Save us from the 'uncharmers,' or permutations thereof, the Rosensteins or Oldenquists to come!"[25] Stanley Kunitz was more dramatic in stating his perception of the art scene: "Confronting this sudden and rather staggering proliferation of 'pop art' in our midst, I am tempted to echo the exclamation of the French artist Paul Delaroche when in 1839 he saw a daguerreotype for the first time: 'From today,' he said, 'painting is dead.'"[26] Perhaps the bleakest and most severe picture was painted by Herbert Read, who wrote in 1965: "The genuine arts of today are engaged in a heroic struggle against mediocrity and mass values, and if they lose, then art, in any meaningful sense, is dead. If art dies, then the spirit of man becomes impotent and the world relapses into barbarism."[27]

With the benefit of hindsight, we know now that rather than wither and die, the Pop movement flourished during the 1960s due largely to the efforts of dealers and the visibility of the artists. Like the boy who cried wolf, the critics' dire predictions failed to come about, dealing a severe blow to the credibility of the critical establishment.

Not all critics were of a singular mind—there were those who actively supported Pop. The critics who were quick to embrace the appearance of Pop tended to be young, neophyte critics such as Lawrence Alloway, Gene R. Swenson, and curator Alan R. Solomon. It is conceivable that these critics saw Pop art, in its embryonic stage, as an opportunity to break into the highly structured and hierarchical realm of art criticism by promoting a style that was already under attack by the established corps of critics.

As products of a consumer culture, these young critics were themselves imbued with the ideology of consumption and were well aware of the importance of promotion, marketing, and advertising. Lawrence Alloway, the originator of the term *Pop art,* demonstrated such comprehension and a keen entrepreneurial instinct in the opening paragraph of *American Pop Art*: "In 1964, Bob Watts embarked on a project to copyright the words *Pop Art,* thereby taking the term off the market and preventing its use, perhaps in anticipation of its extensive use as a marketing label on a variety of products. I used to wish that I had copyrighted the term myself, not to restrict its use but to collect royalties. . . . However since Pop art had already become part of art criticism, it was judged to be a generic term and thus not subject to copyright."[28] Alloway's concerns expanded beyond the realm of the academic to the profit that was possible from his contribution to the Pop movement.

The role of the critic in the establishment of Pop art presents an interesting situation. Most of the established corps of critics actively lobbied against Pop, which they deemed to be regressive, infantile, and not engaged in serious formal problems. Yet Pop succeeded in spite of this. More than anything, what this demonstrates is that the dealers, collectors, and artists—those most involved in marketing and publicity—had come to the fore in a society dominated by consumption.

# CHAPTER 8
# *THE LEGACY OF POP ART:*
## *THE ROOTS OF POSTMODERNISM*

*Because of Andy Warhol, it's no longer possible to do what you do and not have to act it out 24 hours a day. . . . As a result, there's this self-consciousness going on everywhere, this use of the media. It's not just what you do now, it's what you say about it, the way you behave, who your friends are. Your life has to reflect it.*

*—Steve Piccolo, New Wave rock singer* [1]


Through their incisive selection of images from the contemporary environment, the Pop artists provided immediately recognizable references to the highly organized consumer society of the 1960s. The predominance of Keynesian economic theory and the attempts by the government and corporations to promote consumption served as a fertile breeding ground for Pop art. Pop works addressed the many facets of the mature consumer culture, from corporate advertising campaigns to the mass-media vehicles that disseminated such promotional material. Studies of this art movement have tried to establish whether Pop's "message" about American consumer society was affirmative or critical. While the individual works are often cryptic and ambiguous with regard to any direct statement, the total immersion of the Pop movement into the apparatuses and strategies of consumer culture through its presentation by artists and dealers and reception by collectors and public surely rendered any potential for critique futile and invalid.

Beyond the literal references to American consumer society in the works themselves, the production and distribution of Pop art was dependent upon the same ideology of consumption that produced the images for its subject matter. The appropriation of mass-production techniques for the creation of the works and the thematic presentations of Pop in exhibitions emphasized the assembly-line characteristics of the art and were an integral part of the movement. In addition, the institutional apparatus for the presentation and distribution of art had matured. Through careful utilization of mechanisms such as the mass media and publicity, the artists, dealers, and collectors ensured the success of Pop.

That a fully developed consumer culture was necessary for the ascendancy of Pop is revealed by two examples of related art. One example lies in the visual correspondence of Pop to the work of Stuart Davis and Gerald

Murphy, American artists whose paintings of the 1920s and 1930s are especially well known. Both artists present consumer objects from the urban environment in their works, complete with labels and slogans in distinctly legible form. Art historian Abraham A. Davidson noted that during the first few decades of the twentieth century, "Stuart Davis searched more persistently than any other American modernist except Gerald Murphy for subjects in the paraphernalia of consumerism of American industry."[2]

Rather than challenge the contention that the success of Pop art was intrinsically bound to the ideology of consumption, the work of Davis and Murphy confirms this interpretation. Like the 1960s, the 1920s represent a particularly significant period in the history of consumer culture. Rising incomes in the 1920s supported the development of a consumer-oriented society. This growth was reflected not only in the tremendous expansion of the advertising field but also in the development of a consumer-protection movement that anticipated that of the 1960s. *Your Money's Worth: A Study in the Waste of the Consumer's Dollar* (1927) was a best-seller, numerous "Consumer's Clubs" were formed, and in 1929, Consumers' Research, Inc. was organized to perform product testing on a large scale.[3] Consumers Union, which published *Consumer Reports,* was founded a few years later.

The collapse of the stock market in 1929 and, subsequently, of the entire American economy in the 1930s brought this nascent consumer culture to an abrupt halt. The artistic direction of painters such as Stuart Davis and Gerald Murphy was thus put on hold until the 1960s, when a full-blown consumer culture finally emerged.

The necessity of a fully matured consumer culture for the development of Pop art, both as a visual resource as well as for ideological support, is further demonstrated by the history of the British Pop movement of the 1950s. The International Group, a collaboration of British experimental artists, was among the first to incorporate images from the postwar metropolitan environment. It was one of this group's members, critic Lawrence Alloway, who coined the term *Pop art* around 1956. The collages of Richard Hamilton are typical of the artistic endeavors of the International Group. In these works, Hamilton presents a collection of clearly identifiable images from the consumer environment, from appliances to mass-media objects—movie marquees, comic books, and newspapers.

Works by British Pop artists such as Hamilton do presage those by the American Pop artists. Significantly, however, it was not until the late 1950s in the United States that this art style flourished. The British Pop movement was short-lived and limited in scope. This was largely due to the lack of a highly refined consumer culture to sustain the movement, such as that in the United States. Indeed, the members of the International Group claimed that the inspiration for their work was Hollywood, Detroit, and Madison Avenue, paying homage to America's predominance in the fields of mass media, mass production, and advertising.[4] The advanced state of the consumer system can therefore be seen as imperative for the development of the Pop movement.

All told, the Pop movement was not merely a product of the consumer-oriented environment but contributed to the legitimation of that very system through its aggressive appropriation of the images, techniques, and strategies associated with the ideology of consumption. Certainly, Warhol's service as a spokesperson in advertisements for various products illustrates the extent to which the Pop movement eventually served to legitimize the imperative to consume. Even further, the complete immersion of Pop into consumer culture and the use of Pop art itself as currency in this matured culture is revealed by a recollection of Claes Oldenburg. He describes a "television show . . . where the pop art salesman, or the pop art dealer, was selling pop art in order to get money to buy Picassos."[5] Not only was Pop reduced to one among innumerable consumer products being advertised on television but even further, it was reduced to functioning as mere currency in the unavoidable network of consumer transactions.

Perhaps the most conclusive support for this interpretation is not to be found in the era of the 1960s but rather lies in the legacy of Pop art and its effect on subsequent developments in the art world. The transition from modernism to postmodernism, one of the most prominent developments in twentieth-century art, can be attributed in large part to the ascendancy of Pop. By co-opting images and strategies integral to consumer culture, Pop art undermined many of the tenets fundamental to the perpetuation of modernism. It can, hence, be seen as responsible for ushering in the postmodernist era and for providing the conceptual foundation for much of contemporary art. Theorists such as Fredric Jameson and Andreas Huyssen have commented upon this role (both of them classify Pop as postmodern), but a concrete historical exposition needs to be articulated.[6]

Although the concept of the postmodern has gained currency in the past two decades, there is still no consensus as to the definition of postmodernism. This is partially due to the fact that the term has surfaced in the academic and critical discourse in many fields—most notably art, architecture, music, and literature—and thus, the term has acquired specific and differing connotations in each area. Moreover, any attempt to define postmodernism must take into account not just aesthetic issues but the political and social role of art as well. These additional variables make arriving at any concrete definition a formidable task.

More significantly, this lack of consensus can be attributed to the problematic nature of modernism. The term *postmodernism* implies that it is being defined in terms of its relationship to modernism. Modernism is itself an extremely elusive term because it has been applied to a broad range of art over an extended historical span and thus has its own shifting, historically determined connotations.[7] In the twentieth century, it generally involved the rejection of accepted, entrenched art forms and a belief in art as a pure and segregated realm. Over time, modernism came to be identified with avant-gardism.[8] Given the undisguised admiration for the new and innovative that was fundamental to avant-gardism, this confluence of modernism and avant-gardism is understandable. By the 1950s, modernism (as embodied by the avant-garde) became increasingly formulaic and dogmatic largely as a result of the pronouncements of critics such as Clement Greenberg in the 1930s and 1940s.

The earlier discussion on the role of the critic demonstrates that the focus of critical attention was on formal aspects of art production. Postmodernism has been discussed in formal terms as well. In contrast to the overwhelming predominance of abstraction and the preoccupation with asserting the flat, two-dimensional quality of the picture plane that became characteristic of modernism in the years preceding Pop, postmodernism has been character-ized by a lack of a stringent stylistic agenda and encompasses a wide variety of visual modes of representation. The adjectives that surface most often in descriptions of postmodern art are *pluralistic* and *eclectic*.[9]

Beyond this definitive stylistic contrast, however, the art community has not agreed on the eventual outcome of the modernist agenda. This percep-tion of the outcome affects how one defines postmodernism. Because mod-ernism serves as a reference point for postmodernism, an outline of the vari-ous modernist scenarios will help us map out the different perceptions of postmodernism and will clarify the role of Pop in the transition between the two. The views on modernism can be reduced to three basic schemes, and in turn, postmodernism can be defined as a chronological continuation of mod-ernism, a rejection of modernism, or a retrospective reading of modernism.

In reviewing the historical continuum of art during the past century, one might perceive modernism as a well-defined program and the history of mod-ernism as a logical, linear progression of artistic opposition against estab-lished art forms. According to this first scenario, recent postmodern art can be seen as simply a new phase of modernism—a continuation rather than a break with the modernist tradition—and the term *postmodernism* functions as a temporal and philosophical designation.[10] The emergence of Pop fits nicely into this construct. By the late 1950s, Abstract Expressionism had become entrenched as the reigning art movement. Pop challenged many of the tenets underlying this movement that championed purity of form and expression. Such adversarial stances were fundamental to the perpetuation of the avant-garde, which was based on an uncompromising admiration for the new, novel, and innovative. The banal nature and familiarity of Pop images, derived verbatim from mass culture and presented in serial fashion, contrasted sharply with the abstract, highly personal canvases of the Abstract Expressionists. From this standpoint, then, Pop epitomized the ideals of modernism but developed during a later period—hence, the label "postmodern."

Much of recent postmodernist art has amplified the challenges that Pop introduced to the accepted canon. For example, one of the aspects that characterized Abstract Expressionism and made it so avant-garde was its complete rejection of any narrative structure. Pop and subsequent postmodernist movements have challenged that stance, not by returning to a narrative format but by defying the whole rhetoric or mechanism of narrative. We are confronted not with the absence of narrative but with the breakdown of narrative. In Pop art works such as Johns' *Alley Oop,* the visual format informs us that we are viewing a comic strip, but the strip is presented in such simplified and abstracted fashion that we are prevented from actually comprehending the story line. Similarly, Lichtenstein and Warhol painted single comic-strip frames, which makes it difficult to piece together a coherent narrative thread, despite the predictability of the comic-strip plot structures. The wide range of images and references within each painting of Rosenquist and Wesselmann also makes arriving at a convincing and definitive conclusion about narrative intent a formidable task.

This challenge to the traditional narrative format surfaces in the work of many of the neo-Expressionists, the most publicized artists of the recent postmodern era. David Salle, for instance, produces paintings that are conglomerations of seemingly unrelated images. These works are visually similar to the work of James Rosenquist. The various figures and objects overlap and interact as they float on planes of varying depths. The relationship between the component images is always unclear and mystifying and adds an air of intrigue that often ends in frustration for the viewer because the expectation of coherent narrative has been denied. The challenge that this disintegration of narrative structure represents to the established canon can be considered another step in the avant-garde tradition.

However, this contrast to preceding art styles can also be interpreted as clear evidence of an antimodern sentiment. According to this second scenario, postmodernism is the result of the death or exhaustion of the modernist doctrine, which was either undermined by Pop or merely played itself out.[11] Some scholars have asserted that the challenges that movements such as Pop represented to modernism were so disruptive and profound as to render modernism nonviable. Others believe that modernism, as embodied by the avant-garde, placed such a premium on innovation and novelty that a point was reached in the 1960s with Performance art and Conceptual art after which nothing new was possible. Regardless of whether one believes that Pop actively contributed to the demise of modernism or that modernism exhausted itself, this interpretation emphasizes rupture and discontinuity rather than conceptual continuity.

According to this view, one of the major transgressions committed by the Pop artists that rendered modernism invalid or precluded the possibility of its resurrection was their destruction of the boundaries between the avant-garde and kitsch. This separation, as articulated by Clement Greenberg, was sacred to and passionately defended by champions of modernist canon. By introducing elements and sensibilities from mass culture into high art, the Pop artists were destroying the very pedestal upon which traditional high art rested, however precariously. Many postmodern artists have utilized this re-pudiation of the distinction between high art and kitsch. The Super Realists, for example Audrey Flack and Duane Hanson, use mundane subject matter from mass culture, such as household items and middle-class lifestyles, as a means of combatting what they perceive to be the incomprehensibility of abstract art. More recently, artist Jeff Koons has created sculptures that are large-scale presentations of dime-store memorabilia and resort souvenirs that, by most standards, are undeniably kitsch. Other artists no longer look down upon using their artistic talents in the realm of mass culture. Artist Robert Longo, whose paintings are located in important collections (including that of the Museum of Modern Art), has recently begun making MTV music videos for groups such as New Order and the heavy-metal band Megadeth.[12] This disregard for what had, up until Pop, been clearly defined and separate categories was intolerable to those who wanted to maintain the purity of modernist high art. The blurring of those boundaries that Pop encouraged led many staunch supporters of modernism to accuse Pop of bringing about the death of modernism. With this logic, postmodernism can be seen as the antithesis not of a specific historical moment in modernism, but of the entire conceptual framework.

Increasingly, scholars, artists, and critics have acknowledged that far from being a clear-cut and straightforward progression of art movements, the development of modernism was comprised of contradictions, internal challenges, and unfinished agendas. This assessment has led to a third defini-tion of postmodernism as a retrospective reading of modernism—a historical analysis of the program.

While earlier modernist artists had immersed themselves in the actual processes of art production, the Pop artists ushered in an era of far greater awareness and consciousness about their role in the historical continuum of art. They translated this awareness into a self-consciousness and reflexivity that surfaces in their work, and it is this feature that many scholars have posited as the most defined characteristic of postmodern art. Pop art and subsequent postmodern art are, in a sense, comments on the production of art. Lichtenstein, for example, produced a series of "brushstroke" paintings in 1965 and 1966. The subject matter of these works is the fluid application of pigment to the canvas in large, lyrical brushstrokes. Yet Lichtenstein filters the image in a very calculated fashion through his signature style of BenDay dots to create a rigorously contained, stenciled image of a brushstroke that negates the spontaneity and looseness of the original gesture. Coming on the heels of the Abstract Expressionist movement and the predominance of the works of Gestural Abstractionists like Jackson Pollock and Willem de Kooning, these brushstroke paintings are specific referents to, and comments on, the different means of art production.

This appropriation of previous styles, elements, and images has become a mainstay of recent postmodern art and reveals a continued interest in the self-conscious attitude cultivated by the Pop artists. This postmodern interest in citation is perhaps best illustrated by the work of Sherrie Levine. Levine's photographs are faithful reproductions of well-known photographs by such photographers as Edward Weston and Walker Evans. Levine does not transform or in any way alter the image, so her photographs appear to be mere duplicates of the "original." This strategy of appropriation does provide a comment on issues of authorship, mechanical reproduction, and the exhaustion of the modernist penchant for innovation.[13] Beyond that, however, its staying power has been the subject of debate. Regardless, Levine has created an art form that is a measured comment on the process of art production.

This self-conscious mining of previous art forms for recycling can also be seen as support for the assertion that modernism did in fact exhaust itself. The past two decades have witnessed a spate of movements that involve resurrections of previous styles. The ascendancy of neo-Expressionism, Neo Geo, neo-Miminalism, and neo-Pop, among others, can be interpreted as an admission that everything has been done and that the avant-garde has exhausted itself. Although it seems that circumscribed avant-garde gestures are still viable, large-scale ruptures that can be considered revolutionary no longer appear possible.

These differing perceptions of the modernist program and its outcome have led to various assessments of postmodernism. While the focus of many of the discussions about modernism and postmodernism has revolved around the aesthetic concerns just presented, this study of Pop demonstrates that any examination of such wide-ranging phenomena must necessarily extend beyond formal issues. Accordingly, the legacy of Pop for postmodern art practices also involves the changed dynamics of the institutional matrix of the art world.

The rise and acceptance of Pop was inextricably linked to facets of consumer culture—promotion, publicity, and advertising. This occurred not only through the content of the works but also through the activities of the artists, dealers, and collectors. Theorists such as Andreas Huyssen and Fredric Jameson have suggested that it is this consumer orientation that provides the most decisive characteristic of the postmodern art world.[14] Jameson asserts that the "emergence of postmodernism is closely related to the emergence of this new moment of late, consumer or multinational capitalism."[15] This situation can be easily attributed to Pop.

The changes in dynamics of the institutional matrix that were the legacy of Pop art have become more pronounced in recent postmodernist art and have now become the rules rather than the exceptions in the art world. Critic Suzi Gablik describes the art world as now being "mediated by a bureaucratic megastructure that is impersonal, increasingly powerful, and potentially sinister" and that is "controlled by means of corporate-management techniques, public relations, and professional marketing."[16]

One of the major components of this institutional matrix is the artist, who, as demonstrated, played an integral role in the establishment of Pop. In the postmodern era, the role of the artist has become even more crucial in the presentation of art to a public. As publicists, contemporary artists realize the importance of promoting both themselves and their art. Claims artist Robert Longo: "I'm a good salesman, and I transfer my enthusiasm about my work to other people. I convince them that I'm going to be an artist forever and an important one."[17] In the footsteps of Pop artists like Warhol, many of these artists have managed to transcend the realm of the mundane to celebrity status. A number of young, contemporary artists have had feature articles written about them in *People* magazine, the mass-publication bible of celebrity news.

Artists have also continued the trend begun by the Pop artists of explaining their own work, rather than leaving the interpretation to critics. The Neo Geo artists, for example, feel that the explication of the theoretical basis of their art is too important a matter to be left to nonartists. These artists, like the Pop artists, have assumed the critic's function.

Contemporary artists have become especially proficient in the entrepreneurial aspects of art production and distribution. The Environmental art movement of the late 1960s and 1970s provides a definitive illustration of the importance of such aspects in ensuring the success of art movements. Many of the Environmental artists assert that their large-scale earthworks, often constructed in remote areas of the country, are intended as statements against the machinations of the gallery system and the concept of art as commodity. Yet the most successful of the Environmental artists is the Bulgarian-born Christo, who established a private corporation and issued stock that was redeemable in his works of art.[18]

More recently, a new generation of young artists in their thirties, such as the highly touted Robert Longo, Keith Haring, Jean-Michel Basquiat, and Jeff Koons, have mastered the art of business. Robert Longo, whose works were commanding over $40,000 by the time he was thirty-one, has demonstrated his awareness of the business facet of the art world. Rather than changing styles for formal or aesthetic reasons, Longo switches for business reasons: "The whole idea is not to get stuck [with a tired-out product] like Atari," he says.[19] Longo employs assistants, as the Pop artists did, in order to keep his production on schedule. He occasionally interferes with the efforts of his assistants: "If I don't touch my works, they slip out of my hands. I'm like the guy who puts a number in your underwear so you know there's quality control."[20] This statement reveals that Longo sees the whole production process as analogous to that of mass manufacturing and sees himself as functioning in a supervisory capacity. Longo has exhibited his business acumen in other ways as well. He retains a special copyright on all of the drawings he sells, which enables him to borrow the work back from the owner at will.[21]

Keith Haring, who became "almost as well known as his mentor, . . . Andy Warhol," before his early death in 1990 at the age of thirty-eight, started his career drawing outline figures on, appropriately enough, blank advertising spaces in New York subway stations.[22] Since his discovery by dealers and collectors, Haring's prices skyrocketed to over $40,000 per painting.[23] Like Warhol, Haring reveled in the nightlife of New York and was frequently seen in the company of celebrities. He painted rock and movie star Grace Jones' skin, a backdrop for a Brooke Shields poster, and on the back of Madonna's leather jacket.[24] Not only did Haring realize the value of maintaining a high visibility profile, but he also took advantage of the destruction of the distinction between the realms of high art and mass culture that was effected by Pop art. He designed watches with his signature style, which were sold at Bloomingdale's, and he opened his own store, The Pop Shop, which sells T-shirts, sheets, watches, inflatable toys, magnets, and caps imprinted with Haring's familiar logos.

Like Haring, Jean-Michel Basquiat was a friend of Andy Warhol. Enamoured by Warhol's success, Basquiat followed him around until the opportunity arose to introduce himself. "I just wanted to meet him," declared Basquiat. "He was an art hero of mine."[25] This meeting was fortuitous for

Basquiat, most observers of the art scene agree, since Warhol stamped "the newcomer Basquiat with approval and has probably been able to give him excellent business advice. In social circles and through his magazine, *Interview,* he has given Basquiat a good deal of exposure."[26] As a result of this publicity, Basquiat, like Haring and Longo, achieved celebrity status and was an active figure in the art world until his untimely death in 1989 at the age of twenty-eight.

Jeff Koons is an often-cited example of the degree to which the emphasis on marketing skills now dominates the postmodern art world. Koons gave up a career as a commodities broker in 1984 to become an artist. By 1989, his sculptures were selling for up to $250,000 each. Like Longo, Koons' participation in the actual construction of his works is limited. "I manage production," Koons states.[27] Koons is clear about his goal: "I want to be as big an art star as possible."[28] Toward this end, Koons carefully controls the sale of his works to ensure that the works will end up in collections that will enhance his career. "Not everyone can enhance the works," he claims. "It's very important to place them. It's like a company choosing a franchisee: You want one on a busy corner, not in the middle of nowhere."[29] Koons' strategy includes extensive advertising in art journals, featuring photographs of himself rather than of the art works. Koons is straightforward about the need for such advertising: "Advertising and film use every means they can to seduce and manipulate the audience. If the art world doesn't do that too, we won't build a power base for our art."[30]

Contemporary art dealers, as well, have come to acknowledge the consequences of Pop art and to adjust their orientation accordingly. Many new, successful dealers agree with Janelle Reiring, cofounder of the Metro Pictures gallery in the Soho district of New York, who stated: "I feel strongly about recognizing that this is a business we're in—not the pursuit of a nineteenth-century gentleman. Artists want galleries that are more progressive—that will promote their careers."[31] This increased pressure is partially due to the fact that artists' expectations of dealers' efforts on their behalf have risen sharply. In a vivid display of this mentality, Mary Boone, one of the more prominent young dealers, stated that Jeff Koons ended his professional relationship with her after eight months because he claimed that "you haven't made me famous yet."[32] In addition, dealers must now compete with public-relations consultants, investment advisers, and legal and tax experts for the attention of the artist.

Those dealers who have been able to master the necessary marketing skills have been well rewarded, not only financially and with respect in the art world but also appropriately, with celebrity status. Leo Castelli, still considered the most influential dealer as a result of his success in the 1960s with

Pop, has appeared on television talk shows, such as "The Dick Cavett Show." Mary Boone, a young New York dealer, has achieved fame and financial stability due to her keen understanding and use of corporate techniques. Intent on breaking into the competitive field of art dealership, Boone became Castelli's protégée when she opened her own gallery in 1977 in the same building that housed Castelli Gallery. Relying on "a classic corporate strategy," Boone utilized "an aggressive brand of marketing, publicity and salesmanship to establish herself—and neo-expressionist artist Julian Schnabel (both barely past thirty at the time)—as the first and foremost art 'stars' of the decade." [33] As a "public persona in her own right," Boone epitomizes the contemporary art dealer—aggressive and very business oriented. [34]

The role of the collector in affecting the direction of art has expanded during the postmodern era. The importance of the collector was demonstrated by the inaugural exhibition at the Museum of Contemporary Art in Los Angeles in 1983, The First Show: Painting and Sculpture from Eight Collections, 1940–1980. As the inaugural exhibition of a museum that hopes to have great impact on the international art scene, the orientation of this show was crucial in setting the tone for the direction of the museum. It is significant, therefore, that the substantial catalog that accompanied the show was devoted not to the works of art but to the collectors. Essays in the catalog included "Collecting Contemporary Art" and "Collecting in Our Time," along with extensive interviews with the lending collectors; discussions of the art on exhibit were noticeably absent. In viewing the exhibition, then, the audience obtained a sense neither of the aesthetic value nor the historical import of these works, but merely of certain collectors' visions. In her foreword, the senior curator of the show explained: "Portraits of the individual collectors emerge through the cumulative effect of their choices." [35] The emphasis in museum exhibitions has shifted from the art to the collector. This assertion is supported by the increasing number of shows organized around a specific collector's accumulated art—for example, the Armand Hammer collection and the Barry Lowen collection.

It cannot be denied that escalating art prices have made museums increasingly dependent on private collectors for exhibition material and donations. As a result, collectors have come to dominate the art world. Perhaps the most influential collector of contemporary art in recent years has been Charles Saatchi. In light of the movement toward the commodification of art and the emphasis on publicity and promotion in the postmodern era, this is appropriate, given Saatchi's position as founder of the largest advertising agency in the world. [36] His art collection is extensive, as the recent publication of a four-volume catalog raisonné attests. Saatchi's meteoric rise from teaboy at a London advertising agency to ownership of his own agency twelve years later reveals that Saatchi understands the vagaries of the market and possesses keen financial insight. In addition to his business acumen, Saatchi has a firm grasp on the conceptual nature of promotion and publicity, as confirmed by his success in advertising. He demonstrated a thorough comprehension of such concepts when he served as the "image man" behind Margaret Thatcher's sweeping victory in 1979. All of these skills have helped Saatchi in building his art collection, and it is precisely these skills that have prompted criticism from his detractors. Indiana University art economist Leslie Singer made the following charge: "The Saatchis are strictly speculators. . . . They purchase art in large blocks that they hope may appreciate. They expect to corner the market in conjunction with small dealers. They are like the Hunts."[37] Artist Sandro Chia, who was eliminated from Saatchi's collection a few years ago (according to Chia, because he objected to having a single collector buy out one of his exhibitions), concurred: "Mr. Saatchi buys paintings by quantity, with the possibility of promoting his 'product' with his advertising acumen, thereby creating areas of influence and private interest, tantamount to manipulation."[38] Saatchi's influence extends throughout the art world. Dealer Mary Boone attributes much of her success to advice she received from Saatchi.[39] The scale upon which Saatchi and other collectors (such as Count Giuseppe Panza di Biumo, Baron Hans Heinrich Thyssen-Bornemisza, and the Menil family) accumulate art has made the collector a formidable factor in the ongoing dynamics of the art world.

As a result of Pop art, the spheres of influence in the contemporary post-modern art world have shifted, with dealers, collectors, and the artists themselves becoming more prominent, while the role of the critic has diminished. The proof of this changed dynamic is demonstrated not just by the heightened visibility of dealers and collectors like Castelli and Saatchi but also by the burgeoning involvement of critics in new theoretical modes of discourse.

It can be argued that this interest in theory, particularly French critical theory, is logical given the breakdown of narrative structure in art. Much of the French critical theory now popular in academic circles focuses on the strategy of deconstruction, in which individual elements in the image are analyzed as signifiers. Because much of postmodern art is devoid of a clear, linear narrative, this theoretical construct can be useful as an interpretive methodology.

However, this interest in theory can also be interpreted as a historically grounded strategy to reprivilege the role of the critic. Theoretical discourse affords the critic the opportunity to discuss art in a larger, more-complex arena. This arena is one in which most other participants in the art world—

artists, dealers, and collectors—are incapable of competing or which they view as outside the parameters of their respective professions. In this manner, critics have carved out a new, unchallenged niche.

This assertion is supported by the predominance of French poststructural theory in recent years. So pervasive has this approach become that many art observers interchange the terms *poststructuralism* and *postmodernism,* although they are not synonymous terms.[40] This complex network of ideas has been disseminated through the work of Michel Foucault, Jacques Derrida, and the later work of Jean Baudrillard, among others. Poststructural theory constitutes a repriviledging of the critic's role because of the challenge that it represents to the authority of the author-artist as producer of text-image.[41] Poststructural theory revolves around the notion that images are by nature polysemic rather than univocal, and therefore to arrive at an understanding of the image is not a straightforward or simple process. According to these theorists, the artist's intention is just one of a myriad of variables from which meaning is derived. The input of the viewer, historical circumstances, and ideological reverberations contribute to the "meaning" and make the image multidimensional. In fact, theorist Roland Barthes went so far as to assert: "It is necessary to overthrow the myth: the birth of the reader must be at the cost of the death of the Author."[42] In this construct, interpretation is accorded greater importance, whether by the viewer or by critics.

The predominance of poststructural theory in the postmodern era ultimately serves to challenge the commercial orientation of the art world and the dominance of marketing strategy by shifting the equilibrium within the institutional matrix. The wildly fluctuating market of recent years and the plurality of styles are evidence of this unstable dynamic in the art world, in which the actions of any one sector ultimately influence the others. The commodification of art is so entrenched, however, that the possibility of such a challenge bringing about substantial change in the art world is questionable.

The impact that Pop art has had on both the direction of art and the institutional matrix of the art world cannot be understated. Pop art succeeded against the expectations of the established critics and despite their vitriolic assessments of the art. The predominance of Keynesian economic theory and the maturation of consumer culture in the 1960s provided a fertile breeding ground for the Pop movement. Pop entered into the process of negotiation between the ideology of consumption, the growing ethos of self-fulfillment, and governmental and corporate imperatives by appropriating images from the consumer environment. This, in conjunction with the absorption of Pop into an institutional matrix of dealers, critics, and collectors that was itself shifting toward corporate models, contributed to the legitimation of consumer culture. This has been Pop's legacy. So dramatic and resonant was this development that it brought about the dawn of postmodernism. The significance of Pop art thus lies not just in its historical position as an art movement but, more importantly, in the profound effect it has had on the direction of subsequent art.

# NOTES

## INTRODUCTION

1. "le Pop'Art . . . n'est-il qu'un effet de mode, et donc lui-même un pur objet de consommation?," in Jean Baudrillard. *La Société de Consommation: Ses mythes, ses structures,* p. 175.

2. E.g., Sidney Tillim, "In the Galleries: The New Realists," *Arts Magazine* 37, no. 3 (December 1962): 44.

3. Max Kozloff, "'Pop' Culture, Metaphysical Disgust, and the New Vulgarians," *Art International* 6, no. 2 (March 1962): 36.

4. Peter Selz, "Pop Goes the Artist," *Partisan Review* 30, no. 2 (Summer 1963): 314.

5. *Time* magazine presented Warhol to the general public: "Of all the artists, Andy Warhol . . . best plays the part of what a pop artist might expectably be" ("Pop Art—Cult of the Commonplace," *Time,* 3 May 1963, p. 72), and such critics as Thomas B. Hess proclaimed that Warhol was "the brightest of the Pop artists" ("Reviews and Previews: Andy Warhol," *Artnews* 63, no. 9 [January 1965]: 11).

6. Robert Hughes, "A Caterer of Repetition and Glut," *Time,* 9 March 1987, p. 90.

7. While general public usage of the term *consumerism* has rendered it synonymous with *consumption,* in economic circles *consumerism* refers specifically to the consumer-protection movement and not to general activities of consumption. Such a distinction in definitions will be applied throughout this study.

8. In this study, I use the term *Keynesian economics* in a general manner, to include both Keynes' own theories as well as the application of these ideas by followers. However, it is important to note, as Martin Feldstein correctly observes in his essay "The Retreat from Keynesian Economics," in *Public Interest,* no. 64 (Summer 1981): 94, that, precisely speaking, such a distinction does exist (e.g., see Axel Leijonhofvud, *On Keynesian Economics and the Economics of Keynes*).

9. Paul Craig Roberts, "The Breakdown of the Keynesian Model," *Public Interest*, no. 52 (Summer 1978): 21; and E. Ray Canterbery, *Economics on a New Frontier*, preface.

10. David Horowitz, "Capitalism and the Crisis of Abundance," in *In the Marketplace: Consumerism in America*, ed. Editors of *Ramparts* with Frank Browning, p. 224. Given that Keynesian ideas had been disseminated since the 1930s, it is not surprising that previous administrations, including those of Franklin Roosevelt, Harry Truman, and Dwight Eisenhower, did enact legislation that adhered to Keynesian principles. Kennedy was by no means the first to implement Keynesian policies; he was, however, the first to embrace the underlying philosophy and appoint a full slate of Keynesian economists as his advisers, thereby initiating a more unified and systematic utilization of Keynesian doctrine than had heretofore been the case.

11. Kennedy's closest economic advisers included Walter Heller (chair of Kennedy's Council of Economic Advisers), James Tobin, Kermit Gordon, Seymour Harris, Paul Samuelson, Gardner Ackley, and John Lewis, all of whom not only believed in Keynesian economics but also actively advocated such policies (Seymour Harris, *Economics of the Kennedy Years and a Look Ahead*, pp. 21–22; and Robert M. Collins, *The Business Response to Keynes, 1929–1964*, pp. 178, 260 n).

12. Christopher Tugendhat, *The Multinationals*, p. 28.

13. Walter W. Heller, *New Dimensions of Political Economy*, pp. 9, 2.

14. The attempt to "keep up with the Joneses" was by no means unique to this period. Indeed, economist Adam Smith utilized this concept as the basis of his whole theory of "emulation," which he articulated in his 1776 publication *The Wealth of Nations*.

15. Eric Gelman, "They Live to Buy," *Newsweek*, 31 December 1984, p. 28.

16. Ibid.

17. Introduction, *The Culture of Consumption: Critical Essays in American History, 1880–1980*, ed. Richard Wightman Fox and T. J. Jackson Lears, p. xii.


## *1. THE RAPID SUCCESS STORY: THE ESTABLISHMENT OF POP ART*

1. Calvin Tomkins, *Off the Wall: Robert Rauschenberg and the Art World of Our Time*, p. 179.

2. Barbara Haskell, *Blam! The Explosion of Pop, Minimalism, and Performance, 1958–1964*, p. 85.

3. Tomkins, *Off the Wall*, p. 143.

4. Calvin Tomkins, "Profiles: A Good Eye and a Good Ear," *New Yorker*, 26 May 1980, p. 57.

5. Judith Goldman, *James Rosenquist*, pp. 30–31.

6. Barbara Rose, *Claes Oldenburg*, p. 70.

7. Tomkins, *Off the Wall*, p. 215.

8. Ibid., p. 85.

9. Calvin Tomkins, *The Bride and the Bachelors: Five Masters of the Avant-Garde,* p. 195.

10. Tullia Zevi, "The Biennale: How Evil Is Pop Art?" *New Republic,* 19 September 1964, p. 32.

11. Calvin Tomkins, "The Big Show in Venice," *Harper's Magazine* 230, no. 1379 (April 1965): 98. Generally, the Biennale jury awarded one of the international grand prizes to a painter and the other to a sculptor. The only other American ever to win the international grand prize was the sculptor Alexander Calder in 1952. Two other Americans did win other Biennale painting prizes—James Abbot McNeill Whistler in 1895 and Mark Tobey in 1958.

12. The U.S. pavilion had been built by Grand Central Art Galleries in 1929, which sponsored the pavilion until the Museum of Modern Art took over in 1948. The Museum of Modern Art relinquished the sponsorship of the pavilion after the 1962 Biennale due to funding problems (Tomkins, "The Big Show in Venice," pp. 98–99; and Lawrence Alloway, *The Venice Biennale, 1895–1968: From Salon to Goldfish Bowl,* p. 149). For an in-depth study of the American participation in the 1964 Venice Biennale, see Laurie J. Monahan, "Cultural Cartography: American Designs at the 1964 Venice Biennale," in *Reconstructing Modernism: Art in New York, Paris, and Montreal, 1945–1964,* ed. Serge Guilbaut, pp. 369–416.

13. Charles S. Spencer, "Documenta III: Creative Individuality in Contemporary Art Surveyed at Kassel," *Studio International* 168, no. 857 (September 1964): 111.

14. Comparisons between the Venice Biennale and the Kassel Documenta were inevitable, as both were major international exhibitions, and they ran concurrently. The Biennale was scheduled from 20 June to 18 October 1964, while the Documenta ran from 27 June to 5 October 1964.

15. Spencer, "Documenta III," p. 116.

16. John Anthony Thwaites, "Documenta: The Self-Saboteurs," *Arts Magazine* 38, no. 10 (September 1964): 40.

17. "Schade, dass kaum Pop-Art und Neue Realisten . . . zu sehen sind" (Adam Seide, "Documenta III: Eine Umfrage," *Das Kunstwerk* 18, no. 1–3 [July–September 1964]: 16).

18. "Diese dritte documenta wird vielleicht einmal als ein Höhepunkt in der ganzen Reihe gelten. Selbstverständlich werden Neigungen und Abneigungen der Kommissionen sichtbar. . . . die Organisatoren haben zum Beispiel auf den neuen Realismus wie auf die Combine paintings und die vulgäreren Formen von Pop Art verzichtet" (Heinz Keller, "Kassel: Documenta III," *Werk* 51 [September 1964]: 216*).

19. Stuart Preston, "Letter from New York: The 'Czar's' Veto," *Apollo* 79, no. 27 (May 1964): 434.

20. G. S. Whittet, "The Dynamic of Brazil: The VIII Bienal of São Paulo," *Studio International* 170, no. 870 (October 1965): 137.

21. Pierre Restany, "L'Ottava Biennale di San Paolo—Huitieme Biennale de Sao Paulo: Comment Va la Cousine Australe de Venise?" *Domus,* no. 432 (November 1965): 48.

22. Alain Jouffroy, "Le grand jeu de la Biennale," *L'Oeil,* nos. 139–140 (July–

August 1966): 49; and Norman Narotsky, "The Venice Biennale: Pease Porridge in the Pot Nine Days Old," *Arts Magazine* 40, no. 9 (September/October 1966): 42.

23. Jouffroy, "Le grand jeu," p. 45; and Jasia Reichardt, "The Fairness and Unfairness of Prizes," *Studio International* 172, no. 880 (August 1966): 62.

24. Ettore Sottsass, Jr., "Whipped Cream Memoires," *Domus*, no. 444 (November 1966): 43, 44.

25. Alan Bowness, "São Paulo: Impressions of the Bienal," *Studio International* 174, no. 894 (November 1967): 218.

26. Jeanne Siegel, "Documenta IV: Homage to the Americans?" *Arts Magazine* 43, no. 1 (September/October 1968): 37; and Robert Kudielka, "Documenta IV: A Critical Review," *Studio International* 176, no. 903 (September 1968): 77.

27. David Irwin, "The Venice Biennale: The Breaking of Boundaries," *Apollo* 88, no. 80 (October 1968): 293.

28. Tomkins, *The Bride and the Bachelors*, p. 195.

29. Tomkins, "Profiles: A Good Eye and a Good Ear," p. 61.

30. Tomkins, *Off the Wall*, p. 296; and Michael Crichton, *Jasper Johns*, p. 26.

31. *Art at Auction: The Year at Sotheby's & Parke-Bernet, 1970–71*, p. 158.

32. Cathleen McGuigan, "A Pop Patron's Last Hurrah," *Newsweek*, 17 November 1986, p. 97; and "Contemporary Art Sets Auction Price Records," *Los Angeles Times*, 13 November 1986, pt. 6, p. 8.

33. Eamonn Fingleton, "Portrait of the Artist as Money Man," *Forbes*, 1 February 1982, p. 58.


## 2. POP ART AND CONSUMER CULTURE: CORPORATIONS AND THE IMPERATIVE TO CONSUME

1. Interview with James Rosenquist in Gene R. Swenson, "What Is Pop Art? Part 2: Stephen Durkee, Jasper Johns, James Rosenquist, Tom Wesselmann," *Artnews* 62, no. 10 (February 1964): 63.

2. Christopher Tugendhat, *The Multinationals*, p. 27.

3. Ibid., pp. 33, 34.

4. Joyce Kolko, *America and the Crisis of World Capitalism*, p. 4.

5. Daniel Bell, *The Cultural Contradictions of Capitalism*, p. 68.

6. Vance Packard, *The Hidden Persuaders*, p. 5.

7. Ibid.

8. Bell, *Cultural Contradictions*, pp. 68–69.

9. Mary Gardiner Jones, "The Cultural and Social Impact of Advertising on American Society," in *Consumerism: Search for the Consumer Interest*, ed. David A. Aaker and George S. Day, p. 430.

10. Ibid.

11. James Rorty, *Our Master's Voice: Advertising*, p. 16.

12. Ann Douglas, *The Feminization of American Culture*, p. 68.

13. T. J. Jackson Lears, "From Salvation to Self-Realization: Advertising and the

Therapeutic Roots of the Consumer Culture, 1880—1930," in *The Culture of Consumption: Critical Essays in American History, 1880—1980,* ed. Richard Wightman Fox and T. J. Jackson Lears, p. 31.

14. *National Advertising Investments,* 12, no. 2 (January–December 1960): 12; and 20, no. 2 (January–December 1968): 6.

15. ". . . And Now a Word about Commercials," *Time,* 12 July 1968, p. 55.

16. Emma Rothschild, *Paradise Lost: The Decline of the Auto-Industrial Age,* p. 5.

17. Ibid.

18. Ibid., p. 247.

19. Ibid., p. 42.

20. Ibid., p. 66.

21. John Jerome, *The Death of the Automobile: The Fatal Effect of the Golden Era, 1955–1970,* p. 31.

22. Ibid., p. 13.

23. Interview with James Rosenquist in Swenson, "What Is Pop Art? Part 2," p. 63.

24. Packard, *The Hidden Persuaders,* p. 43.

25. *Sports Illustrated,* 1966.

26. Ibid.

27. Beth L. Bailey, *From Front Porch to Back Seat: Courtship in Twentieth-Century America,* p. 86.

28. Grace and Fred M. Hechinger, "College Morals Mirror Our Society," *New York Times Magazine,* 14 April 1963, p. 22.

29. Packard, *The Hidden Persuaders,* p. 44.

30. Thomas Hine, *Populuxe,* p. 83.

31. Packard, *The Hidden Persuaders,* p. 43.

32. Hine, *Populuxe,* p. 87.

33. Clark C. Spence, *The Sinews of American Capitalism: An Economic History,* p. 336.

34. John M. Logsdon, *The Decision to Go to the Moon: Project Apollo and the National Interest,* p. 72. In its report, which was submitted to President Kennedy, the advisory committee listed five major motivations for the space program. They were: national prestige, national security, scientific observation and experiment, practical nonmilitary applications, and international cooperation.

35. William O'Neill, *Coming Apart: An Informal History of America in the 1960's,* p. 49.

36. Ibid., pp. 59–60.

37. That this painting can be seen as support for the space program despite the disjointed presentation of seemingly disparate photographs and painted passages is further suggested by the invitation extended to Rauschenberg by NASA to participate in that agency's Art Program in 1969. This art program was initiated to increase the visibility of the agency and publicize its programs. Clearly, the selection of Rauschenberg to depict rocket launches suggests that NASA saw his work as effective promotion.

38. Kolko, *America and the Crisis*, p. 4.

39. David Horowitz, "Capitalism and the Crisis of Abundance," in *In the Marketplace: Consumerism in America,* ed. Editors of *Ramparts* with Frank Browning, pp. 221–222.

40. Ibid., p. 222.

41. Kolko, *America and the Crisis,* pp. 5–6.

42. Joseph D. Phillips, "Economic Effects of the Cold War," in *Corporations and the Cold War,* ed. David Horowitz, p. 175.

43. James L. Clayton, ed., *The Economic Impact of the Cold War: Sources and Readings,* p. 193. In "Impact of Vietnam War on American Economy" (background paper prepared by Murray L. Weidenbaum for the Joint Economic Committee, U.S. Congress), it was noted that even before the Vietnam buildup, military spending accounted for 85 percent of all federal government purchases of goods and services.

44. U.S. Congress, Joint Economic Committee, *Economic Effect of Vietnam Spending: Hearings before the Congress of the United States,* 90th Cong., 1st sess., 24–27 April 1967, vol. 1: Statements of Witnesses and Supporting Materials, p. 20. It is also interesting to note that the economic consequences of American involvement in the war would have been glaringly apparent to Kennedy's secretary of defense, Robert McNamara. McNamara was not a career military man but rather came from a business background, having earned an MBA from Harvard. He relinquished the presidency of the Ford Motor Company in order to accept this post in Kennedy's cabinet.

45. Hine, *Populuxe*, p. 128.

46. Ibid.

47. Jerome, *Death of the Automobile*, p. 63.

48. Rothschild, *Paradise Lost*, p. 57.

49. Such cars included the Pontiac GTO, Plymouth Road Runner, Chevrolet Chevelle SS 396, Dodge Charger, Ford Cobra, and Oldsmobile 4-4-2 (Jerome, *Death of the Automobile*, p. 17).

50. Ibid.

51. Many of these particular car disaster paintings were derived from press photos that were never published because the editors considered them too graphic. These images are therefore somewhat anomalous to Warhol's oeuvre; he generally used widely reproduced photographs for his works (Thomas Crow, "Saturday Disasters: Trace and Reference in Early Warhol," in *Reconstructing Modernism: Art in New York, Paris, and Montreal, 1945–1964,* ed. Serge Guilbaut, p. 322).

52. Lawrence J. White, *The Automobile Industry since 1945,* p. 18.

53. That Pop art's focus on cars and association with consumer culture was recognized is revealed by projects that were commissioned during the 1970s and 1980s. BMW commissioned Andy Warhol, Roy Lichtenstein, and Robert Rauschenberg to decorate its cars. Displayed at the corporate headquarters in Munich, the impetus for this project was BMW's reasoning that "an eyecatching exterior would be a great way to ensure publicity" (T. Nicholas Dawidoff, "Art in the Fast Lane," *Sports Illustrated,* 20 April 1987, p. 115).

54. Jennifer Cross, *The Supermarket Trap: The Consumer and the Food Industry*, p. 33.

55. Packard, *The Hidden Persuaders*, pp. 91–92.

56. Cross, *The Supermarket Trap*, p. 15. One example outlined by Cross is Armour, which is known to the public primarily as a meatpacking company but which also makes dairy and poultry products, soap, household waxes and cleaners, chemicals, adhesives, agricultural chemicals, heavy industrial equipment, and pharmaceuticals.

57. Jim Hightower, *Eat Your Heart Out: Food Profiteering in America*, p. 20.

58. Cross, *The Supermarket Trap*, pp. 14–15.

59. Hightower, *Eat Your Heart Out*, p. 21.

60. Cross, *The Supermarket Trap*, p. 166.

61. Ibid., p. 30.

62. Barbara Rose, *Claes Oldenburg*, p. 64.

63. Ibid.

64. Ibid.

65. Although relatively little seems to have been made of the fact that the Pop artists were appropriating actual design concepts (albeit from the commercial world), the Brillo soap pad boxes did cause somewhat of a stir. James Harvey, the designer of the original cartons (and himself an artist who painted in an Abstract Expressionist style), objected to Warhol's use of his design. A press release issued by the industrial design firm for which Harvey worked, stated: "This makes Jim scream, 'Andy is running away with my box'" (Lawrence Campbell, "Reviews and Previews: Andy Warhol," *Artnews* 63, no. 4 [Summer 1964]: p. 16).

66. Grace Glueck, "Art Notes: Boom?," *New York Times*, 10 May 1964, sec. 2, p. 19.

67. Sidney Tillim, "In the Galleries: Andy Warhol," *Arts Magazine* 38, no. 10 (September 1964): 62.

68. Campbell, "Reviews and Previews," p. 16.

69. Patrick S. Smith, *Warhol: Conversations about the Artist*, p. 203.

70. Hightower, *Eat Your Heart Out*, p. 137.

71. Ibid., p. 195.

72. Ibid., p. 30.

73. Ibid., p. 138.

74. Alvin Toffler, "The Competition That Refreshes," *Fortune* 63, no. 5 (May 1961): 125.

75. Ibid.

76. Ibid., p. 200.

77. Ibid., p. 202.

78. Personal communication, Philip F. Mooney, manager, Archives Department, Coca-Cola Company, 2 May 1989.

79. Craig Gilborn, "Pop Pedagogy: Looking at the Coke Bottle," *Museum News* 47, no. 4 (December 1968): 17; and Pat Watters, *Coca-Cola: An Illustrated History*, p. 1.

80. Cross, *The Supermarket Trap*, p. 37.

81. "Nous ne somme plus que de pauvres nègres arriérés, tout juste bons à être colonisés. Le premier commando est sur place: il s'appelle le Pop'Art" (Pierre Cabanne, "L'Amérique proclame la fin de l'Ecole de Paris et lance le Pop'Art pour coloniser l'Europe," *Arts* [Paris], no. 968 [24–30 June 1964]: 16).

82. John Maughan, "The Great Soup War," *Dun's Review and Modern Industry* 78, no. 3 (September 1961): 29.

83. Ibid.

84. Cross, *The Supermarket Trap*, pp. 32–33.

85. Interview with Tom Wesselmann in Swenson, "What is Pop Art? Part 2," p. 64.

## 3. POP ART AND CONSUMER CULTURE:
## THE MASS MEDIA IN AN AGE OF PUBLICITY

1. Andy Warhol, Kasper König, Pontus Hultén, and Olle Granath, eds., *Andy Warhol.*

2. Although the film and recording industries have historically reaped their profits solely from the sale of their products, that situation has begun to change, and they are increasingly deriving income from advertising, like the other forms of media. In recent years, film production companies have received substantial remuneration from various corporations in exchange for what are, for all intents and purposes, ads—prominent displays of their products in movies. Advertisements have even invaded those areas traditionally considered off-limits: home videos and record albums. Viewers now have to endure ads for Pepsi-Cola when watching *Top Gun* on video cassette, and Tony James, a punk rocker, has formed the "first totally corporate rock-and-roll band" whose first album, *Sigue Sigue Sputnik Flaunt It,* contains paid advertisements between the song tracks ("Do Top Guns Swig Diet Pop?" *Time,* 9 March 1987, p. 65; and Penelope Wang, "A Rock and Roll Marketing Whiz Plays for Pay," *Newsweek,* 11 August 1986, p. 39).

3. ". . . And Now a Word about Commercials," *Time,* 12 July 1968, p. 55.

4. Jennifer Cross, *The Supermarket Trap: The Consumer and the Food Industry,* p. 22.

5. Robert Sobel, *The Manipulators: America in the Media Age,* p. 348.

6. Ibid., pp. 350–351; and Melvin L. DeFleur and Sandra Ball-Rokeach, *Theories of Mass Communication,* p. 9.

7. Sobel, *The Manipulators,* p. 343.

8. Ibid., p. 338.

9. Ibid., p. 340.

10. National Collection of Fine Arts, Smithsonian Institution, *Robert Rauschenberg,* p. 123.

11. Erik Barnouw, *Tube of Plenty: The Evolution of American Television,* p. 363.

12. Perhaps the ultimate example of the power of television to endorse government positions was the cancellation of "The Smothers Brothers Comedy Hour" in

1972 despite high ratings in large part because of the Smothers' refusal to cease their satirical attacks on the Vietnam War.

13. Interview with Tom Wesselmann in Gene R. Swenson, "What Is Pop Art? Part 2: Stephen Durkee, Jasper Johns, James Rosenquist, Tom Wesselmann," *Artnews* 62, no. 10 (February 1964): 64–65.

14. Geoffrey Gorer, *The American People: A Study in National Character*, p. 47.

15. David Manning White, "Comics and the American Image Abroad," in *The Funnies: An American Idiom*, ed. David Manning White and Robert H. Abel, p. 77.

16. "The Administration: Telling the World," *Time*, 16 March 1962, p. 17.

17. White, "Comics and the American Image Abroad," p. 78.

18. For an extensive discussion of the foreign dissemination of Disney comics, see Ariel Dorfman and Armand Mattelart, *How to Read Donald Duck: Imperialist Ideology in the Disney Comic*.

19. It is difficult to gauge accurately the widespread impact that Walt Disney Productions had on American culture during this period, but it was considerable. Even beyond cartoons and comic strips, Disney Productions produced television shows that contributed to the acceptance of government activities, such as the space program. For example, Disney orchestrated the production of the "Man in Space" show and received a congratulatory call from President Eisenhower the day after the show aired. No doubt he expected the show to solidify support for his nascent space program. When Apollo 8 landed on the moon a few years later, Wernher von Braun, who had collaborated on the program with the Disney staff, called the show's director and said, "Well, Ward, it looks as though they are following our script" (Leonard Mosley, *Disney's World*, p. 265).

20. Walt Disney Productions was one of the most profitable studios during this period in large part because it did not maintain a large stable of stars for its movies, as was the practice at other Hollywood studios. Rather, they simply hired actors as necessity demanded. Thus, their most famous stars were, in fact, their cartoon characters. For more information on the structure of the Disney studio and its history, see Leonard Mosley, *Disney's World*.

21. John Rublowsky, *Pop Art*, p. 43.

22. The original comic-strip frame that provided the source for *Takka Takka* is illustrated in Lawrence Alloway, *Roy Lichtenstein*, p. 28.

23. Diane Waldman, *Roy Lichtenstein*, p. 26.

24. Alloway, *Roy Lichtenstein*, p. 110.

25. Leo Bogart, "Comic Strips and Their Adult Readers," in *The Funnies: An American Idiom*, ed. White and Abel, p. 240.

26. David Manning White and Robert H. Abel, "Introduction: Comic Strips and American Culture," in *The Funnies*, ed. White and Abel, p. 22.

27. Hortense Powdermaker, *Hollywood, the Dream Factory: An Anthropologist Looks at the Movie-makers*.

28. Bernard Rosenberg and David Manning White, "Motion Pictures," in *Mass Culture: The Popular Arts in America*, ed. Bernard Rosenberg and David Manning White, p. 254.

29. While the 1960s saw the demise of magazines such as *Life, Look,* and *Saturday Evening Post,* the magazine that was to register the highest circulation figures during that decade (and which continues to maintain this domination of the field) was *TV Guide,* a publication designed to give readers an inside glimpse into the entertainment industry (George N. Gordon, *The Communications Revolution: A History of Mass Media in the United States,* pp. 292–293).

30. Lincoln Kirstein, "Marilyn Monroe: 1926–1962." *Nation,* 25 August 1962, p. 72; and "'I Love You . . . I Love You. . . ,'" *Newsweek,* 20 August 1962, p. 30.

31. "The Growing Cult of Marilyn," *Life,* 25 January 1963, pp. 89–91+.

32. "Stars: A Funny Thing Happened on the Way to Decorum," *Time,* 2 January 1964, p. 56.

33. "Star's Illness Costs Insurers $2 Million," *Business Week,* 28 October 1961, p. 104; and "'Boss' Makes $150,000, 'Employe' [*sic*] 2.4 Million," *U.S. News & World Report,* 3 June 1963, p. 10.

34. "Stars: Miracle on 46th Street," *Time,* 12 June 1964, pp. 86, 90.

35. Wilbur Schramm, "Communication in Crisis," in *The Kennedy Assassination and the American Public,* ed. Bradley S. Greenberg and Edwin B. Parker, pp. 14–15.

36. Curtis Prendergast, with Geoffrey Colvin, *The World of Time Inc.: The Intimate History of a Changing Enterprise,* vol. 3, *1960–1980,* p. 121; and Loudon Wainwright, *The Great American Magazine: An Inside History of Life,* p. 314.

37. Ibid., p. 129.


## 4. POP ART AND CONSUMER CULTURE:
## THE CULT OF DOMESTICITY AND CONSUMPTION IN THE HOME

1. John Loring, "Oldenburg on Multiples," *Arts Magazine* 48, no. 8 (May 1974): 45.

2. For discussion of this transition see T. J. Jackson Lears, "From Salvation to Self-Realization: Advertising and the Therapeutic Roots of the Consumer Culture, 1880–1930," in *The Culture of Consumption: Critical Essays in American History, 1880–1980,* ed. Richard Wightman Fox and T. J. Jackson Lears, pp. 1–38.

3. William H. Whyte, Jr., *The Organization Man,* p. 4.

4. Ibid.

5. David Riesman with Nathan Glazer and Revel Denney, *The Lonely Crowd: A Study of the Changing American Character,* p. 157.

6. For discussion of the effects of social and geographical mobility on the development of consumer culture, see "Historical Roots of Consumer Culture," in Michael Schudson, *Advertising, the Uneasy Persuasion: Its Dubious Impact on American Society,* pp. 147–177.

7. "The Era of Predigestion," *Atlantic* 104 (November 1909): 715–716.

8. Lears, "From Salvation to Self-Realization," p. 7.

9. Thomas Luckmann and Peter Berger, "Social Mobility and Personal Identity," *Archives Européennes de Sociologie* 5, no. 2 (1964): 339.

10. Ronald Berman, *Advertising and Social Change*, p. 107.

11. "Into the Red Shadowland," *Newsweek*, 27 July 1959, p. 41.

12. Ibid.

13. "Setting Russia Straight on Facts about the U.S.," *U.S. News & World Report*, 3 August 1959, p. 70.

14. "Encounter," *Newsweek*, 3 August 1959, p. 17.

15. Ibid., p. 15.

16. E. Ray Canterbery, *Economics on a New Frontier*, p. 150.

17. Thomas Hine, *Populuxe*, pp. 128, 133.

18. This association between high technology and housewares was not limited to the push button but extended to other products and other national concerns. For example, atomic and rocket imagery was especially pervasive in the post-Sputnik years, when the United States launched a major effort in space exploration. The design of many products, such as table lamps, vacuum cleaners, china, glassware, and electric razors mimicked the forms of satellites, atoms, and rockets.

19. Although extensive research was being undertaken during the 1960s in the development of computer-chip-driven technology and microwave technology, this research was not translated into new high-tech appliances and housewares that were readily available to the average American consumer until the late 1970s and 1980s.

20. Hine, *Populuxe*, pp. 128–129.

21. Earl Lifshey, *The Housewares Story: A History of the American Housewares Industry*, p. 273.

22. For discussion of the technological development of the electric blender in America, see Lifshey, *The Housewares Story*, p. 273.

23. Ibid., p. 274.

24. Ibid., p. 159.

25. Armon Glenn, "Thriving Drive-Ins: They Are the Hottest Thing in the Restaurant Business Today," *Barron's*, 5 June 1961, pp. 11, 13; and "Doesn't Anyone Cook at Home Any More?," *Printers Ink*, 16 October 1964, p. 3.

26. Jim Hightower, *Eat Your Heart Out: Food Profiteering in America*, pp. 96–97.

27. Margaret J. King, "Empires of Popular Culture: McDonald's and Disney," in *Ronald Revisited: The World of Ronald McDonald*, p. 109.

28. A. A. Berger, "Berger vs. Burger: A Personal Encounter," in *Ronald Revisited: The World of Ronald McDonald*, p. 126; and King, "Empires of Popular Culture," p. 109.

29. Paul Boyer, *By the Bomb's Early Light: American Thought and Culture at the Dawn of the Atomic Age*, p. 353.

30. For discussion on the proposed tax cut and the rationale for this legislation, see Canterbery, *Economics on a New Frontier*, pp. 150, 263–278.

31. Ibid., p. 263.

32. Ibid., pp. 271, 272.

33. Robert M. Collins, *The Business Response to Keynes, 1929–1964,* p. 15.

34. Alvin H. Hansen, *Economic Issues of the 1960s,* p. 66.

35. Steven Mintz and Susan Kellogg, *Domestic Revolutions: A Social History of American Family Life,* pp. 217–218.

36. For discussion on the changing structure of the American family in the 1960s, see ibid., pp. 203–237.

37. For discussion of the use of sexual innuendo in advertising during this period, see "The Built-In Sexual Overtone," in Vance Packard, *The Hidden Persuaders,* pp. 71–82.

38. For a detailed discussion of both the history and engineering design of the F-III, see Robert F. Coulam, *Illusions of Choice: The F-III and the Problem of Weapons Acquisition Reform.*

39. Ibid., pp. 37, 89.

40. Ibid., pp. 68, 69.

41. Ibid., p. 3.

42. Gene R. Swenson, "F-III: An Interview with James Rosenquist," *Partisan Review* 32, no. 4 (Fall 1965): 589–590.

43. For example, see "The TFX Plane—What the Fight Is About," *U.S. News & World Report,* 25 March 1963, pp. 61–63; "F-III, in model form, spreads . . . its 'switchblade' wings," *Business Week,* 30 May 1964, p. 27; "Aerodynamics: A Fighter for All Speeds," *Time,* 23 October 1964, p. 52; "Plane and Fancy," *Newsweek,* 26 October 1964, p. 99; "Why the TFX Plane Is Still under Fire," *U.S. News & World Report,* 26 October 1964, p. 8; "TFX Flies . . . But Questions Remain," *U.S. News & World Report,* 4 January 1965, pp. 6, 8; "F-III Breaks Another Barrier," *Business Week,* 13 March 1965, p. 34; "The $7 Billion 'Goody,'" *Newsweek,* 24 May 1965, pp. 103–104.

44. Packard, *The Hidden Persuaders,* p. 65.

45. Lifshey, *The Housewares Story,* p. 357.

## 5. THE POP MOVEMENT AND THE INSTITUTIONAL MATRIX: THE ARTISTS

1. Andy Warhol, *The Philosophy of Andy Warhol (From A to B and Back Again),* p. 92.

2. The information about this incident was collected from J. Morris International Gallery Ltd. press releases and letters from the National Gallery of Canada and the National Revenue, Customs and Excise, as well as from numerous reports in various newspapers.

3. Information about Roy Lichtenstein's dinnerware was obtained from the advertisements in periodicals, brochures, and the order form.

4. Carter Ratcliff, *Andy Warhol,* pp. 12–13.

5. For discussion of the window displays of Matson Jones, see Calvin Tomkins, *Off the Wall: Robert Rauschenberg and the Art World of Our Time,* pp. 111–114.

6. Judith Goldman, *Windows at Tiffany's: The Art of Gene Moore,* p. 19.

7. There are, of course, exceptions to this generalization. Abstract Expressionist

Barnett Newman expounded widely on the theoretical and philosophical bases of his art, while Pop artist Jasper Johns has become notorious for his reticence and low profile.

8. Tomkins, *Off the Wall*, p. 180.

9. Alan Solomon, *Andy Warhol*, p. 2.

10. Although this incident has been recounted by some of the scholars who have studied Warhol's career, the most complete account of this incident (and, ironically, the one that I have chosen to utilize) comes from Warhol himself in Andy Warhol and Pat Hackett, *POPism: The Warhol '60s*, pp. 247–248.

11. Judith Goldman, *James Rosenquist*, p. 45.

12. Ibid., p. 44.

13. Tomkins, *Off the Wall*, p. 216.

14. Warhol and Hackett, *POPism*, pp. 131–132.

15. Ibid., p. 133.

16. Patrick S. Smith, *Warhol: Conversations about the Artist*, p. 220.

17. George H. Roeder, Jr., *Forum of Uncertainty: Confrontation with Modern Painting in Twentieth-Century American Thought*, p. 220.

18. Calvin Tomkins, "Raggedy Andy," in *Andy Warhol*, by John Coplans, p. 12.

19. Ibid.

20. Warhol and Hackett, *POPism*, p. 24.

21. Grace Glueck, "Robert C. Scull, Prominent Collector of Pop Art," *New York Times*, 3 January 1986, sec. B, p. 5; and Tomkins, *Off The Wall*, p. 296.

22. Roberta B. Gratz, "Artist's a Study in Blue at Scull's SRO Auction," *New York Post*, 19 October 1973, p. 3.

23. Ibid.; and Tomkins, *Off The Wall*, p. 296.

24. Barbaralee Diamonstein, "Pop Art, Money, and the Present Scene: An Interview With Roy Lichtenstein and Leo Castelli," *Partisan Review* 45, no. 1 (1978): 93.

25. "Contemporary Art Sets Auction Price Records," *Los Angeles Times*, 13 November 1986, pt. 6, p. 8.

26. Barbara Rose, *Claes Oldenburg*, p. 102; and Barbara Haskell, *Claes Oldenburg: Object into Monument*, p. 85.

27. Rose, *Claes Oldenburg*, p. 102.

## 6. THE POP MOVEMENT AND THE INSTITUTIONAL MATRIX: THE DEALERS AND COLLECTORS

1. Warhol and Hackett, *POPism*, p. 21.

2. Calvin Tomkins, "Profiles: A Good Eye and a Good Ear," *New Yorker*, 26 May 1980, p. 40.

3. Ibid., p. 58.

4. Ibid., p. 67.

5. Ibid.

6. Judith Goldman, *James Rosenquist*, p. 43.

7. Ibid.

8. Richard F. Shepard, "To What Lengths Can Art Go?" *New York Times,* 13 May 1965, p. 1; and "Art: Pop," *Time,* 28 May 1965, p. 80.

9. Tomkins, "Profiles," p. 68.

10. Calvin Tomkins, *Off the Wall: Robert Rauschenberg and the Art World of Our Time,* p. 184.

11. John Tancock, "The Robert C. Scull Auction," in *Art at Auction: The Year at Sotheby Parke Bernet, 1973–74,* p. 143.

12. John Rublowsky, *Pop Art,* p. 159.

13. Personal communication, 24 May 1989.

14. Laura de Coppet and Alan Jones, *The Art Dealers,* p. 125.

15. Rublowsky, *Pop Art,* p. 157.

16. Ibid.

17. "You Bought It—Now Live with It," *Life,* 16 July 1965, p. 59.

18. Ibid., p. 58.

19. Joyce Kolko, *America and the Crisis of World Capitalism,* p. 80. For further information, see also Frank Vogl, *German Business after the Economic Miracle;* and Volker R. Berghahn, *The Americanisation of West German Industry, 1945–1973.*

20. Tomkins, "Profiles," p. 70.

21. An interview with Robert Scull exists in the Oral History Collection of the Archives of American Art; however, it was not consulted for this study. Unfortunately, because Mr. Scull's estate was in litigation during the years that this study was researched and written, scholarly access to this interview was denied.

22. "At Home with Henry," *Time,* 21 February 1964, p. 68.

23. Ibid.; and Rublowsky, *Pop Art,* p. 155.

24. Tomkins, "Profiles," p. 61.

25. Barbara Rose, "Profit without Honor," *New York Magazine,* 5 November 1973, pp. 80–81.

26. "At Home with Henry," p. 68.

27. Grace Glueck, "Robert C. Scull, Prominent Collector of Pop Art," *New York Times,* 3 January 1986, sec. B, p. 5.

28. Tomkins, "Profiles," p. 61.


## 7. THE POP MOVEMENT AND THE INSTITUTIONAL MATRIX: THE CRITICS

1. Max Kozloff, "Art," *Nation,* 20 January 1964, p. 79.

2. Clement Greenberg, "After Abstract Expressionism," *Art International,* 25 October 1962, p. 32.

3. Herbert Read, "Disintegration of Form in Modern Art," *Studio International* 169, no. 864 (April 1965): 153.

4. Peter Plagens, "Present-Day Styles and Ready-Made Criticism," *Artforum* 5, no. 4 (December 1966): 36.

5. Ibid., pp. 36–37.

6. Harold Rosenberg, "The Art World: Marilyn Mondrian," *New Yorker,* 8 November 1969, p. 167.

7. Ibid., p. 170.

8. Ibid., p. 169.

9. Barbara Rose, "Problems of Criticism, V: The Politics of Art, Part II," *Artforum* 7, no. 5 (January 1969): 46.

10. Ibid., p. 47.

11. Kozloff, "Art," p. 78.

12. Max Kozloff, "'Pop' Culture, Metaphysical Disgust, and the New Vulgarians," *Art International* 6, no. 2 (March 1962): 36.

13. Barbara Haskell, *Blam! The Explosion of Pop, Minimalism, and Performance, 1958–1964,* p. 89.

14. Kozloff, "'Pop' Culture," p. 36.

15. Sidney Tillim, "New York Exhibitions: Month in Review," *Arts Magazine* 37, no. 6 (March 1963): 61.

16. Clement Greenberg, "Avant-Garde and Kitsch," *Partisan Review* 6, no. 5 (Fall 1939): 39–40.

17. Erle Loran, "Pop Artists or Copy Cats?," *Artnews* 62, no. 5 (September 1963): 48–49, 61.

18. Peter Selz, "Pop Goes the Artist," *Partisan Review* 30, no. 2 (Summer 1963): 314.

19. Eva Cockcroft, "Abstract Expressionism: Weapon of the Cold War," *Artforum* 12, no. 10 (June 1974): 40.

20. Ibid.

21. Hilton Kramer, statement in "A Symposium on Pop Art," *Arts Magazine* 37, no. 7 (April 1963): 38.

22. Ibid.

23. Henry Geldzahler, "The Art Audience and the Critic," *Hudson Review* 18, no. 1 (Spring 1965): 106.

24. Barbara Rose, "Problems of Criticism, VI: The Politics of Art, Part III," *Artforum* 7, no. 9 (May 1969): 48.

25. Kozloff, "'Pop' Culture," p. 36.

26. Stanley Kunitz, statement in "A Symposium on Pop Art," *Arts Magazine* 37, no. 7 (April 1963): p. 41.

27. Read, "Disintegration of Form in Modern Art," p. 155.

28. Lawrence Alloway, *American Pop Art,* p. 1.


## 8. THE LEGACY OF POP ART: THE ROOTS OF POSTMODERNISM

1. Mary Harron, "Pop Art/Art Pop: The Warhol Connection," *Melody Maker,* 16 February 1980, p. 21.

2. Abraham A. Davidson, *Early American Modernist Painting, 1910–1935,* p. 257.

3. For more information on the history of consumer protection, see Robert O.

Herrmann, "The Consumer Movement in Historical Perspective," in *Consumerism: Search for the Consumer Interest,* ed. David A. Aaker and George S. Day, pp. 10–18.

4. Lawrence Alloway, "The Development of British Pop," in *Pop Art,* by Lucy R. Lippard, p. 32.

5. Interview with Claes Oldenburg in Alan R. Solomon Papers, Archives of American Art, Smithsonian Institution, Washington, D.C.

6. Fredric Jameson, "Postmodernism and Consumer Society," in *The Anti-Aesthetic: Essays on Postmodern Culture,* ed. Hal Foster, pp. 111–125; and Andreas Huyssen, "The Cultural Politics of Pop," in *After the Great Divide: Modernism, Mass Culture, Postmodernism,* pp. 141–159.

7. It is not the goal of this chapter to engage in a detailed, comprehensive discussion of modernism and postmodernism, but rather, to sketch out some of the overriding aspects that characterize modernism and postmodernism. Thus, given the limited scope of this treatment and the clear lack of consensus with regard to definitional parameters of the terms, no attempt will be made to discuss the various and often subtle social and political positions that are frequently ascribed to the numerous modernist and postmodernist agendas (and which are still the subjects of debate).

8. For discussion of this equation between avant-gardism and modernism, see Jürgen Habermas, "Modernity versus Postmodernity," *New German Critique* 8, no. 1 (Winter 1981): 3–14; and Andreas Huyssen, "The Search for Tradition: Avant-Garde and Postmodernism in the 1970s," *New German Critique* 8, no. 1 (Winter 1981): 23–40.

9. For example, see Kim Levin, "Farewell to Modernism," *Arts Magazine* 54, no. 2 (October 1979): 90–92; Hal Foster, "(Post)Modern Polemics," *New German Critique* 11, no. 3 (Fall 1984): 67–78; and Andreas Huyssen, "Mapping the Postmodern," *New German Critique* 11, no. 3 (Fall 1984): 5–52.

10. For discussion of this interpretation, see Huyssen, "The Search for Tradition," pp. 23–40; and Huyssen, "Mapping the Postmodern," pp. 5–52.

11. For discussion of this interpretation, see Habermas, "Modernity versus Postmodernity," pp. 3–14; Foster, "(Post)Modern Polemics," pp. 67–78; and Huyssen, "Mapping the Postmodern," pp. 5–52.

12. Patrick Goldstein, "Disc-graces Grace Annual Bottom 10," *Los Angeles Times Calendar,* 11 January 1987, p. 80.

13. For discussion on the strategy of appropriation in photography and its relationship to modernism and postmodernism, see Douglas Crimp, "The Photographic Activity of Postmodernism," in *Postmodern Perspectives: Issues in Contemporary Art,* ed. Howard Risatti, pp. 131–139.

14. Jameson, "Postmodernism and Consumer Society," pp. 111–125; and Huyssen, "The Cultural Politics of Pop," pp. 141–159.

15. Jameson, "Postmodernism and Consumer Society," p. 125.

16. Suzi Gablik, *Has Modernism Failed?* p. 13.

17. Kim Foltz and Maggie Malone, "Golden Paintbrushes: Artists Are Developing a Fine Eye for the Bottom Line," *Newsweek,* 15 October 1984, p. 82.

18. Calvin Tomkins, *Off the Wall: Robert Rauschenberg and the Art World of Our Time,* p. 284.

19. Foltz and Malone, "Golden Paintbrushes," p. 82.

20. Michael Small, "Already a Big Man on Canvas, Robert Longo Goes Multimedia," *People,* 10 November 1986, p. 135.

21. Foltz and Malone, "Golden Paintbrushes," p. 82.

22. Michael Small, "For a Few Fleeting Hours Keith Haring Makes a Bright Canvas of the Berlin Wall," *People,* 10 November 1986, p. 54.

23. Ibid.

24. Ibid.

25. Cathleen McGuigan, "New Art, New Money: The Marketing of an American Artist," *New York Times Magazine,* 10 February 1985, p. 34.

26. Ibid., p. 35.

27. Meg Cox, "Feeling Victimized? Then Strike Back: Become an Artist," *Wall Street Journal,* 13 February 1989, sec. A, p. 1.

28. Ibid.

29. Ibid.

30. Ibid.

31. Foltz and Malone, "Golden Paintbrushes," p. 82.

32. Cox, "Feeling Victimized?," p. 8.

33. Foltz and Malone, "Golden Paintbrushes," p. 83.

34. McGuigan, "New Art, New Money," p. 32.

35. Julia Brown and Bridget Johnson, eds., *The First Show: Painting and Sculpture from Eight Collections, 1940–1980,* p. 5.

36. With its purchase of Ted Bates Worldwide in May 1986, Saatchi & Saatchi Co. P.L.C. moved into the position of the largest ad agency in the world (Richard W. Stevenson, "Ad Agency Mergers Changing the Business," *New York Times,* 13 May 1986, sec. A, p. 1).

37. "Cornering the Contemporary Art Market with an Eye on Profit," *Insight,* 31 March 1986, p. 13.

38. Ibid.

39. Foltz and Malone, "Golden Paintbrushes," p. 83.

40. For discussion of the relationship between poststructuralism and postmodernism, see Huyssen, "Mapping the Postmodern," pp. 36–47; and Foster, "(Post)Modern Polemics," pp. 67–78.

41. I have included the terms *author* and *text* because French critical theory, particularly poststructuralism, has been the most clearly articulated and developed in the area of literary theory. Much of the current application to the field of art is derived from the interdisciplinary nature of poststructuralism.

42. Roland Barthes, *Image-Music-Text,* p. 148.

# BIBLIOGRAPHY

## UNPUBLISHED MATERIAL

Archives of American Art, Smithsonian Institution, Washington, D.C.
    Oral History Collection
        Henry Geldzahler
        Ivan C. Karp
        Nelson Rockefeller
    Alan R. Solomon Papers
        Biennale notes, correspondence
        Interviews with
            Jasper Johns
            Roy Lichtenstein
            Claes Oldenburg
            Robert Rauschenberg
            Andy Warhol
Castelli Archives, Leo Castelli Gallery, New York, N.Y.
    Reviews, announcements, press clippings, correspondence, exhibition catalogs on
        Jasper Johns
        Roy Lichtenstein
        Claes Oldenburg
        James Rosenquist
        Andy Warhol
Personal communication with
    Selma P. Kessler, Campbell Soup Company
    Philip Mooney, manager, Archives Department, the Coca-Cola Company
Personal interview with
    Leo Castelli, 24 May 1989
    Ivan Karp, 18 May 1989
    Gene Moore, 16 May 1989

## PUBLISHED MATERIAL

Aaker, David A., and George S. Day, eds. *Consumerism: Search for the Consumer Interest.* 2d ed. New York: Free Press, 1974.

"The Administration: Telling the World." *Time,* 16 March 1962, p. 17.

"Aerodynamics: A Fighter for All Speeds." *Time,* 23 October 1964, p. 52.

Alfieri, Bruno. "U.S.A.: Towards the End of 'Abstract' Painting?" *Metro,* nos. 4–5 (1962): 4–13.

Allen, James Sloan. *The Romance of Commerce and Culture: Capitalism, Modernism, and the Chicago-Aspen Crusade for Cultural Reform.* Chicago: University of Chicago Press, 1983.

Allen, Jane Addams. "Speculating: A Fine Art." *Insight,* 31 March 1986, pp. 6–15.

Alloway, Lawrence. *American Pop Art.* New York: Macmillan, 1974.

―――. "The Development of British Pop." In *Pop Art,* by Lucy R. Lippard, pp. 27–67. New York: Oxford University Press, 1966.

―――. *Roy Lichtenstein.* New York: Abbeville Press, 1983.

―――. *Six Painters and the Object.* New York: Solomon R. Guggenheim Foundation, 1963.

―――. *The Venice Biennale, 1895–1968: From Salon to Goldfish Bowl.* Greenwich, Conn.: New York Graphic Society, 1968.

Alsop, Joseph. "Art into Money." *New York Review of Books,* 17 July 1986, pp. 42–45.

Alvard, Julien. "Paris." *Artnews* 67, no. 5 (September 1968): 24, 67.

Amaya, Mario. *Pop Art . . . and After.* New York: Viking Press, 1965.

*Amerikansk pop-konst.* Stockholm: Moderna Museet, 1964.

Ammann, Jean-Christophe. "Kassel: IV. Documenta." *Werk* 55, no. 8 (August 1968): 566–567.

". . . And Now a Word about Commercials." *Time,* 12 July 1968, pp. 55–60.

*Andy Warhol.* Paris: Ileana Sonnabend, 1965.

Armand, Miriam. "Biennale Winners Reflect Contemporary Trends." *Arts Magazine* 43, no. 2 (November 1968): 14.

*Art at Auction: The Year at Sotheby's & Parke-Bernet.* New York: Viking Press, Inc., [various years].

"Art: Pop." *Time,* 28 May 1965, p. 80.

Ashbery, John. "The Venice Biennale Begins To Show Its Changing Face." *New York Herald Tribune* (Paris), 16 June 1964, p. 5.

―――. "Venice Biennale Center of Controversy." *New York Herald Tribune* (Paris), 23 June 1964, p. 5.

Ashton, Dore. "IX Bienal de São Paulo: Notes from an Innocent Abroad." *Arts Magazine* 42, no. 2 (November 1967): 24–29.

*Aspetti dell'Arte Contemporanea.* Roma: Edizioni dell'Ateneo, 1963.

"At Home with Henry." *Time,* 21 February 1964, pp. 68–71.

Bailey, Beth L. *From Front Porch to Back Seat: Courtship in Twentieth-Century America.* Baltimore: Johns Hopkins University Press, 1988.

Baker, Elizabeth C. "Brazilian Bouillabaisse." *Artnews* 64, no. 8 (December 1965): 30–31, 56–58.

Barnouw, Erik. *Tube of Plenty: The Evolution of American Television*. Rev. ed. New York: Oxford University Press, 1982.

Baro, Gene. "The Venice Biennale." *Arts Magazine* 38, no. 10 (September 1964): 32–37.

Barthes, Roland. *Image-Music-Text*. Translated by Stephen Heath. New York: Noonday Press, 1977.

———. *Mythologies*. Translated by Annette Lavers. New York: Hill and Wang, 1972.

Battcock, Gregory. "Andy Warhol: New Predictions for Art." *Arts Magazine* 48, no. 8 (May 1974): 34–37.

Baudrillard, Jean. *La Société de Consommation: Ses mythes, ses structures*. Paris: Gallimard, 1970.

Bauer, Raymond A., and Stephen A. Greyser. *Advertising in America: The Consumer View*. Boston: Division of Research, Graduate School of Business Administration, Harvard University, 1968.

Bell, Daniel. *The Cultural Contradictions of Capitalism*. New York: Basic Books, 1976.

Benjamin, Walter. "The Work of Art in the Age of Mechanical Reproduction." In *Illuminations*, edited and with an introduction by Hannah Arendt, pp. 219–253. New York: Harcourt, Brace & World, 1968.

Berger, A. A. "Berger vs. Burger: A Personal Encounter." In *Ronald Revisited: The World of Ronald McDonald*, pp. 125–128. Bowling Green, Ohio: Bowling Green University Popular Press, 1983.

Berghahn, Volker R. *The Americanisation of West German Industry, 1945–1973*. Leamington Spa: Berg Publishers, 1986.

Berman, Ronald. *Advertising and Social Change*. Beverly Hills: Sage Publications, 1981.

Bernstein, Roberta. *Jasper Johns' Paintings and Sculptures, 1954–1974: "The Changing Focus of the Eye."* Ann Arbor: UMI Research Press, 1985.

Best, Michael H., and William E. Connolly. *The Politicized Economy*. Lexington, Mass.: D. C. Heath and Company, 1976.

"The Best of the Best." *Time*, 6 July 1962, pp. 46, 49.

Birmingham, Nan Tillson. *Store*. New York: G. P. Putnam's Sons, 1978.

Bogart, Leo. "Comic Strips and Their Adult Readers." In *The Funnies: An American Idiom*, edited by David Manning White and Robert H. Abel, pp. 232–246. New York: Free Press, 1963.

Boime, Albert. "Roy Lichtenstein and the Comic Strip." *Art Journal* 28, no. 2 (Winter 1968–1969): 155–159.

Bongard, Willi. "When Rauschenberg Won the Biennale." *Studio International* 175, no. 901 (June 1968): 288–289.

"'Boss' Makes $150,000, 'Employe' [*sic*] 2.4 Million." *U.S. News & World Report*, 3 June 1963, p. 10.

Bowness, Alan. "Reflections on the Biennale 1." *Studio International* 172, no. 880 (August 1966): 77–78.

———. "São Paulo: Impressions of the Bienal." *Studio International* 174, no. 894 (November 1967): 218–219.

Boyer, Paul. *By the Bomb's Early Light: American Thought and Culture at the Dawn of the Atomic Age*. New York: Pantheon Books, 1985.

Brady, Maxine. *Bloomingdale's*. New York: Harcourt Brace Jovanovich, 1980.

Brown, Julia, ed. *The Museum of Contemporary Art: The Panza Collection*. Los Angeles: Museum of Contemporary Art, 1985.

——, and Bridget Johnson, eds. *The First Show: Painting and Sculpture from Eight Collections, 1940–1980*. Los Angeles: Museum of Contemporary Art, 1983.

Bruggen, Coosge van. *Claes Oldenburg: Mouse Museum/Ray Gun Wing*. Cologne: Museum Ludwig, 1979.

Butler, Joseph T. "The American Way with Art." *Connoisseur* 169, no. 681 (November 1968): 200–201.

Cabanne, Pierre. "L'Amérique proclame la fin de l'Ecole de Paris et lance le Pop'Art pour coloniser l'Europe." *Arts* (Paris), no. 968 (24–30 June 1964): 16.

Calas, Nicholas. "Why Not Pop Art?" *Art and Literature*, no. 4 (Spring 1965): 178–184.

Campbell, Lawrence. "Reviews and Previews: Andy Warhol." *Artnews* 63, no. 4 (Summer 1964): 16.

Canaday, John. "Pop Art Sells On and On—Why?" *New York Times Magazine*, 31 May 1964, pp. 1, 48, 52–53.

Canterbery, E. Ray. *Economics on a New Frontier*. Belmont, Calif.: Wadsworth Publishing Co., 1968.

——. "The Fine Line Between Politics and Economics." *Challenge* 11, no. 10 (July 1963): 28–31.

Carlson, Walter. "Pavilion At Fair to Show Fine Art." *New York Times*, 13 May 1964, p. 35.

Carluccio, Luigi. "Alla XXXII Biennale." *Domus* 418 (September 1964): 45, 55.

*Catalogo della XXXII Esposizione Biennale Internationale d'Arte, Venezia*. Venezia: Stamperia di Venezia, 1964.

Celant, Germano. "F-111, Rosenquist a Roma." *La Biennale di Venezia* 17, no. 61 (March 1967): 61.

Chafe, William Henry. *The American Woman: Her Changing Social, Economic, and Political Roles, 1920–1970*. New York: Oxford University Press, 1972.

Chevalier, Denys. "La sculpture à la Biennale de Venise." *Aujourd'hui* 8, no. 47 (October 1964): 36–39.

*Claes Oldenburg*. London: Arts Council of Great Britain, 1970.

*Claes Oldenburg*. Paris: Galerie Ileana Sonnabend, 1964.

*Claes Oldenburg: Tekeningen, Aquarellen en Grafiek*. Amsterdam: Stedelijk Museum, 1977.

Clark, T. J. "Clement Greenberg's Theory of Art." In *Pollock and After: The Critical Debate*, edited by Francis Frascina, pp. 47–63. New York: Harper & Row, 1985.

Clayton, James L., ed. *The Economic Impact of the Cold War: Sources and Readings*. New York: Harcourt, Brace & World, 1970.

Cockcroft, Eva. "Abstract Expressionism: Weapon of the Cold War." *Artforum* 12, no. 10 (June 1974): 39–41.

Collins, Robert M. *The Business Response to Keynes, 1929–1964.* New York: Columbia University Press, 1981.

Compton, Michael. *Pop Art.* London: Hamlyn Publishing Group, 1970.

"Contemporary Art Sets Auction Price Records." *Los Angeles Times,* 13 November 1986, pt. 6, p. 8.

Coplans, John. *Andy Warhol.* New York: New York Graphic Society, 1970.

———. "Early Warhol: The Systematic Evolution of the Impersonal Style." *Artforum* 8, no. 7 (March 1970): 52–59.

———. *Serial Imagery.* Pasadena, Calif.: Pasadena Art Museum, 1968.

Corcoran, Farrell. "Television as Ideological Apparatus: The Power and the Pleasure." In *Television: The Critical View,* edited by Horace Newcomb, pp. 533–552. 4th ed. New York: Oxford University Press, 1987.

"Cornering the Contemporary Art Market with an Eye on Profit." *Insight,* 31 March 1986, pp. 12–13.

Coulam, Robert F. *Illusions of Choice: The F-111 and the Problem of Weapons Acquisition Reform.* Princeton: Princeton University Press, 1977.

Cox, Meg. "Feeling Victimized? Then Strike Back: Become an Artist." *Wall Street Journal,* 13 February 1989, sec. A, pp. 1, 8.

Crichton, Michael. *Jasper Johns.* New York: Harry N. Abrams, 1977.

Crimp, Douglas. "The Photographic Activity of Postmodernism." In *Postmodern Perspectives: Issues in Contemporary Art,* edited by Howard Risatti, pp. 131–139. Englewood Cliffs, N.J.: Prentice-Hall, 1990.

Crone, Rainer. *Andy Warhol.* New York: Praeger Publishers, 1970.

———. *Andy Warhol: Das zeichnerische Werk, 1942–1975.* Stuttgart: Württembergischer Kunstverein, 1976.

Cross, Jennifer. *The Supermarket Trap: The Consumer and the Food Industry.* Bloomington: Indiana University Press, 1970.

Crow, Thomas. "Modernism and Mass Culture in the Visual Arts." In *Pollock and After: The Critical Debate,* edited by Francis Frascina, pp. 233–266. New York: Harper & Row, 1985.

———. "Saturday Disasters: Trace and Reference in Early Warhol." In *Reconstructing Modernism: Art in New York, Paris, and Montreal, 1945–1964,* edited by Serge Guilbaut, pp. 311–326. Cambridge, Mass.: MIT Press, 1990.

Davidson, Abraham A. *Early American Modernist Painting, 1910–1935.* New York: Harper & Row, 1981.

Davis, John H. *The Kennedys—Dynasty and Disaster, 1848–1983.* New York: McGraw-Hill Book Co., 1984.

Dawidoff, T. Nicholas. "Art in the Fast Lane." *Sports Illustrated,* 20 April 1987, p. 115.

de Coppet, Laura, and Alan Jones. *The Art Dealers.* New York: Clarkson N. Potter, 1984.

DeFleur, Melvin L., and Sandra Ball-Rokeach. *Theories of Mass Communication.* 3d ed. New York: David McKay Co., 1975.

Deroudille, René. "A Venise Santé et tonus de 'l'Hourloupe' de Dubuffet." *Aujourd'hui* 8, no. 47 (October 1964): 42.

Diamonstein, Barbaralee. "Pop Art, Money, and the Present Scene: An Interview with Roy Lichtenstein and Leo Castelli." *Partisan Review* 45, no. 1 (1978): 80–93.

Dickstein, Morris. *Gates of Eden: American Culture in the Sixties*. New York: Basic Books, 1977.

Dienst, Rolf-Gunter. "Die documenta IV." *Das Kunstwerk* 21, nos. 11–12 (August–September 1968): 36–55.

———. *Pop-Art: Eine kritische Information*. Wiesbaden: Limes Verlag, 1965.

"Doesn't Anyone Cook at Home Any More?" *Printers Ink*, 16 October 1964, p. 3.

Dorfman, Ariel, and Armand Mattelart. *How to Read Donald Duck: Imperialist Ideology in the Disney Comic*. Translated by David Kunzle. New York: International General, 1975.

"Do Top Guns Swig Diet Pop?" *Time*, 9 March 1987, p. 65.

Douglas, Ann. *The Feminization of American Culture*. New York: Alfred A. Knopf, 1977.

Dubreuil-Blondin, Nicole. *La Fonction critique dans le Pop Art américain*. Montreal: Les Presses de l'Université de Montréal, 1980.

Eckstein, Otto. "The Economics of the 1960's—A Backward Look." *Public Interest*, no. 19 (Spring 1970): 86–97.

Editors of *Ramparts* with Frank Browning, eds. *In the Marketplace: Consumerism in America*. San Francisco: Canfield Press, 1972.

Emerson, Robert L. *Fast Food: The Endless Shakeout*. New York: Chain Store Publishing Corp., 1979.

"Encounter." *Newsweek*, 3 August 1959, pp. 15–19.

"The Era of Predigestion." *Atlantic* 104 (November 1909): 715–716.

*An Exhibition of New Work by Claes Oldenburg*. New York: Sidney Janis Gallery, 1967.

*An Exhibition of New Work by Tom Wesselmann*. New York: Sidney Janis Gallery, 1968.

*An Exhibition of Recent Work by Claes Oldenburg*. New York: Sidney Janis Gallery, 1964.

"Exhibitions: Pop Goes the Biennale," *Time*, 3 July 1964, p. 54.

Ewen, Stuart. *Captains of Consciousness: Advertising and the Social Roots of the Consumer Culture*. New York: McGraw-Hill Book Co., 1976.

Ewen, Stuart, and Elizabeth Ewen. *Channels of Desire: Mass Images and the Shaping of American Consciousness*. New York: McGraw-Hill Book Co., 1982.

"F-111 breaks another barrier." *Business Week*, 13 March 1965, p. 34.

"F-111, in model form, spreads . . . its 'switchblade' wings." *Business Week*, 30 May 1964, p. 27.

Farr, Dennis. "Documenta III, Kassel, 1964." *Apollo* 80, no. 31 (September 1964): 241–242.

Feldstein, Martin. "The Retreat from Keynesian Economics." *Public Interest*, no. 64 (Summer 1981): 92–105.

Fingleton, Eamonn. "Portrait of the Artist as Money Man." *Forbes*, 1 February 1982, pp. 58–60, 62.

Fitz-Gibbon, Bernice. "DepARTment Stores . . . Meet Me among the Matisses, Maggie." *Art in America* 44, no. 2 (Spring 1956): 18–25, 61–62.

Flamant, Maurice, and Jeanne Singer-Kérel. *Modern Economic Crises and Recessions.* Translated by Pat Wardroper. New York: Harper and Row, 1970.

Flash, Edward S., Jr. *Economic Advice and Presidential Leadership—The Council of Economic Advisers.* New York: Columbia University Press, 1965.

Foltz, Kim, and Maggie Malone. "Golden Paintbrushes: Artists Are Developing a Fine Eye for the Bottom Line." *Newsweek,* 15 October 1984, pp. 82–83.

Foster, Hal. *The Anti-Aesthetic: Essays on Postmodern Culture.* Port Townsend, Wash.: Bay Press, 1983.

————. "(Post)Modern Polemics." *New German Critique* 11, no. 3 (Fall 1984): 67–78.

————. *Recodings: Art, Spectacle, Cultural Politics.* Port Townsend, Wash.: Bay Press, 1985.

*4 Documenta.* Katalog I & II. Kassel: Druck & Verlag GmbH Kassel, 1968.

Fox, Richard Wightman, and T. J. Jackson Lears, eds. *The Culture of Consumption: Critical Essays in American History, 1880–1980.* New York: Pantheon Books, 1983.

Fox, Stephen. *The Mirror Makers: A History of American Advertising and Its Creators.* New York: William Morrow and Co., 1984.

França, José-Augusto. "Dix huit musées se confessent à Venise." *Aujourd'hui* 8, no. 47 (October 1964): 40–41.

Francis, Richard. *Jasper Johns.* New York: Abbeville Press, 1984.

Frascina, Francis, ed. *Pollock and After: The Critical Debate.* New York: Harper & Row, 1985.

Fried, Michael. "How Modernism Works: A Response to T. J. Clark." In *Pollock and After: The Critical Debate,* edited by Francis Frascina, pp. 65–88. New York: Harper & Row, 1985.

Frigerio, Simone. "La 32ᵉ Biennale de Venise: La peinture dans quelques sections étrangères." *Aujourd'hui* 8, no. 47 (October 1964): 26–29.

Gablik, Suzi. *Has Modernism Failed?* New York: Thames & Hudson, 1984.

Galbraith, John Kenneth. *The Affluent Society.* 2d ed. Boston: Houghton Mifflin Co., 1969.

Garrels, Gary, ed. *The Work of Andy Warhol.* Seattle: Bay Press, 1989.

Gassiot-Talabot, Gérald. "La panoplie de l'oncle Sam à Venise." *Aujourd'hui* 8, no. 47 (October 1964): 30–33.

Geelhaar, Christian. *Jasper Johns Working Proofs.* London: Petersburg Press, 1980.

Geldzahler, Henry. "The Art Audience and the Critic." *Hudson Review* 18, no. 1 (Spring 1965): 105–109.

————. *Pop Art, 1955–70.* Sydney, Australia: International Cultural Corporation of Australia Limited, 1985.

Gelman, Eric. "They Live to Buy." *Newsweek,* 31 December 1984, pp. 28–29.

Genauer, Emily. "The Merchandise of Venice." *Sunday Herald Tribune Magazine* (New York), 12 July 1964, p. 21.

Gendel, Milton. "Hugger-mugger in the Giardini." *Artnews* 63, no. 5 (September 1964): 32–35, 53.

————. "Venice." *Artnews* 67, no. 5 (September 1968): 25.

————. "Venice: Miniskirts or Miniart?" *Artnews* 65, no. 5 (September 1966): 52–54, 64–67.

Gilborn, Craig. "Pop Pedagogy: Looking at the Coke Bottle." *Museum News* 47, no. 4 (December 1968): 12–18.

Gitlin, Todd. "Prime Time Ideology: The Hegemonic Process in Television Entertainment." In *Television: The Critical View,* edited by Horace Newcomb, pp. 507–532. 4th ed. New York: Oxford University Press, 1987.

Glenn, Armon. "Thriving Drive-Ins: They Are the Hottest Thing in the Restaurant Business Today." *Barron's,* 5 June 1961, pp. 11, 13.

Glueck, Grace. "Art Notes: Boom?" *New York Times,* 10 May 1964, sec. 2, p. 19.

————. "Robert C. Scull, Prominent Collector of Pop Art." *New York Times,* 3 January 1986, sec. B, p. 5.

Goldman, Eric F. *The Crucial Decade—And After: America, 1945–1960.* New York: Vintage Books, 1960.

Goldman, Judith. *James Rosenquist.* New York: Viking Penguin, 1985.

————. *Windows at Tiffany's: The Art of Gene Moore.* New York: Harry N. Abrams, 1980.

Goldstein, Patrick. "Disc-Graces Grace Annual Bottom 10." *Los Angeles Times Calendar,* 11 January 1987, pp. 80–81.

Gordon, George N. *The Communications Revolution: A History of Mass Media in the United States.* New York: Hastings House, 1977.

Gordon, John. "Exhibition Preview: Business Buys American Art." *Art in America* 48, no. 1 (Spring 1960): 88–93.

Gorer, Geoffrey. *The American People: A Study in National Character.* Rev. ed. New York: W. W. Norton & Co., 1964.

Gratz, Roberta B. "Artist's a Study in Blue At Scull's SRO Auction." *New York Post,* 19 October 1973, pp. 3, 16.

Greenberg, Bradley S., and Edwin B. Parker, eds. *The Kennedy Assassination and the American Public.* Stanford, Calif.: Stanford University Press, 1965.

Greenberg, Clement. "After Abstract Expressionism." *Art International,* 25 October 1962, pp. 24–32.

————. "Avant-Garde and Kitsch." *Partisan Review* 6, no. 5 (Fall 1939): 34–49.

"The Growing Cult of Marilyn." *Life,* 25 January 1963, pp. 89–91 +.

Gruen, John. "Roy Lichtenstein: From Outrageous Parody to Iconographic Elegance." *Artnews* 75, no. 3 (March 1976): 39–42.

Guilbaut, Serge. *How New York Stole the Idea of Modern Art: Abstract Expressionism, Freedom and the Cold War.* Translated by Arthur Goldhammer. Chicago: University of Chicago Press, 1983.

Haacke, Hans. *The Chocolate Master.* Toronto: Art Metropole, 1982.

Habermas, Jürgen. "Modernity versus Postmodernity." *New German Critique* 8, no. 1 (Winter 1981): 3–14.

Hansen, Alvin H. *Economic Issues of the 1960s.* New York: McGraw-Hill Book Co., 1960.

Harris, Seymour E. "Economic Policies under Kennedy in 1962 and Fiscal Year 1963:

Introduction and Summary." *Review of Economics and Statistics* 44, no. 1 (February 1962): 1–3.

———. *Economics of the Kennedy Years and a Look Ahead.* New York: Harper & Row, 1964.

Harron, Mary. "Pop Art/Art Pop: The Warhol Connection." *Melody Maker,* 16 February 1980, pp. 21–23, 33, 43.

Haskell, Barbara. *Blam! The Explosion of Pop, Minimalism, and Performance, 1958–1964.* New York: Whitney Museum of American Art, 1984.

———. *Claes Oldenburg: Object into Monument.* Pasadena: Pasadena Art Museum, 1971.

Hechinger, Grace and Fred M. "College Morals Mirror Our Society." *New York Times Magazine,* 14 April 1963, pp. 22, 120, 122.

Heller, Walter W. *New Dimensions of Political Economy.* Cambridge, Mass.: Harvard University Press, 1966.

Hendrickson, Robert. *The Grand Emporiums: The Illustrated History of America's Great Department Stores.* New York: Stein and Day, 1979.

Heren, Louis. *The Power of the Press?* London: Orbis Publishing, 1985.

Hess, Thomas B. "Editorial: Moses the Art Slayer Wins One Round." *Artnews* 63, no. 2 (April 1964): 25.

———. "Reviews and Previews: Andy Warhol." *Artnews* 63, no. 9 (January 1965): 11.

Hightower, Jim. *Eat Your Heart Out: Food Profiteering in America.* New York: Vintage Books, 1976.

Hine, Thomas. *Populuxe.* New York: Alfred A. Knopf, 1986.

Hoctin, Luce. "Documenta III." *L'Oeil,* no. 117 (September 1964): 24–31, 47.

Hodgson, Godfrey. *America in Our Time.* Garden City, N.Y.: Doubleday & Co., 1976.

Holsworth, Robert D. *Public Interest Liberalism and the Crisis of Affluence: Reflections on Nader, Environmentalism, and the Politics of a Sustainable Society.* Boston: G. K. Hall & Co., 1980.

Holub, Robert C. *Reception Theory: A Critical Introduction.* New York: Methuen, 1984.

Honour, Hugh. "Biennales of Other Days: A Cautionary Tale." *Apollo* 84, no. 53 (July 1966): 24–33.

Horowitz, David, ed. *Corporations and the Cold War.* New York: Monthly Review Press, 1969.

———. "Capitalism and the Crisis of Abundance." In *In The Marketplace: Consumerism in America,* edited by Editors of *Ramparts* with Frank Browning, pp. 213–228. San Francisco: Canfield Press, 1972.

Howard, Gerald, ed. *The Sixties.* New York: Pocket Books, 1982.

Huber, Carlo. *Jasper Johns Graphik.* Bern: Kornfeld und Klipstein, 1971.

Hughes, Robert. "Careerism and Hype amidst the Image Haze." *Time,* 17 June 1985, pp. 78–83.

———. "A Caterer of Repetition and Glut." *Time,* 9 March 1987, p. 90.

———. "On Art and Money." *New York Review of Books,* 6 December 1984, pp. 20–27.

Hunter, Sam. *Masters of the Sixties: From New Realism to Pop Art.* New York: Marisa del Re Gallery, 1984.

Huyssen, Andreas. *After the Great Divide: Modernism, Mass Culture, Postmodernism.* Bloomington: Indiana University Press, 1986.

———. "Mapping the Postmodern." *New German Critique* 11, no. 3 (Fall 1984): 5–52.

———. "The Search for Tradition: Avant-Garde and Postmodernism in the 1970s." *New German Critique* 8, no. 1 (Winter 1981): 23–40.

"'I Love You . . . I Love You. . . .'" *Newsweek,* 20 August 1962, pp. 30–31.

"Into the Red Shadowland." *Newsweek,* 27 July 1959, pp. 39–42.

Irwin, David. "The Venice Biennale: The Breaking of Boundaries." *Apollo* 88, no. 80 (October 1968): 292–294.

*James Rosenquist.* Ottawa: National Gallery of Canada, 1968.

Jameson, Fredric. "The Politics of Theory: Ideological Positions in the Postmodernist Debate." *New German Critique* 11, no. 3 (Fall 1984): 53–65.

———. "Postmodernism and Consumer Society." In *The Anti-Aesthetic: Essays on Postmodern Culture,* edited by Hal Foster, pp. 111–125. Port Townsend, Wash.: Bay Press, 1983.

———. "Postmodernism, or The Cultural Logic of Late Capitalism." *New Left Review,* no. 146 (July–August 1984): 53–92.

*Jasper Johns.* New York: Jewish Museum, 1964.

*Jasper Johns: Die Graphik.* Hannover: Ludwigshafen am Rhein, 1971.

*Jasper Johns: Drawings.* London: Arts Council of Great Britain, 1974.

*Jasper Johns Paintings, Drawings & Sculpture, 1954–1964.* London: Whitechapel Gallery, 1964.

Jerome, John. *The Death of the Automobile: The Fatal Effect of the Golden Era, 1955–1970.* New York: W. W. Norton & Co., 1972.

Johns, Jasper. *Jasper Johns.* Edited by Max Kozloff. New York: Harry N. Abrams, 1969.

———, and Max Kozloff. *Jasper Johns.* New York: Harry N. Abrams, 1972.

Johnson, Ellen H. *Claes Oldenburg.* Baltimore: Penguin Books, 1971.

Johnson, Philip. "Young Artists at the Fair and at Lincoln Center." *Art in America* 52, no. 4 (1964): 112–121.

Jones, Mary Gardiner. "The Cultural and Social Impact of Advertising on American Society." In *Consumerism: Search for the Consumer Interest,* edited by David A. Aaker and George S. Day, pp. 430–433. 2d ed. New York: Free Press, 1974.

Jouffroy, Alain. "Le grand jeu de la Biennale." *L'Oeil,* nos. 139–140 (July–August 1966): 44–51, 61.

Jürgen-Fischer, K. "Deutsche Kunst in Quarantäne? Zum documenta—streit." *Das Kunstwerk* 21, nos. 1–2 (October–November 1967): 35.

———. "Kunstkritisches Tagebuch IV." *Das Kunstwerk* 21, nos. 11–12 (August–September 1968): 6–33, 83, 84.

Kassalow, Everett M. "U.S. Ideology vs. European Pragmatism." *Challenge* 11, no. 10 (July 1963): 22–25.

Katona, George. *The Mass Consumption Society.* New York: McGraw-Hill Book Co., 1964.

Keller, Heinz. "Kassel: Documenta III." *Werk* 51 (September 1964): 216*–217*.

Kellner, Douglas. "TV, Ideology and Emancipatory Popular Culture." In *Television: The Critical View,* edited by Horace Newcomb, pp. 471–503. 4th ed. New York: Oxford University Press, 1987.

King, Margaret J. "Empires of Popular Culture: McDonald's and Disney." In *Ronald Revisited: The World of Ronald McDonald,* pp. 106–119. Bowling Green, Ohio: Bowling Green University Popular Press, 1983.

Kirstein, Lincoln. "Marilyn Monroe: 1926–1962." *Nation,* 25 August 1962, pp. 70–73.

Kolko, Joyce. *America and the Crisis of World Capitalism.* Boston: Beacon Press, 1974.

Kornbluth, Jesse. "Andy: The World of Warhol." *New York,* 9 March 1987, pp. 38–49.

Kozloff, Max. "Art." *Nation,* 2 November 1963, pp. 284–287.

———. "Art." *Nation,* 20 January 1964, pp. 77–80.

———. "Art." *Nation,* 29 April 1968, pp. 578–580.

———. "Art: Dissimulated Pop." *Nation,* 30 November 1964, pp. 417–419.

———. "Art: Review of the Season." *Nation,* 7 June 1965, pp. 623–625.

———. "'Pop' Culture, Metaphysical Disgust, and the New Vulgarians." *Art International* 6, no. 2 (March 1962): 34–36.

Kramer, Hilton. "Art." *Nation,* 17 November 1962, pp. 334–335.

Kudielka, Robert. "Documenta IV: A Critical Review." *Studio International* 176, no. 903 (September 1968): 76–78.

———. "Documenta IV: The German Contribution." *Studio International* 176, no. 902 (July/August 1968): 29–32.

Kunzle, David. "Pop Art as Consumerist Realism." *Studies in Visual Communication* 10, no. 2 (Spring 1984): 16–33.

Kuspit, Donald B. "Pop Art: A Reactionary Realism." *Art Journal* 36, no. 1 (Fall 1976): 31–38.

Larson, Gary O. *The Reluctant Patron: The United States Government and the Arts, 1943–1965.* Philadelphia: University of Pennsylvania Press, 1983.

Lears, T. J. Jackson. "From Salvation to Self-Realization: Advertising and the Therapeutic Roots of the Consumer Culture, 1880–1930." In *The Culture of Consumption: Critical Essays in American History, 1880–1980,* edited by Richard Wightman Fox and T. J. Jackson Lears, pp. 1–38. New York: Pantheon Books, 1983.

Leijonhofvud, Axel. *On Keynesian Economics and the Economics of Keynes.* New York: Oxford University Press, 1970.

Levin, Kim. "Farewell to Modernism." *Arts Magazine* 54, no. 2 (October 1979): 90–92.

Lewis, Jo Ann. "The Mind & Heart of the Master Art Dealer." *Washington Post,* 12 April 1990, sec. C, pp. 1–2.

Lichtenstein, Roy. "Bobby Kennedy." *Time,* 24 May 1968, cover.

———. "The Gun in America." *Time,* 21 June 1968, cover.

Lifshey, Earl. *The Housewares Story: A History of the American Housewares Industry.* Chicago: National Housewares Manufacturers Association, 1973.

Lipman, Jean. "Coca-Cola." *Art and Artists* 3, no. 7 (October 1968): 36–41.

Lippard, Lucy R. *Pop Art.* New York: Oxford University Press, 1966.

Logsdon, John M. *The Decision to Go to the Moon: Project Apollo and the National Interest.* Cambridge, Mass.: MIT Press, 1970.

Lohr, Steve. "'Uppity Pups' At Saatchi's Helm." *New York Times,* 13 May 1986, sec. D, p. 4.

Longford, Lord. *Nixon: A Study in Extremes of Fortune.* London: Weidenfeld and Nicolson, 1980.

Loran, Erle. "Pop Artists or Copy Cats?" *Artnews* 62, no. 5 (September 1963): 48–49, 61.

Loring, John. "Graphic Arts: Comic Strip Pop." *Arts Magazine* 49, no. 1 (September 1974): 48–50.

———. "Oldenburg on Multiples." *Arts Magazine* 48, no. 8 (May 1974): 42–45.

Love, John F. *McDonald's: Behind the Arches.* New York: Bantam Books, 1986.

Luckmann, Thomas, and Peter Berger. "Social Mobility and Personal Identity." *Archives Européennes de Sociologie* 5, no. 2 (1964): 331–343.

Lyotard, Jean-François. *The Postmodern Condition: A Report on Knowledge.* Minneapolis: University of Minnesota Press, 1984.

"'Made in U.S.A.'—in Red Capital." *U.S. News & World Report,* 3 August 1959, pp. 38–39.

Mahsun, Carol Anne. *Pop Art and the Critics.* Ann Arbor: UMI Research Press, 1987.

———. *Pop Art: The Critical Dialogue.* Ann Arbor: UMI Research Press, 1989.

Marabini, Jean. *Marcuse & McLuhan et la nouvelle révolution mondiale.* Tours: Maison Mame, 1973.

Marchand, Roland. *Advertising the American Dream: Making Way for Modernity, 1920–1940.* Berkeley: University of California Press, 1985.

Marcus, Leonard S. *The American Store Window.* New York: Whitney Library of Design, 1978.

Marcuse, Herbert. *The Aesthetic Dimension: Toward a Critique of Marxist Aesthetics.* Boston: Beacon Press, 1978.

———. *One-Dimensional Man: Studies in the Ideology of Advanced Industrial Society.* Boston: Beacon Press, 1964.

Maughan, John. "The Great Soup War." *Dun's Review and Modern Industry* 78, no. 3 (September 1961): 29–31.

May, Elaine Tyler. *Homeward Bound: American Families in the Cold War Era.* New York: Basic Books, 1988.

Mayne, Richard. *The Community of Europe.* London: Victor Gollancz, 1962.

McGrath, Peter. "A New Voting Bloc." *Newsweek,* 31 December 1984, pp. 30–31.

McGuigan, Cathleen. "New Art, New Money: The Marketing of an American Artist." *New York Times Magazine,* 10 February 1985, pp. 20–28, 32, 34–35, 72.

———. "A Pop Patron's Last Hurrah." *Newsweek,* 17 November 1986, p. 97.

Meyer, Karl E. *The Art Museum: Power, Money, Ethics.* New York: William Morrow and Co., 1979.

Mintz, Steven, and Susan Kellogg. *Domestic Revolutions: A Social History of American Family Life.* New York: Free Press, 1988.

Monahan, Laurie J. "Cultural Cartography: American Designs at the 1964 Venice Biennale." In *Reconstructing Modernism: Art in New York, Paris, and Montreal, 1945–1964,* edited by Serge Guilbaut, pp. 369–416. Cambridge: MIT Press, 1990.

Morphet, Richard. *Roy Lichtenstein.* London: Tate Gallery, 1968.

Morucchio, Berto. "La section Italienne à la Biennale de Venise." *Aujourd'hui* 8, no. 47 (October 1964): 34–35.

Mosley, Leonard. *Disney's World.* New York: Stein and Day, 1985.

Murken-Altrogge, Christa. *Werbung Mythos Kunst am Beispiel Coca-Cola.* Tübingen: Verlag Ernst Wasmuth, 1977.

Myers, John Bernard. "Junkdump Fair Surveyed." *Art and Literature,* no. 3 (Autumn–Winter 1964): 122–141.

———. *Tracking the Marvelous: A Life in the New York Art World.* New York: Random House, 1983.

Narotzky, Norman. "The Venice Biennale: Pease Porridge in the Pot Nine Days Old." *Arts Magazine* 40, no. 9 (September/October 1966): 42–44.

*National Advertising Investments* 12, no. 2 (January–December 1960); and 20, no. 2 (January–December 1968).

National Collection of Fine Arts. Smithsonian Institution. *Robert Rauschenberg.* Washington, D.C.: National Collection of Fine Arts, Smithsonian Institution, 1976.

*New Paintings by Wesselmann.* New York: Sidney Janis Gallery, 1966.

*New Work by Oldenburg.* New York: Sidney Janis Gallery, 1966.

Nystrom, J. Warren, and Peter Malof. *The Common Market: The European Community in Action.* Princeton: D. Van Nostrand Company, 1962.

Okun, Arthur M. *The Political Economy of Prosperity.* Washington, D.C.: Brookings Institution, 1970.

Oldenburg, Claes. *Injun & Other Histories (1960).* New York: Something Else Press, 1966.

O'Neill, William L. *Coming Apart: An Informal History of America in the 1960's.* New York: New York Times Book Co., Quadrangle Books, 1971.

Opotowsky, Stan. *The Kennedy Government.* New York: E. P. Dutton Co., 1961.

Packard, Vance. *The Hidden Persuaders.* New York: Pocket Books, 1958.

———. *The Waste Makers.* New York: Pocket Books, 1963.

*Painting/Sculpture: Dine, Oldenburg, Segal.* Toronto: Art Gallery of Ontario, 1967.

"Painting: The Great American Nude." *Time,* 14 June 1968, p. 60.

Phillips, Joseph D. "Economic Effects of the Cold War." In *Corporations and the Cold War,* edited by David Horowitz, pp. 173–203. New York: Monthly Review Press, 1969.

Plagens, Peter. "Present-Day Styles and Ready-Made Criticism." *Artforum* 5, no. 4 (December 1966): 36–39.

"Plane and Fancy." *Newsweek,* 26 October 1964, p. 99.

"Pop Art—Cult of the Commonplace." *Time,* 3 May 1963, pp. 69–72.

*Pop Art: Evoluzione di una Generazione.* Milano: Electa Editrice, 1980.

*Pop-Sammlung Beck*. Düsseldorf: Rheinland-Verlag, 1970.

*The Popular Image Exhibition*. Washington, D.C.: Washington Gallery of Modern Art, 1963.

Powdermaker, Hortense. *Hollywood, the Dream Factory: An Anthropologist Looks at the Movie-makers*. Boston: Little, Brown & Co., 1950.

Prendergast, Curtis, with Geoffrey Colvin. *The World of Time Inc.: The Intimate History of a Changing Enterprise*. Vol. 3, *1960–1980*. New York: Atheneum, 1986.

Preston, Stuart. "Letter from New York: The 'Czar's' Veto." *Apollo* 79, no. 27 (May 1964): 434.

Rae, John B. *The American Automobile: A Brief History*. Chicago: University of Chicago Press, 1965.

*Raid the Icebox 1 with Andy Warhol*. Providence: Museum of Art, Rhode Island School of Design, 1969.

Ransom, Roger L. *Coping with Capitalism: The Economic Transformation of the United States, 1776–1980*. Englewood Cliffs, N.J.: Prentice-Hall, 1981.

Ratcliff, Carter. *Andy Warhol*. New York: Abbeville Press, 1983.

*Rauschenberg*. Paris: Galerie Ileana Sonnabend, 1963.

*Rauschenberg Graphic Art*. Philadelphia: Institute of Contemporary Art, University of Pennsylvania, 1970.

Read, Herbert. "Disintegration of Form in Modern Art." *Studio International* 169, no. 864 (April 1965): 144–155.

Reese, David A., ed. *The Legacy of Keynes*. New York: Harper & Row, 1987.

Reichardt, Jasia. "The Fairness and Unfairness of Prizes." *Studio International* 172, no. 880 (August 1966): 62–64.

Reif, Rita. "Rosenquist Painting Sells for Record Price." *New York Times*, 12 November 1986, sec. C, p. 28.

———. "Sculls' Art To Be Sold At Auction." *New York Times*, 9 September 1986, sec. C, p. 13.

Reitberger, Reinhold, and Wolfgang Fuchs. *Comics: Anatomy of a Mass Medium*. London: Studio Vista, 1972.

Restany, Pierre. "La IX Biennale de São Paulo." *Domus*, no. 457 (December 1967): 51–55.

———. "'Kulturkampf 1964' a Kassel: L'Espressionismo Storico Contro I Gruppi D'Avanguardia." *Domus*, no. 418 (September 1964): 42–43.

———. "La XXXII Biennale di Venezia, Biennale della Irregolarità." *Domus*, no. 417 (August 1964): 27–42.

———. "L'Ottava Biennale di San Paolo—Huitieme Biennale de Sao Paulo: Comment Va la Cousine Australe de Venise?" *Domus*, no. 432 (November 1965): 47–52.

Revel, Jean-François. "XXXIIᶜ Biennale de Venise: Triomphe du 'Réalisme Nationaliste'." *L'Oeil*, nos. 115–116 (July–August 1964): 2–11.

Richardson, John Adkins. "Dada, Camp, and the Mode Called Pop." *Journal of Aesthetics and Art Criticism* 24, no. 4 (Summer 1966): 549–558.

Riesman, David, with Nathan Glazer and Revel Denney. *The Lonely Crowd: A Study of the Changing American Character.* 3d rev. ed. New Haven: Yale University Press, 1969.

*Robert Rauschenberg.* Krefeld: Museum Haus Lange, 1964.

*Robert Rauschenberg.* Paris: Galerie Daniel Cordier, 1961.

*Robert Rauschenberg: Oeuvres de 1949 à 1968.* Paris: Musée d'art moderne de la Ville de Paris, 1968.

*Robert Rauschenberg: Paintings, 1953–1964.* Minneapolis: Walker Art Center, 1965.

*Robert Rauschenberg: Paintings, Drawings, and Combines, 1949–1964.* London: White-chapel Art Gallery, 1964.

*Robert Rauschenberg: Prints 1948–1970.* Minneapolis: Minneapolis Institute of Arts, 1970.

Roberts, Paul Craig. "The Breakdown of the Keynesian Model." *Public Interest,* no. 52 (Summer 1978): 20–33.

Roeder, George H., Jr. *Forum of Uncertainty: Confrontations with Modern Painting in Twentieth-Century American Thought.* Ann Arbor: UMI Research Press, 1980.

Rogers, John G. "Moses Beotian, Forestiere to Art Lovers." *New York Herald Tribune,* 23 June 1964, p. 14.

*Ronald Revisited: The World of Ronald McDonald.* Bowling Green: Bowling Green University Popular Press, 1983.

Rorty, James. *Our Master's Voice: Advertising.* New York: John Day Co., 1934.

Rose, Barbara. *Claes Oldenburg.* New York: Museum of Modern Art, 1970.

———. "Problems of Criticism, V: The Politics of Art, Part II." *Artforum* 7, no. 5 (January 1969): 44–49.

———. "Problems of Criticism, VI: The Politics of Art, Part III." *Artforum* 7, no. 9 (May 1969): 46–51.

———. "Profit without Honor." *New York Magazine,* 5 November 1973, pp. 80–81.

Rosenberg, Bernard, and David Manning White, eds. *Mass Culture: The Popular Arts in America.* Glencoe, Ill.: Free Press, 1957.

Rosenberg, Harold. "The Art Establishment." *Esquire,* 63, no. 1 (January 1965): 43–46, 114.

———. "The Art World: Marilyn Mondrian." *New Yorker,* 8 November 1969, pp. 167–170, 173–176.

———. "Virtuosos of Boredom." *Vogue,* 1 September 1966, pp. 296–297, 328.

Rosenblum, Robert. "Pop Art and Non-Pop Art." *Art and Literature,* no. 5 (Summer 1965): 80–93.

*Rosenquist.* Paris: Galerie Ileana Sonnabend, 1964.

Rothschild, Emma. *Paradise Lost: The Decline of the Auto-Industrial Age.* New York: Random House, 1973.

Rotzoll, Kim B., James E. Haefner, and Charles H. Sandage. *Advertising in Contemporary Society: Perspectives Toward Understanding.* Columbus, Ohio: Copyright Grid, 1976.

*Roy Lichtenstein.* Hannover: Kestner-Gesellschaft, 1968.

*Roy Lichtenstein.* London: Tate Gallery, 1968.

*Roy Lichtenstein.* Paris: Galerie Ileana Sonnaband, 1965.

*Roy Lichtenstein.* Pasadena, Calif.: Pasadena Art Museum, 1967.

*Roy Lichtenstein: Graphics, Reliefs & Sculpture, 1969–1970.* Irvine: University of California Art Gallery, 1970.

Rowen, Hobart. *The Free Enterprisers: Kennedy, Johnson, and the Business Establishment.* New York: G. P. Putnam's Sons, 1964.

Rublowsky, John. *Pop Art.* New York: Basic Books, 1965.

Russell, John. "Aimez-vous Documenta?" *L'Oeil,* nos. 164–165 (August–September 1968): 32–39.

———, and Suzi Gablik. *Pop Art Redefined.* New York: Frederick A. Praeger, 1969.

Salisbury, Harrison. "Nixon and Khrushchev argue in public as U.S. exhibit opens; accuse each other of threats." *New York Times,* 25 July 1959, pp. 1–2.

*Sammlung 1968 Karl Ströher.* München: Galerie-Verein, 1968.

*São Paulo 9, United States of America: Edward Hopper Environment U.S.A., 1957–1967.* Washington, D.C.: Smithsonian Institution Press, 1967.

Schmied, Wieland. *Notizen zu Roy Lichtenstein.* Hannover: Kestner-Gesellschaft, 1968.

Scholz-Wanckel, Katharina. *Pop Import.* Hamburg: Matari Verlag, 1965.

Schramm, Wilbur. "Communication in Crisis." In *The Kennedy Assassination and the American Public,* edited by Bradley S. Greenberg and Edwin B. Parker, pp. 1–25. Stanford: Stanford University Press, 1965.

Schudson, Michael. *Advertising, the Uneasy Persuasion: Its Dubious Impact on American Society.* New York: Basic Books, 1984.

———. *Discovering the News: A Social History of American Newspapers.* New York: Basic Books, 1978.

Seide, Adam. "Documenta III: Eine Umfrage." *Das Kunstwerk* 18, nos. 1–3 (July–September 1964): 15–16.

Selz, Peter. "Pop Goes the Artist." *Partisan Review* 30, no. 2 (Summer 1963): 313–316.

"Setting Russia Straight on Facts about the U.S." *U.S. News & World Report,* 3 August 1959, pp. 70–72.

*Seven Artists: Dine, Fahlstrom, Kelly, Marisol, Oldenburg, Segal, Wesselmann.* New York: Sidney Janis Gallery, 1969.

"The $7 Billion 'Goody.' " *Newsweek,* 24 May 1965, pp. 103–104.

Shapiro, David. *Jasper Johns Drawings, 1954–1984.* New York: Harry N. Abrams, 1984.

———. "Sculpture as Experience: The Monument That Suffered." *Art in America* 62, no. 3 (May–June 1974): 55–58.

Shepard, Richard F. "To What Lengths Can Art Go?" *New York Times,* 13 May 1965, p. 1.

Siegel, Jeanne. "Documents IV: Homage to the Americans?" *Arts Magazine* 43, no. 1 (September/October 1968): 37–41.

Small, Michael. "Already a Big Man on Canvas, Robert Longo Goes Multimedia." *People,* 10 November 1986, pp. 135–136.

———. "For a Few Fleeting Hours Keith Haring Makes a Bright Canvas of the Berlin Wall." *People,* 10 November 1986, pp. 52–55.

Smith, Patrick S. *Warhol: Conversations about the Artist.* Ann Arbor: UMI Research Press, 1988.

Smith, Robert L. *LeRoy Neiman, Andy Warhol: An Exhibition of Sports Paintings.* Los Angeles: Los Angeles Institute of Contemporary Art, 1981.

Sobel, Robert. *Car Wars: The Untold Story.* New York: E. P. Dutton, 1984.

————. *The Manipulators: America in the Media Age.* Garden City, N.Y.: Doubleday, Anchor Press, 1976.

Solomon, Alan R. "Americans in Venice at the Biennale." *Art Gallery* 7, no. 9 (June 1964): 14–21.

————. *Andy Warhol.* Boston: Institute of Contemporary Art, 1966.

————. *Four Germinal Painters, Four Younger Artists.* New York: Jewish Museum, 1964.

————. *The Popular Image Exhibition.* Washington, D.C.: Washington Gallery of Modern Art, 1963.

————. *Robert Rauschenberg.* New York: Jewish Museum, 1963.

Sottsass, Ettore, Jr. "Whipped Cream Memoires." *Domus,* no. 444 (November 1966): 42—44.

Spence, Clark C. *The Sinews of American Capitalism: An Economic History.* New York: Hill and Wang, 1964.

Spencer, Charles S. "Documenta III: Creative Individuality in Contemporary Art Surveyed at Kassel." *Studio International* 168, no. 857 (September 1964): 110–117.

"Stars: A Funny Thing Happened on the Way to Decorum." *Time,* 3 January 1964, p. 56.

"Star's Illness Costs Insurers $2 Million." *Business Week,* 28 October 1961, p. 104.

"Stars: Miracle on 46th Street." *Time,* 12 June 1964, pp. 86, 88, 90.

Stealingworth, Slim. *Tom Wesselmann.* New York: Abbeville Press, 1980.

Steinberg, Leo. "Contemporary Art and the Plight of its Public." *Harper's Magazine* 224, no. 1342 (March 1962): 31–39.

Sternlieb, George. *The Future of the Downtown Department Store.* Cambridge: Joint Center for Urban Studies of the Massachusetts Institute of Technology and Harvard University, 1962.

Stevens, Mark. *"Like No Other Store in the World": The Inside Story of Bloomingdale's.* New York: Thomas Y. Crowell, 1979.

Stevenson, Richard W. "Ad Agency Mergers Changing the Business." *New York Times,* 13 May 1986, sec. A, p. 1, sec. D, p. 4.

Stich, Sidra. *Made in U.S.A.: An Americanization in Modern Art, the '50s and '60s.* Berkeley: University of California Press, 1987.

Sweezy, Paul M., and Harry Magdoff. *The Dynamics of U.S. Capitalism.* New York: Monthly Review Press, 1972.

"A Symposium on Pop Art." *Arts Magazine* 37, no. 7 (April 1963): 36–45.

Swenson, G. R. "F-111: An Interview with James Rosenquist." *Partisan Review* 32, no. 4 (Fall 1965): 589–601.

————. "What Is Pop Art? Part 1: Jim Dine, Robert Indiana, Roy Lichtenstein, Andy Warhol." *Artnews* 62, no. 7 (November 1963): 24–27, 60–64.

————. "What Is Pop Art? Part 2: Stephen Durkee, Jasper Johns, James Rosenquist, Tom Wesselmann." *Artnews* 62, no. 10 (February 1964): 40–43, 62–67.

Tancock, John. "The Robert C. Scull Auction." In *Art at Auction: The Year at Sotheby Parke Bernet, 1973–74,* pp. 137–145. New York: Viking Press, 1975.

Taylor, Paul. *Post-Pop Art.* Cambridge: MIT Press, 1989.

"TFX Flies . . . But Questions Remain." *U.S. News & World Report,* 4 January 1965, pp. 6, 8.

"The TFX Plane—What the Fight Is About." *U.S. News & World Report,* 25 March 1963, pp. 61–63.

Thompson, David. "Reflections on the Biennale 2." *Studio International* 172, no. 880 (August 1966): 79–81.

Thwaites, John Anthony. "Documenta: The Self-Saboteurs." *Arts Magazine* 38, no. 10 (September 1964): 38–41.

Tillim, Sidney. "In the Galleries: Andy Warhol." *Arts Magazine* 38, no. 10 (September 1964): 62.

———. "In the Galleries: The New Realists." *Arts Magazine* 37, no. 3 (December 1962): 44.

———. "New York Exhibitions: Month in Review." *Arts Magazine* 37, no. 6 (March 1963): 59–62.

Toffler, Alvin. "The Competition That Refreshes." *Fortune* 63, no. 5 (May 1961): 124–28, 200, 202, 207, 209.

———. *The Culture Consumers: A Study of Art and Affluence in America.* New York: St. Martin's Press, 1964.

Tomkins, Calvin. "The Big Show in Venice." *Harper's Magazine* 230, no. 1379 (April 1965): 98–104.

———. *The Bride and the Bachelors: Five Masters of the Avant-Garde.* Harmondsworth, Middlesex, England: Penguin Books, 1976.

———. *Off the Wall: Robert Rauschenberg and the Art World of Our Time.* Harmondsworth, Middlesex, England: Penguin Books, 1981.

———. "Profiles: A Good Eye and a Good Ear." *New Yorker,* 26 May 1980, pp. 40–44, 47–48, 51–52, 57–58, 61–63, 66–72.

———. "Raggedy Andy." In *Andy Warhol,* by John Coplans, pp. 8–14. New York: New York Graphic Society, 1970.

*Tom Wesselmann.* Paris: Galerie Ileana Sonnabend, 1966.

"Toys in the Gallery." *Time,* 20 December 1963, p. 60.

Tuchman, Phyllis. "American Art in Germany: The History of a Phenomenon." *Artforum* 9, no. 3 (November 1970): 58–69.

Tucker, Marcia. *James Rosenquist.* New York: Whitney Museum of American Art, 1972.

Tugendhat, Christopher. *The Multinationals.* New York: Random House, 1972.

Tunstall, Jeremy. *The Media Are American: Anglo-American Media in the World.* London: Constable and Company, 1977.

Turner, Louis. *Multinational Companies and the Third World.* New York: Hill and Wang, 1973.

"The Two Worlds: A Day-Long Debate." *New York Times,* 25 July 1959, pp. 1, 3.

United Nations. Economic Commission for Europe. *Economic Survey of Europe in 1966: The European Economy in 1966.* Geneva: United Nations, 1967.

U.S. Congress. Joint Economic Committee. *Economic Effect of Vietnam Spending: Hearings before the Congress of the United States.* 90th Cong., 1st sess., 24–27 April 1967. Vol. 1: Statements of Witnesses and Supporting Materials. Washington: U.S. Government Printing Office, 1967.

Vernon, Raymond. *Storm over the Multinationals: The Real Issues.* Cambridge: Harvard University Press, 1977.

Vogl, Frank. *German Business after the Economic Miracle.* London: Macmillan, 1973.

Wainwright, Loudon. *The Great American Magazine: An Inside History of Life.* New York: Alfred A. Knopf, 1986.

Waldberg, Patrick. "A la VIIIme Biennale de São Paolo." *Quadrum,* no. 19 (1965): 180.

Waldman, Diane. *Roy Lichtenstein.* New York: Harry N. Abrams, 1971.

———. *Roy Lichtenstein: Drawings & Prints.* New York: Chelsea House Publishers, 1970.

Walker, John A. *Art Since Pop.* London: Thames and Hudson, 1975.

"Wall Street Treasure." *Time,* 30 June 1961, pp. 42, 47.

Wang, Penelope. "A Rock and Roll Marketing Whiz Plays for Pay." *Newsweek,* 11 August 1986, p. 39.

Warhol, Andy. *The Andy Warhol Diaries.* Edited by Pat Hackett. New York: Warner Books, 1989.

———. *The Philosophy of Andy Warhol (From A to B and Back Again).* New York: Harcourt Brace Jovanovich, 1975.

———. *Time,* 29 January 1965, cover.

Warhol, Andy, and Pat Hackett. *POPism: The Warhol '60s.* New York: Harper & Row, 1983.

Warhol, Andy, Kasper König, Pontus Hultén, and Olle Granath, eds. *Andy Warhol.* Stockholm: Moderna Museet, 1968.

Watters, Pat. *Coca-Cola: An Illustrated History.* Garden City, N.Y.: Doubleday, 1978.

Weil, Gordon L., ed. *A Handbook on the European Economic Community.* New York: Frederick A. Praeger, 1965.

Westecker, Dieter, Carl Eberth, Werner Lengemann, and Erich Muller. *Documenta— Dokumente: 1955–1968.* Kassel: Georg Wenderoth Verlag, 1972.

"When Nixon Took On Khrushchev." *U.S. News & World Report,* 3 August 1959, pp. 36–37.

White, David Manning. "Comics and the American Image Abroad." In *The Funnies: An American Idiom,* edited by David Manning White and Robert H. Abel, pp. 73–80. New York: Free Press, 1963.

———, ed. *Pop Culture in America.* Chicago: Quadrangle Books, 1970.

———, and Robert H. Abel, eds. *The Funnies: An American Idiom.* New York: Free Press, 1963.

White, Lawrence J. *The Automobile Industry since 1945.* Cambridge: Harvard University Press, 1971.

Whitford, Frank. "Les origines britanniques du Pop Art." *Revue de l'art,* no. 30 (1975): 77–81, 110–111.

————. "Documenta 4: A Critical Review." *Studio International* 176, no. 903 (September 1968): 74–76.

Whittet, G. S. "Sculpture Scoops the Lagoon." *Studio International* 168 no. 857 (September 1964): 96–103.

————. "The Dynamic of Brazil: The VIII Bienal of São Paulo." *Studio International* 170, no. 870 (October 1965): 136–143.

"Why the TFX Plane Is Still under Fire." *U.S. News & World Report*, 26 October 1964, p. 8.

Whyte, William H., Jr. *The Organization Man.* New York: Simon and Schuster, 1956.

Wicker, Tom. *JFK and LBJ: The Influence of Personality upon Politics.* Harmondsworth, Middlesex, England: Penguin Books, 1969.

Willard, Charlotte. "Dealers-Eye View." *Art in America* 52, no. 2 (April 1964): 120, 122–23, 125–127, 130, 132, 134.

Wissman, Jürgen. *Robert Rauschenberg: Black Market.* Stuttgart: Philipp Reclam Jun., 1970.

Wofford, Harris. *Of Kennedys and Kings: Making Sense of the Sixties.* New York: Farrar, Straus, Giroux, 1980.

Wolff, Janet. *The Social Production of Art.* New York: New York University Press, 1984.

Wolff, Janet L. *What Makes Women Buy: A Guide to Understanding and Influencing the New Woman of Today.* New York: McGraw-Hill Book Co., 1958.

Wood, Barry James. *Show Windows: 75 Years of the Art of Display.* New York: Congdon & Weed, 1982.

Wood, Michael. *America in the Movies, or "Santa Maria, It Had Slipped My Mind."* New York: Dell Publishing Co., 1975.

Yates, Brock. *The Decline and Fall of the American Automobile Industry.* New York: Empire Books, 1983.

Yarwood, Doreen. *Five Hundred Years of Technology in the Home.* London: B. T. Batsford, 1983.

"You Bought It—Now Live with It." *Life,* 16 July 1965, pp. 56–61.

Zahn, Leopold. "Biennale 1964." *Das Kunstwerk* 18, nos. 1–3 (July–September 1964): 31–48.

*Zeichnungen von Claes Oldenburg.* Tubingen: Kunsthalle, 1975.

Zemter, Wolfgang. "Robert Rauschenberg: Untersuchungen zur Bildstruktur." Ph.D. diss., Ruhr-Universität Bochum, 1974.

Zevi, Tullia. "The Biennale: How Evil Is Pop Art?" *New Republic,* 19 September 1964, pp. 32–34.

Zinn, Howard. *Postwar America: 1945–1971.* Indianapolis, Ind.: Bobbs-Merrill Co., 1973.

# INDEX